Children and Young People's Workforce

Janet Stearns, Clare Schmieder,
Elaine Millar
(Edited by Janet Stearns and
Mark Walsh)

Level 3 Diploma

Candidate Handbook

Published by Collins Education
An imprint of HarperCollins Publishers
77-85 Fulham Palace Rd
Hammersmith
London
W68JB

Browse the complete Collins Education catalogue at
www.collinseducation.com

10 9 8 7 6 5 4 3 2 1

ISBN 978 00 0 741843 5

British Library Cataloguing in Publication Data.
A Catalogue record for this publication is available from the British Library.

Commissioned by Charlie Evans
Project Managed by Jo Kemp
Design and typesetting by Joerg Hartsmannsgruber and Q2A
Cover design by Angela English

Index by Indexing Specialists Ltd

Printed and bound by L.E.G.O.S.p.a

Contents

Acknowledgements

Alamy: 6, 7, 8, 9, 15, 17, 18, 21, 28, 29, 37, 48, 49, 56, 59, 64, 66, 71, 73, 74, 75, 78, 81, 82, 84, 86, 87, 87, 87, 87, 88, 90, 91, 92, 93, 102, 108, 113, 115, 121, 127, 129, 131, 132, 139, 146, 147, 148, 150, 152, 154, 157, 166, 171, 173, 174, 187, 190, 193, 199, 206, 214, 217, 218, 221, 222, 223, 224, 227, 228, 229, 230, 231, 232, 234, 234, 238, 238, 239, 242, 244, 246, 247, 248, 250, 253, 255, 261, 263, 268, 270, 271, 272, 276, 277, 278, 280, 287, 288, 288, 291, 291, 292, 293, 294, 295, 296, 297, 298, 298, 298, 299, 300, 301, 304, 306, 314, 320, 324, 326, 327, 337, 343, 348, 362, 373, 377, 380, 382, 393, 402, 405, 407, 409, 410, 411, 412, 414, 419, 420

Crown copyright: 185, 334, 339, 377

Getty Images: 143, 319

iStock: 2, 13, 26, 27, 32, 40, 42, 43, 50, 52, 55, 60, 62, 68, 75, 79, 91, 97, 99, 120, 124, 126, 129, 130, 133, 134, 135, 136, 137, 138, 140, 141, 142, 144, 149, 151, 155, 158, 160, 161, 162, 165, 168, 168, 170, 177, 180, 183, 185, 189, 194, 198, 199, 200, 202, 204, 209, 212, 215, 216, 227, 249, 251, 256, 258, 258, 262, 264, 266, 281, 282, 300, 301, 302, 302, 305, 306, 310, 313, 332, 341, 342, 350, 352, 353, 354, 360, 365, 368, 370, 374, 378, 388, 390, 392, 395, 404, 416

Shutterstock: 5, 10, 23, 30, 31, 34, 45, 105, 106, 110, 111, 112, 112, 114, 118, 123, 128, 172, 175, 176, 196, 207, 207, 208, 240, 241, 243, 245, 283, 303, 323, 331, 344, 346, 357, 362, 364, 371

Introduction

Welcome to the Level 3 Diploma for the Children and Young People's Workforce.

The material in this book covers all of the mandatory units required for the Early Learning and Childcare Pathway, which combine to give you 49 credits towards your qualification. You need a total of 65 credits to achieve the full qualification and your tutor or assessor will help you to choose relevant optional units in order to do this.

Each chapter of the book covers a specific Level 3 unit. You will see that the chapters are divided into different sections, which are exactly matched to the specifications for the Level 3 qualification. Each section provides you with a focused and manageable chunk of learning and covers all of the content areas that you need to know about in a particular unit.

In order to achieve your Level 3 qualification, you need to provide evidence of your knowledge and understanding as well as your practical competence in the real work environment. Each chapter in this book begins with a summary of 'What you need to know' and 'What you need to do' in order to successfully complete the unit. The checklist at the end of each chapter will help you to keep track of your progress.

The suggested assessment tasks in each chapter will help you to gather the evidence you need for each unit. These are based on both Knowledge Assessment Tasks to assess your understanding and Practical Assessment Tasks to assess your competence in the real work environment. Your tutor or assessor will help you to plan your work in order to meet the assessment requirements.

There is a strong work-related focus to the materials in this book, using case studies, activities and realistic examples to develop your interest in and understanding of professional practice within the Children and Young People's Workforce. Achieving the Diploma will help you to gain employment in the sector or move on to higher-level training if you wish to do so.

We hope that the material in this book is accessible, interesting and inspires you to pursue a rewarding career with children and young people. Good luck with your course!

Janet Stearns, Clare Schmieder and Elaine Millar

1 | Promote communication in health, social care or children and young people's settings (SHC 31)

Assessment of this unit

This unit highlights the central importance of communication in work with children and young people. It focuses on the reasons why people communicate in childcare settings, the methods they use and the importance of ensuring that communication in care settings is effective. You will need to:

1. understand why effective communication is important in the work setting

2. be able to meet the communication and language needs, wishes and preferences of individuals

3. be able to overcome barriers to communication

4. be able to apply principles and practices relating to confidentiality.

You will be assessed on both your knowledge of effective communication and your ability to apply this in practical work with children and young people. To complete this unit successfully, you will need to produce evidence of your knowledge, as shown in the 'What you need to know' chart opposite, and evidence of your practical competence, as shown in the 'What you need to do' chart. The 'What you need to do' criteria must be assessed in a real work environment by a vocationally competent assessor. Your tutor or assessor will help you to prepare for your assessment and the tasks suggested in the chapter will help you to create the evidence that you need.

CHAPTER 1

AC   What you need to know

1.1   The different reasons people communicate

1.2   How communication affects relationships in the work setting

AC   What you need to do

2.1   Demonstrate how to establish the communication and language needs, wishes and preferences of individuals

2.2   Describe the factors to consider when promoting effective communication

2.3   Demonstrate a range of communication methods and styles to meet individual needs

2.4   Demonstrate how to respond to an individual's reactions when communicating

3.1   Explain how people from different backgrounds may use and/or interpret communication methods in different ways

3.2   Identify barriers to effective communication

3.3   Demonstrate ways to overcome barriers to communication

3.4   Demonstrate strategies that can be used to clarify misunderstandings

3.5   Explain how to access extra support or services to enable individuals to communicate effectively

4.1   Explain the meaning of the term confidentiality

4.2   Demonstrate ways to maintain confidentiality in day-to-day communication

4.3   Describe the potential tension between maintaining an individual's confidentiality and disclosing concerns

---

This unit also links to some of the other mandatory units:

CYP 3.1   Understand child and young person development

CYP 3.5   Develop positive relationships with children, young people and others involved in their care

CYP 3.6   Working together for the benefit of children and young people

EYMP 2   Promote learning and development in the early years

Some of your learning will be repeated in these units and will give you the chance to review your knowledge and understanding.

Why do people communicate?

Communication is a central part of everyday life for most people and is particularly important when you work with children and young people in a care setting. You must understand:

▶ what communication involves

▶ the different reasons for communication

▶ the way communication affects how practitioners work.

Communication means making contact with others *and* being understood. We all communicate continuously, through a two-way process of sending and receiving messages. These messages can be:

▶ **verbal communication**, using spoken or written words

▶ **non-verbal communication**, using body language such as gestures, eye-contact and touch.

People who work with children and young people may communicate with the people they are caring for, with relatives and visitors, with colleagues and with practitioners from other care agencies for a variety of different reasons, as shown in Figure 1.1.

Making and developing relationships

People communicate to make new relationships. The way you first speak and listen to a newcomer can make them feel welcome or overlooked. As you speak and comment, listen and watch, take an interest, smile and nod to a child, a young person, a colleague or a visiting practitioner you are building and developing your relationship with them. Communication will continue to be the main way you nurture and develop your relationships at work.

Giving and receiving information

At work you will be expected to give and receive different types of information. Perhaps a child tells you some news, or a parent asks a question. A colleague might give you instructions or a visiting practitioner might make an observation. The information you give, receive and pass on will help you to carry out your work effectively.

Your assessment criteria:

1.1 Identify the different reasons people communicate

Key terms

Non-verbal communication: ways of communicating without using words (for example, through body language such as gestures, eye-contact and touch)

Verbal communication: forms of communication that use (spoken or written) words

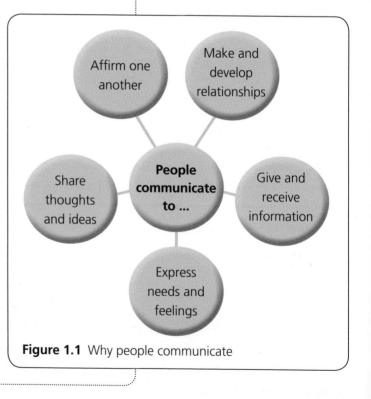

Figure 1.1 Why people communicate

People communicate to ...
- Affirm one another
- Make and develop relationships
- Give and receive information
- Express needs and feelings
- Share thoughts and ideas

Expressing needs and feelings

Expressing needs and feelings is part of being human and these are communicated through behaviour as well as speech. A baby cries to tell you, 'I'm hungry!' and a child wriggles with excitement when they tell you about their new puppy. Adults also need to share needs and feelings with each other and in this way build up a sense of trust with the person they confide in.

Sharing thoughts and ideas

Humans process many of their thoughts by discussing them. If you have ideas, questions and opinions about your work, sharing them with colleagues helps to clarify, develop and even change the way you think and act. This process is equally true of children and young people as they learn about their world. The way in which you respond can encourage or discourage the development of this important form of communication.

Affirming one another

Affirmation is about acknowledging and encouraging each other and reassuring individuals of their worth and value. Affirmation is communicated through positive words, praise and gestures. This is important in all relationships, but particularly with children and young people who are still developing a sense of who they are and how they fit in with others.

Users of children's and young people's care services and their relatives often seek reassurance from practitioners as a way of developing their self-confidence. In response, practitioners use praise and touch, and give time and attention as a way of rewarding a person's efforts and achievements and to reassure them. Some care settings also use support groups, staff meetings and appraisals as ways of providing practitioners with support and reassurance about their work performance.

Key terms

Affirmation: a positive statement declaring a quality about something or someone

Over to you!

Think about the ways in which you were welcomed when you first started in your placement or work setting.

▶ *What forms of communication helped you to settle and made you feel at ease?*

▶ *Share with a colleague the similarities and differences in your experiences.*

Knowledge Assessment Task　　1.1

Read the statements and match each one to the relevant reason (A to E) for communicating.

1. Fahim praised Sylvie because she managed to tie her own shoelaces for the first time.
2. Tanya confides to her social worker that she was upset by her weekend visit to her father, because he spent most of the time playing football with her stepbrothers.
3. Lisbet and Matthew discuss different ways to record staff meetings.
4. Ken asks the new carer, Ghalib, what his name means in African.
5. The playground assistant explains to Mrs Dale that her son grazed his knee at playtime.

　　A　To give or receive information　　B　To make and maintain relationships　　C　To express needs and feelings

　　D　To share thoughts and ideas　　E　To affirm a person

Keep your notes as evidence towards your assessment.

How does communication affect relationships in care settings?

The ability to communicate well is a key skill that enables you to work effectively with others. Always remember that the communication process is as much about listening and receiving messages as it is about talking and giving messages. As a care worker you need to be skilled in both aspects. In general, you will use communication effectively as part of your work role if you:

▶ get the other person's attention before you begin communicating with them

▶ communicate clearly and directly so that you get your message across

▶ adapt the way you communicate so that the child or adult is able to understand you

▶ use empathy to try to understand the other person's needs, point of view or the way they might be affected by what you are saying to them

▶ listen carefully to what the child or adult communicates to you

▶ use your own non-verbal communication skills effectively

▶ summarise what the other person has said as a way of checking and confirming your understanding of what they mean.

Your communication skills will develop and become more effective as you gain experience in your work role, learning from observing more experienced colleagues. Learning from others, seeking advice and using support are all part of this process.

Why skilled communication is needed

During your work with children and young people there will be specific situations where good communication skills are particularly necessary. Some of these are illustrated in Figure 1.2.

Your assessment criteria:

1.2 Explain how communication affects relationships in the work setting

Key terms

Empathy: understanding another person's feelings as if they are your own

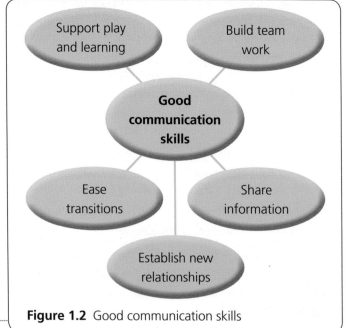

Figure 1.2 Good communication skills

Support play and learning

Build team work

Good communication skills

Ease transitions

Share information

Establish new relationships

Building teamwork

Working in a care setting usually means working in a team. Members of the team may have different roles, but the wellbeing of the children and young people you care for is a common focus for all. A team with members who communicate well with each other is a strong team.

Sharing information

In a care setting it is vital that information is shared appropriately to enable each member to carry out their role effectively. In the course of your work you will need to find out information, pass on information and listen to information.

Establishing new relationships

When a person – a child, a young person or an adult – arrives in a new environment, their may feel apprehensive. The ability to empathise, that is, to imagine how the person is feeling, is a key communication skill. It helps you understand what the person needs in order to feel at ease, such as a warm welcome, information and reassurance.

Helping children and young people with transitions

A transition is a change from one state or stage to another. It might be a small change, such as a child being taken home from playgroup by a childminder, or a big change, such as a child starting school, or a young person leaving home for the first time. If you are supporting a child or young person through a transition, your sensitive communication will help the individual cope with both the losses and the gains that the change will involve.

Supporting play and learning

Despite the fact that babies cannot speak, they are excellent communicators. To play with a baby, good eye contact and physical closeness are essential. You will notice that a baby holds your gaze and communicates with sounds. Communicating with a child at their level can literally mean getting down on your hands and knees, as well as using more simple language and gestures to communicate your interest and involvement as they explore the world around them. For a young person beginning to learn about their place in the adult world, it is often most helpful to be a reliable presence alongside, who is there when needed to encourage, support and advise.

Key terms

Transition: moving from one state or stage to another

Effective communication with relatives and visitors

Children's and young people's care service users and their relatives need to be able to trust you and have confidence in your ability to support and care for them. Communication with relatives and visitors is more likely to be effective if you:

▶ establish a good rapport with each individual

▶ show people respect by using their preferred names (e.g. 'Mrs Griffiths' rather than 'Jenny', if preferred) and make sure you consult them about anything that affects them

▶ speak directly and clearly, using positive body language and good eye contact when interacting

▶ give each individual enough time to understand what you are saying and listen carefully to what they say to you

▶ respond quickly and in an appropriate way to an individual's communication by phone, email or in person

▶ respect **confidentiality** by communicating personal, sensitive or private information about individuals in an appropriate, private area of the care setting

▶ adapt your communication skills to meet the needs of people who have hearing or visual impairments or whose first language is not English.

People will trust and respect you if you adopt a consistent, professional and respectful approach when you communicate with them. They need to be confident that you value them as people and that you are able to communicate with them about their particular needs, wishes and preferences relating to children's and young persons' care.

Effective communication with colleagues

Effective communication with colleagues is an essential part of your work role as you will be in a team-working environment. Communication is more likely to affect relationships positively with colleagues in the work setting if you:

▶ establish an appropriate work-related rapport with each of your colleagues

▶ show that you respect your colleagues' skills, abilities and professional approach towards their work role

Your assessment criteria:

1.2 Explain how communication affects relationships in the work setting

Key terms

Confidentiality: ensuring information is only accessible to people who are authorised to know about it

- talk to your colleagues clearly and directly, using positive body language and giving them enough time to absorb what you are saying

- always listen to your colleagues' point of view, making sure you are polite and constructive if you disagree

- check that colleagues understand what you are trying to communicate when you are passing on important information

- clarify any points or ask questions whenever you don't fully understand what you have been told or are being asked to do

- demonstrate that you understand and respect confidentiality and the feelings of your colleagues by communicating about sensitive, personal or private issues in an appropriately private place

- ask someone to check any emails, letters or notes that you write on behalf of the care setting to ensure that your language is professional and is presented appropriately.

Effective communication with work colleagues is based on establishing a friendly but professional working relationship where you can give and receive support. Communication with colleagues should revolve around your shared goal of promoting the health and wellbeing of the children and young people you provide care and support for.

Case study

The Parent Staff (Home–School) Association at Elm Lea primary school wants to improve communication with parents whose children are moving up from nursery to the reception class. They decide to put together an information leaflet. They have asked for staff input to help them think about relevant matters to help new parents support their children through this transition stage.

1. Give two examples of information you think should be communicated to parents, explaining how each would ease transition.

2. Suggest other activities or events that could be put on by the nursery and school to help the children and their parents with this transition.

Over to you!

Think of an example of communication that regularly takes place with colleagues at your placement or work setting, such as a handover report or a team meeting.

- *What enables good communication on these occasions?*

- *What interferes with or interrupts the communication process?*

Knowledge Assessment Task   1.2

Think of two practical examples from your work setting or placement that illustrate how you have used communication to affect relationships positively. Describe each scenario, explaining how different types of communication were used to build teamwork successfully, or to share information, establish new relationships, ease transitions or support play and learning.

Keep the written work that you produce as evidence for your assessment.

Your assessment criteria:

2.1 Demonstrate how to establish the communication and language needs, wishes and preferences of individuals

How do you establish the communication and language needs, wishes and preferences of individuals?

When you work with children or young people in a care setting an important part of your role is to **facilitate** communication. This means enabling individuals to express themselves and understand the communication of others. To be effective in this role you must first recognise that each person is unique, meaning there will be differences in the way each person communicates.

Key terms

Facilitate: to encourage and enable

Different influences affecting communication

There are many different influences that affect communication. Figure 1.3 shows some of the main reasons for these differences.

Facilitating communication

As well as different influences affecting the communication of individuals such as their culture, ethnicity, nationality and any particular needs, there will be different conditions in the environment of a care setting, for example, to do with levels of noise or different types of activity going on. You will need to modify your methods of communication according to who you are speaking with and the conditions you are in. This requires a flexible approach.

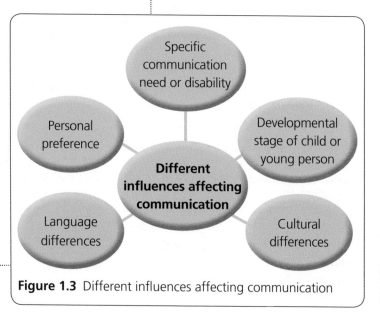

Figure 1.3 Different influences affecting communication

Working with adults

When working with adults (colleagues, family members, other practitioners) you can usually speak directly to ask about language and communication needs and preferences; for example, how to address a person, whether by their first name or more formally, and whether a woman wishes to be called Miss, Mrs or Ms. Remember that it is not possible to tell just by outward appearances whether a person has literacy needs to do with reading and writing. You may need to question directly how a person wishes to receive information.

Working with babies and children

Children who haven't yet learned to speak use **non-verbal** forms of communication (there is more about non-verbal communication on page 16). A baby will express a range of needs through crying, such as hunger, thirst, whether too hot or cold, wet or soiled, tired or bored, or just in need of comfort. Younger children will require some interpretation of speech, with patience on both sides because it can be a frustrating process. Let the child know you are listening and suggest different methods, such as showing or pointing to communicate. Be aware that children may use made-up or 'baby' words for significant items, such as comforters, or parts of the body which you need to become familiar with in order to understand their needs.

Working with young people

Adolescence can be a self-conscious time for young people and also for parents, all of whom commonly report difficulties maintaining effective communication. It can be useful to draw on your own experience and remember with empathy how your teenage self felt. Knowledge of youth culture will help you understand the ways some young people speak and the words and gestures used, but adopting the same style yourself may not be welcomed and it is never appropriate to swear or use aggressive or sexually explicit language at work.

Working with people who are hearing impaired or visually impaired

If you are working with children or young people who are hearing impaired, face the person you are speaking to at all times and speak slowly and clearly. Use your eyes, facial expressions and gestures to communicate, as appropriate, and do not be tempted to shout into a person's ear or hearing aid. If you are working with people who are visually impaired, say who you are and introduce anyone with you. Explain if anything might affect the communication, such as people joining or leaving, and end the conversation clearly so they know you are leaving.

Key terms

Non-verbal: communicating without using words

Over to you!

Think back over the last few years about the particular expressions of speech or buzz words that everyone in your peer group used.

▶ *Can you link your experience then to the ways in which children and young people communicate today?*

▶ *How does this use of language help to make a person feel part of a group?*

What factors promote effective communication?

When you are communicating with others the content of the message needs to be clear, but it also needs to be said in a clear way. When receiving messages it is necessary to be alert to both verbal (spoken) and non-verbal (without speech) messages.

Promoting effective communication

To communicate effectively keep in mind the factors illustrated in Figure 1.4. There is no one combination of factors that provides the ideal way to communicate a message. It will differ according to the message, the recipient and the situation.

Figure 1.4 Factors that affect communication

Environment	Proximity	Orientation	Posture	Touch
Location	Physical distance	Body positioning	Behaviour	Type and appropriateness
Are noise and activity levels too high? Do you need privacy? Would it be easier to have this conversation while carrying out an activity together? Walking side by side can ease the flow of conversation.	The better you know a person the closer you are likely to be physically. Closeness can encourage sharing. Positioning chairs at an angle rather than side by side makes it physically easier to talk to another person. Sitting directly opposite is more formal and can feel confrontational. Sometimes a table between you helps a person to feel protected. Yelling from one room to another doesn't aid communication!	Leaning forward can communicate that you are interested, but getting too close might invade **body space**. Turning away can show lack of interest but standing directly opposite a person can be too direct, whereas being at an angle can provide a helpful space.	Folded arms can look defensive and discourage communication. Friends and family, without realising, often mirror the other person's posture, which is thought to increase a sense of familiarity. Standing over a person who is seated might make the person feel patronised or threatened.	Holding a baby close and holding hands with a child can communicates care and security. A light touch on a person's arm or hand can communicate caring and understanding, but sometimes touch can feel intrusive, even threatening. Touch is a **safe-guarding** issue and you must never impose yourself physically on a child or young person. (See Chapter 7, page 180 for more about this)

Case study

It is raining and cold so the children at Busy Bees nursery cannot play outside as usual. Bruno, aged three, is full of energy and boisterously careers around the nursery crashing a tambourine off the walls and furniture, laughing loudly. Molly, aged four, who is in the book corner, puts her hands over her ears as he passes, saying loudly, 'That boy is a naughty, rough boy.' The next day Molly's mother asks to speak to the nursery nurse because she is concerned that her daughter might be being bullied by Bruno.

1. How might you respond to Molly's mother's concerns?
2. What would you do to help to improve communication between Bruno and Molly?

Active listening

Communication is as much about listening and observing as it is about talking. **Active listening** means more than just hearing a message – it is about really tuning in and taking in what is being communicated. Active listening requires you to understand non-verbal communication, which is explored further on page 16.

Allow time to communicate

When working with children and young people, allow time for communication to take place. Children may need you to repeat, explain and give examples in order to understand your message fully. Young people may need to question, challenge and negotiate. Each individual needs time to take in what has been said and to formulate an answer. In a busy care setting you may have to respond quickly to a range of communications and, at times, these might be urgent. Try to find some quiet moments to stop and review whether you have communicated clearly and understood correctly the communication of others.

Key terms

Active listening: close listening, accompanied by an awareness of non-verbal communication of self and others

Body space: also known as interpersonal space, refers to the physical space between two people that feels comfortable and which is smaller when the intimacy between them is greater

Safeguarding: the protection of children, young people and vulnerable adults from harm and abuse and the promotion of their health and wellbeing

Over to you!

Think about the last time you felt you were really listened to.

▶ *What did the person do and say to make you feel heard? Now think about the last time you felt overlooked and not listened to.*

▶ *What did the person do and say to make you feel dismissed?*

Routes of communication

In your work role you will use a number of routes to communicate information. Each time you communicate you need to decide on the most appropriate route. Sometimes you will use more than one route, such as a conversation followed up by a letter, or a committee meeting followed up with written minutes. Figure 1.5 summarises the aspects of different forms of communication.

Your assessment criteria:

2.2 Describe the factors to consider when promoting effective communication

Figure 1.5 Positive and negative aspects of different communication routes

Spoken word

Face-to-face conversation

Positive aspects	Negative aspects
+ Able to observe body language	− May take time to arrange a meeting
+ Able to observe non-verbal responses of others	− May not have privacy
+ Able to question and clarify	

Conversation over telephone

+ Quick method of communication	− Cannot observe body language responses of others
+ Immediate method of communication	
+ Able to hear tone of voice	− Person might not be in to receive call

Written word

Letters and reports

+ Able to relay long or complex messages	− Takes time to compose letter
+ Able to expand on thoughts without interruption	− Need literacy skills
+ Able to present information in a formal way	− Letter could get lost in the post
+ Recipient has time to absorb information	− Person may take a long time to respond, or not do so at all

Emails and texts

+ Fast, easy way to send messages	− Recipient could misinterpret abbreviated messages
+ Able to send information in an abbreviated form	
+ Able to send one message to many recipients	− Need the technology to use these methods
+ Able to edit and change message before sending	− Have to wait for recipient's response

Case study

Roseanne is a learning support assistant working closely with Stevie, who experiences communication difficulties associated with autism. Stevie is to return to school after a three-week absence due to illness and Roseanne suspects it won't be easy for him to adapt back into the school routine. She needs to find out how he is feeling about his return and if he is fully fit, or whether he needs to ease back gradually into a full day's work. Roseanne knows it is difficult to provide reassurance for Stevie, especially as he doesn't like to be touched, and she also worries that the noisy bustle of the classroom will be a shock after the quiet of home and that he will find it difficult to focus.

1. What difficulties with communication does Stevie experience?
2. How do you suggest Roseanne prepares for Stevie's return?
3. What factors might faciliate effective communication between Roseanne and Stevie?

Over to you!

Think about the different routes you use to communicate.

▶ *What is your preferred way of communicating?*
▶ *Why is this?*

How can you use a range of communication methods and styles to meet individual needs and respond to an individual's reactions when communicating?

Communication is a complex process made up of many different elements to do with verbal and non-verbal language. These are reflected in a range of communication styles and methods. Communication is also a two-way process that must take into consideration the reactions of others and respond appropriately. To be a skilled communicator and interpreter of communication you must pay close attention to your words and actions, as well as the words and actions of others.

Non-verbal communication

Non-verbal communication is a form of communication that takes place almost **subconsciously**, that is, without being aware of thinking. It provides clues about the meaning of spoken language. You have already looked at some aspects related to non-verbal communication to do with proximity, orientation, posture and touch. The main aspects of non-verbal communication are illustrated in Figure 1.6 and described on the next page.

Your assessment criteria:

2.3 Demonstrate a range of communication methods and styles to meet individual needs

2.4 Demonstrate how to respond to an individual's reactions when communicating

Key terms

Subconsciously: happening at a level without conscious thought or full awareness

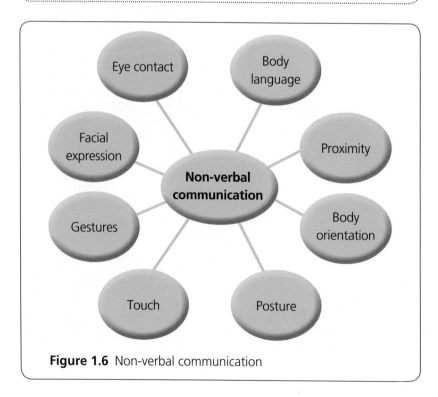

Figure 1.6 Non-verbal communication

Body language

Body language is the way your body reflects your thoughts and feelings. This can add emphasis to your words, but if you don't really mean what you are saying it can also reveal a truer and contradictory message beneath your words. For example, exclaiming, 'How fascinating,' might sound as though you are interested, but your body language, such as tapping fingers, poor eye contact and stifled yawns betrays that you are actually bored.

Gestures

Gestures are signs made with the hands and arms to illustrate or emphasise your words or to stand in place of words. People often gesticulate during conversations without really thinking about it. You may see someone gesticulating while talking on a phone, even though the person receiving the call cannot see these actions. It is difficult to find a single gesture which is universally acceptable; for example, the thumbs-up sign, seen as positive across many countries, is an offensive gesture in Ghana, South America, Iran and Iraq. You must be careful because not all gestures are universal and, instead of clarifying a message, a gesture could create confusion.

Facial expression

Facial expression reveals a great deal about our feelings. Think of a grimace of pain, a wide grin of happiness, a worried frown. In fact, a blank facial expression makes it much harder to interpret what is being said.

Eye contact

Eye contact is very important and sometimes it is difficult to know if a person is telling the truth unless you can look into their eyes. Holding someone's gaze is a sign of intimacy, but to do so with a person you don't know well can feel uncomfortable, even threatening. During most conversations your gaze will flit to and from another's face.

When working with babies and very young children it helps to exaggerate elements of non-verbal communication to provide more clues about your spoken message.

Key terms

Body language: communication expressed through gestures, poses and posture

Over to you!

Take some time to watch people in conversation with each other and notice their non-verbal communication. Be aware of body language, gestures, facial expression, eye contact, proximity, orientation, posture and touch.

Verbal communication

Verbal communication is about the choice of words being spoken and also the way the words are said.

Vocabulary

Choosing words that are appropriate to a child's age and stage is important. If you use complicated words your meaning might be lost. Equally, if you speak in very simple terms to a young person or adult this may come across as being patronising.

Tone of voice

Tone of voice often reveals the emotional message being conveyed. A parent may scold, 'Don't use that tone of voice with me,' to a child speaking disrespectfully. Babies and children are particularly sensitive to tone of voice and will, for example, pick up if a person is angry, even if angry words aren't being spoken.

Pitch of voice

Pitch of voice relates to how low or high your voice is. Speaking in a low voice can be calming and soothing, but too low and you can sound boring. A high pitch can sound shrill, but you will probably find that when talking to young children you naturally raise the pitch of your voice as this has been found to appeal to babies and attract their attention more.

Responding appropriately

The following qualities will help you respond appropriately to the communication of others.

▶ Awareness of how your communication is being received. Look for non-verbal cues that indicate the recipient's interest and understanding and, equally, those that indicate misunderstanding or boredom.

▶ Sensitivity to tune in to your recipient's emotional responses to your words.

▶ Flexibility to change the way you say something in order to clarify your meaning and increase understanding.

Over to you!

Make a point of listening to yourself and others when speaking. Notice the tone and pitch of voice and how this contributes to the message being communicated. Make notes about your observations.

Communication techniques

Some communication techniques assist in the process of responding to the reactions of others.

Echoing

Echoing is a technique whereby you repeat back what a person has said in a way that both checks your understanding of their words and also affirms the underlying feeling being expressed. For example, if a child is crying and tells you another child ruined their painting, you might say, 'I'm sorry Jonah splashed water on your picture making you feel it is spoilt.'

Mirroring

Mirroring is a communication technique used to improve **rapport** with another person. In many cases it happens naturally, where one person imitates the other person's physical positions and mannerisms, their tone of voice, word use and communication style.

Asking questions

If you want a person to express their ideas and feelings it is best to ask **open questions** that invite broader responses. 'What would you like to do after lunch?' is an example, where a child is free to choose a response. If you ask a **closed question** the answer is usually reduced to one word. For example, 'Would you like to go to the park after lunch?' invites a 'yes' or 'no' response.

Key terms

Closed questions: questions that are worded in a way that invites a one word, yes or no answer

Open questions: questions that are worded in a way that invites a full response in answer

Rapport: a relationship of mutual understanding or trust and agreement between people

Over to you!

Think about people you know who you would judge to be good communicators.

- ▶ *What is it about the words they use and the way they say them that makes their communication successful?*
- ▶ *Have you noticed them using any particular communication techniques to good effect?*

Practical Assessment Task   2.1 2.2 2.3 2.4

Direct contact and face-to-face work with the children, young people and families provide ideal opportunities for demonstrating that you are able to establish and adapt to individual's communication and language needs, wishes and preferences. To complete this assessment task you need to think about how you communicate with children or young people, parents, carers, colleagues and other professionals. You need to show that you are able to do the following.

1. Establish the individual's communication and language needs, wishes and preferences.
2. Describe factors that influence the effectiveness of communication with the person.
3. Use a range of communication methods (verbal and non-verbal) and styles to meet the individual's communication needs, wishes and preferences.
4. Respond to individuals' reactions appropriately when communicating with them.

Your evidence for this task must be based on your practice in a real work environment and must be in a format that is acceptable to your assessor.

How do people from different backgrounds use and interpret communication methods differently?

Communication is all about sharing with one another and yet each person communicates slightly differently according to their different backgrounds and experiences.

The impact of differences

Diversity is something to be celebrated and enjoyed, but our differences can also lead to misunderstandings and different interpretations of the same communication. Have a look at Figure 1.7 for some of the major causes of difference.

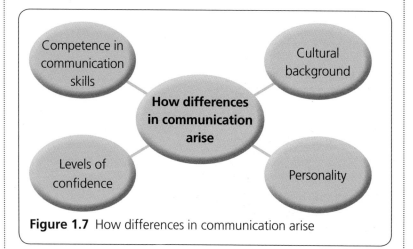

Figure 1.7 How differences in communication arise

Cultural background

Cultural differences refer to a variety of different influences, such as family background, peer group religion and ethnicity. These all play a part in shaping the way a person views the world and responds to it. Cultural differences are revealed by particular attitudes, values and practices, all of which have a bearing on how a person communicates and understands the communication of others. For example, if an individual comes from a family where it is usual to make decisions through noisy and heated discussions, this person might find it difficult to accept an order without question.

Personality

Although individuals share personality traits in common with others, the unique make-up of these and the way they operate together is individual to that person. One individual might be quiet and reserved, another enthusiastic and bubbly and this will affect the way each communicates and responds to communication.

Levels of confidence

All communication requires a certain amount of confidence to speak up, or make a statement, or share with others through spoken or written words. Sometimes a person has had their confidence undermined by a previous experience of communication, such as being laughed at for using a word wrongly, or always coming last in spelling tests. Confidence can be built up over time but can be knocked down in seconds, by a thoughtless or unkind response.

Competence in communication skills

Literacy skills refer to a person's competence in reading, writing and speaking in a particular language. Children and young people will be at different levels of competence in literacy and need to be communicated with at a level they can cope with. Remember too that some adults struggle with literacy and may feel embarrassed by their difficulties. As well as literacy skills, some individuals will have better access to and be more competent using information and computer technology (ICT) than others. You should not assume that everyone you have dealings with at work has access to the internet and email, or mobile phones, or that they are competent in using such technology.

Over to you!

Think about the different influences on your communication, in terms of cultural background, personality, confidence and competence.

▶ Can you work out what might have shaped the way you communicate and respond to the communication of others?

▶ How is this similar and different to the experiences of friends and colleagues?

Practical Assessment Task

3.1

The children, young people and families who use the services of your work setting may have very different backgrounds and a diverse range of communication needs and preferences. To complete this assessment task you need to focus on a child, young person or family with whom you work and explain how their background leads them to use and/or interpret communication methods in different ways.

The evidence for this task must be assessed in a real work environment and must result from your practice. You should ensure that you protect the confidentiality of the people you refer to in any discussion or written work you produce.

Identifying and overcoming barriers to communication

Your assessment criteria:

3.2 Identify barriers to effective communication

3.3 Demonstrate ways to overcome barriers to communication

Communication is a complex process and can be interrupted at any stage by a number of different barriers. These might be to do with forming a coherent message, or relaying it to another person. Problems may also be encountered with reliably receiving a message, or making sense of its content.

Where communication goes wrong

It is useful to look at different barriers to communication in relation to each stage of the communication process, as shown in Figure 1.8.

Figure 1.8 Communication process and barriers

Stage	Barrier	Example
Selection of information to be relayed in a message	• Sender speaks a different language • Sender cannot speak well • Poor or incomplete information selection	Clara's baby has a high fever, but she forgets to mention to the doctor that he was given his vaccination that morning.
Encode message by deciding on method of transfer: via conversation or written means	• Sender chooses an inappropriate method • Sender cannot express message clearly, in speech or writing	The predictive text function on Ralph's new mobile phone means his message, 'Cool' gets sent as 'Book'.
Transfer message speak face to face speak by phone write an email, text message or letter	• Equipment may fail • May be interrupted • May be interfered with • May go astray	Leta's mum finds the head teacher's newsletter crumpled in the bottom of her school bag, weeks out of date!
Receive message	• Hearing difficulties • Visual difficulties • Distraction • Recipient may not recognise who the message is aimed at	Tobias saw the message from his boss saying, 'Come to my office at 12', but thought it was meant for his colleague.
Decode message	• Wrong interpretation • Difficulties in understanding • Lack of time	Viv was so frightened by her father shouting that she couldn't take in what he was saying.
Respond to message	• Recipient may fail to respond • Response may be late • Response may be inappropriate	Alexi didn't understand that RSVP meant she must reply to the theatre invitation, so her friend didn't book her a ticket.

Finding ways around barriers to communication

As well as written and spoken words there are other routes to communicate information. Some of these can be used alongside spoken or written words to strengthen communication and some can be used in place of words.

▶ *Public information signs* convey important information without any – or many – words, using commonly understood symbols, such as on road and health and safety signs. These are especially vital for those who do not speak English and those who have problems with reading and writing.

▶ *Sign language:* British sign language (BSL) is a recognised language that helps people who are deaf to communicate with others. It uses a sign for each letter of the alphabet and signs for different objects and places, as well as having signs that express ideas and concepts.

▶ *Language support,* which illustrate and therefore emphasise spoken words (There is more about this on pages 26–27.):
   – *Picture Exchange Communication System* (PECS)
   – *Makaton.*

Practical Assessment Task   3.2   3.3

Communication is not always straightforward and a number of barriers can be encountered when working in children's and young people's settings. Think about barriers that occur where you work when communicating with a child or young person, with parents or with colleagues and other practitioners. To complete this assessment task you need to show that you can follow the procedure outlined below.

1. Identify some of the barriers to communication in your work setting.

2. Explain how each barrier makes communication less effective.

3. Demonstrate ways to reduce or overcome each barrier.

Your evidence for this task must be based on your practice in a real work environment and must be witnessed by or be in a format that is acceptable to your assessor.

Over to you!

Can you recall a situation where you experienced a communication 'breakdown'?

▶ *At what stage in the communication process did the break occur?*

▶ *How was it resolved?*

23

What strategies help to clarify misunderstandings?

Communication is a very complex process and working with children and young people is a complex area, so it is inevitable that misunderstandings will arise from time to time.

Strategies to improve understanding

When a misunderstanding is unavoidable it is important to have a range of methods to clarify the situation and improve communication, such as:

▶ adapt your message

▶ change the environment

▶ ask for feedback

▶ allow time

▶ apologise.

Adapt your message

Sometimes the message needs to be said or written in a different way. Perhaps the tone needs to change, or its style. The language you have used might need to be simplified. Maybe a phone conversation has been unsatisfactory in some way, but a face-to-face meeting would help to establish better communication.

Change the environment

It might be necessary to make changes to the environment to enable better communication. For example, if you are conducting a meeting in an office where people are constantly coming in and out, or the phone keeps ringing, you will need to find a quieter place to speak.

Ask for feedback

In most situations it is acceptable to stop the flow of conversation, whether it is with a child, a young person or an adult, to check that you have understood correctly what is being spoken about. Equally, you can check that the person you are communicating with can hear you and understand you.

Allow time

Much of communication happens while we are busy doing other things, but sometimes in order to make sure a message is received and understood you need to make time to have a proper conversation. By doing this you may find you actually save time.

Make an apology

Sometimes it is important to take responsibility for a misunderstanding and say you are sorry. A sincere apology can help to restore confidence and allow for the relationship to continue to build, on a firmer foundation.

Practical Assessment Task   3.4

An awareness of strategies to sort out communication misunderstandings is vital when you work with children and young people and their families. To complete this assessment task you need to focus on situations in which misunderstandings could arise in your work setting, or which you have experienced or witnessed. These might involve a child or young person in your care, their family members or a colleague.

1. Briefly describe two situations where a communication misunderstanding occurred (being careful to change names and maintain confidentiality if these actually occurred in your workplace).
2. Describe the strategies you used, or would use, to clarify the misunderstanding in each case.
3. Explain why you think each strategy would help.

Your evidence for this task must be based on your practice in a real work environment and must be in a format that is acceptable to your assessor.

Over to you!

Think about the last time you apologised about something.

▶ Was a breakdown in communication part of the problem?
▶ What was the effect of your apology?
▶ How did it make you feel?

Your assessment criteria:

3.5 Explain how to access extra support or services to enable individuals to communicate effectively

How can you access support and services to enable effective communication?

There is a range of support available to enable effective communication with the children and young people you work with and the adult members of their family. Importantly, individuals need to be informed about these services and should be able to access them. For example:

▶ Support is available via local authorities and services such as the NHS, education and children and families services.

▶ Help is also available from national charities, such as ICAN, for speech and language needs and for **autistic spectrum disorder (ASD)** with the National Autistic Society.

▶ The Citizens Advice Bureau (CAB) is another source for advice and assistance on advocacy, translation and interpretation.

▶ In addition there may be projects operating in local areas and these are likely to be advertised at a local library or community centre, or in a health centre. See also Chapter 16, page 402.

Key terms

Autistic spectrum disorder (ASD): a developmental disorder which makes it difficult to make sense of the world and affects communication and social interaction

Communication support

Communication support tends to include these categories:

▶ speech and language services

▶ translation and interpreting services

▶ language service professionals (lsps)

▶ advocacy services.

Speech and language services

Speech and language therapy is concerned with the management of disorders of swallowing, speech, language and communication in children and adults. **Speech, language and communication therapists (SLCTs)** work closely with parents, carers and other health and education professionals. They help children who have communication problems due to mild, moderate or severe learning difficulties, physical disabilities, such as cleft palate and spasticity, language delay or impairment, hearing difficulties, speech impediments such as stammering, as well as autistic spectrum disorder and social interaction difficulties.

Children can be referred for speech and language therapy via the GP or health visitor, or through education services. It is also possible for a family to self-refer their child by contacting the local service directly.

As a care worker you might have to work closely with a SLCT. This might mean supporting a child to carry out exercises, or using language aids such as **Makaton**, which is a signing system, or the **Picture Exchange Communication System (PECS)** (Figure 1.9), which is a visual system, both of which support language.

Key terms

Makaton: a system that uses signs and symbols alongside speech to help people with learning and/or communication difficulties to communicate

Picture Exchange Communication System (PECS): a system particularly used to reinforce communication with children who have autistic spectrum disorder for rewarding social interaction, where the child exchanges a picture of an object which they want or need in order to receive the desired object

Speech, language and communication therapists (SLCTs): practitioners who assess and treat speech, language and communication problems in people of all ages

Picture Exchange Communication System (PECS)

Translation and interpreting services

Translation services may be required for children and their parents who speak a language other than English. Information documents about services and benefits are now widely available in different languages.

Similarly interpreters can be brought in to help translate conversation and discussions during meetings. Interpreters are trained not to give their own opinion, but to reflect whatever those present wish to convey.

If meetings are of a specialist nature and particular terms or jargon are likely to be used the interpreter will need notice of this to enable them to prepare.

Language Service Professionals (LSPs)

There are also translation and interpreter services for people with sensory impairment. Local authorities and services, such as the police and National Health Services are obliged to provide communication support for individuals:

▶ when visiting a doctor, optician or hospital

▶ if interviewed by the police

▶ when attending court or at a public meeting.

Support for those with sensory disability includes:

▶ British sign language (BSL) interpreters

▶ deafblind interpreters

▶ lip-speakers

▶ notetakers and speech-to-text reporters (palantypists).

Advocacy services

Children will be assigned an **advocate** in circumstances where there is no other adult, such as a parent, who can speak up for them, for example, children in local authority care or from an asylum seeking family where the parent doesn't speak English.

Key terms

Advocate: a supportive person who speaks in an official capacity on a person's behalf and in their best interests

Practical Assessment Task 3.5

Some people have communication difficulties that require extra support or services to enable them to communicate effectively. To complete this assessment task you need to focus on a child, young person or family you work with and explain how they can access extra support or services to enable them to communicate effectively. You should think about and understand:

1. the nature of the individual's communication difficulty

2. how services, equipment and professional support can be identified and contacted.

Your evidence for this task must be based on your practice in a real work environment and must be in a format that is acceptable to your assessor.

Over to you!

Think about all the resources you know of locally and nationally.

- *Do you know what support and advice is available in your placement or work setting?*
- *What about local authority projects or national charities?*

What does confidentiality mean?

When you work in a care setting you will regularly deal with information to do with the children or young people in your care and their families. Some of this is personal and private. Confidentiality refers to the need to handle personal and private information in ways that are appropriate, safe and professional and meet legal requirements.

Why confidentiality is important

There are three main reasons why confidentiality is an important issue in a care setting.

1. Trust

The relationships you build with children and young people and their families are central to your care role. If you share their personal information with others who have no need or right to know you risk breaking their trust in you. Individuals also need to know that there are secure systems and procedures operating in the care setting to protect confidential information.

Your assessment criteria:

4.1 Explain the meaning of the term confidentiality

Key terms

Confidentiality: the requirement to keep personal information private and only share it with those who need to know

2. Safety

Some information must be kept confidential for safety reasons. For example, a child's wellbeing might be in danger if an estranged parent who has been refused contact because of previous abuse finds out where he or she is now living, through a breach in confidentiality.

3. The law

It is a legal requirement for organisations to manage and safeguard personal information correctly.

Practical Assessment Task 4.1

Confidentiality is an important element of communication when you work with children and young people. To complete this assessment task you need to identify the different types of communication in your work setting and explain how the principle of confidentiality affects each one. Your work for this assessment task should do the following.

1. Explain the meaning of the term 'confidentiality'.

2. Use examples from your own practice in a real work environment.

Your evidence for this task must be based on your own practice and should be in a format that is acceptable to your assessor.

Over to you!

Think about the information you receive and give at work.

▶ Are you aware of the information that is confidential?

▶ Do you know how to handle this information?

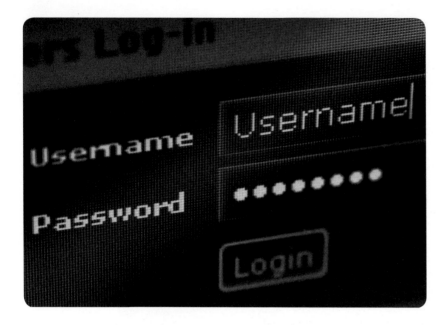

How do you maintain confidentiality at work?

A great deal of information will pass around at your place of work through conversations, hand-over reports, letters, written reports and emails. Some of it will be confidential and you need to know how to manage this appropriately.

Types of confidential information

You will need to deal appropriately with confidential information of various types when working in a care setting. If you are unsure whether information is confidential in nature ask a senior member of staff.

Spoken information

Oral information can be transferred via face-to-face conversations or over the phone. These might take place during meetings or in less formal settings. If you need to discuss a confidential matter with a child, young person or family member, or with a colleague or visiting practitioner, make sure you find somewhere private where you will not be interrupted or overheard. In care settings it is not generally the policy to discuss confidential matters over the telephone, unless you can verify that the person is who they claim to be. Never leave confidential messages on an answering machine. Do not at any time be tempted to gossip about confidential work matters.

Paper information

Personal records including notes, reports and letters concerning individual children or young people and their families, should be kept together in a file which is locked in a safe place. Remember that a lockable filing cabinet is only safe if keys are not left lying around. Equally, rooms with keypads are not secure if the door has been propped open! Avoid leaving documents lying around such as diaries, telephone messages and faxes, if these contain confidential information. Many organisations have a policy that personal records must not be removed from the workplace, because these could be lost, damaged, seen by others, or the information could be taken and used wrongly.

Electronic information

These days a great deal of information is stored and transferred electronically, via computer. Computer files should be protected using passwords which are only shared with authorised individuals. Care must be taken to close private documents after use, to prevent individuals who are passing from catching sight of the screen. Be vigilant when transporting information between computers via memory sticks or discs. Make sure the memory stick doesn't get lost and that the information doesn't remain on the hard drive of the computer on which it was read.

Over to you!

How is confidential information handled where you work? What are the security measures like? Are you careful with computer passwords?

Practical Assessment Task

4.2

When you work with children and young people and their families you will need to communicate different types of information. In doing so, you will need to recognise what is private and how to keep it confidential. Think about these issues in your placement or setting.

1. The types of information concerning a child, young person or family that are confidential, in both paper and electronic format (making sure you consider spoken information such as conversations, in person and over the phone, both casual and more formal and written information in notes, records and assessments).
2. How you keep the information confidential.

Your evidence for this task must be based on your practice in a real work environment and must be in a format that is acceptable to your assessor.

When should information be kept confidential?

There will be a confidentiality policy where you work that includes procedures to guide the way confidential information is recorded, handled, stored and shared. As a care worker you have a responsibility to find out about these and work within the guidelines.

Privacy law

There is no specific privacy law in the UK, but issues related to privacy and confidential information are included in legislation.

▶ Privacy is highlighted as a right in the *United Nations Declaration of Human Rights (Article 8)*.

▶ *The Data Protection Act 1998* concerns the way personal information must be acquired, handled and stored.

▶ *The Freedom of Information Act 2000* protects the rights of individuals to have access to personal data that is held about them (see Figure 1.9 opposite).

The *Information Commissioner's Office* (ICO) is an independent authority set up to ensure that organisations understand their responsibilities and the public their rights about confidential information. Most care settings are required to register with the ICO.

Over to you!

When you work with children and young people you need to make sure you maintain confidentiality during social conversations, both in and out of work.

▶ *What measures do you take when chatting with friends and family about your work, to make sure you do not breach confidentiality?*

▶ *How about when you are socialising with colleagues?*

Confidential information and the law

You will need to follow legal requirements for confidentiality in your children's and young people's setting, as shown in Figure 1.9.

Figure 1.9 Confidential information and the law

Legal requirements	Example
You may only obtain information that is relevant to your requirements.	Carly was told it breached privacy to record whether the teenagers in her support group were sexually active.
You may only use information for the purpose for which it was collected.	Aibileen cannot use information from paediatric medical records for her research study unless she approaches the parents for permission.
Do not disclose information to others unless there is a legitimate reason.	Jake passed his reading test, but his teacher would not say how well his friend did, because it was confidential.
You must keep personal information up to date and not keep records longer than necessary.	The new playgroup treasurer shredded a letter to a parent about unpaid fees because the debt had been settled.
You must keep information in a safe place.	The youth group purchased a lockable filing cabinet in which to keep service users' contact details.
You must keep to guidelines about transferring information out of the country.	When Alfie emigrated his primary school contacted Ofsted and the ICO for advice about transferring educational records.
Individuals have a right to know what information is held about them and in most cases may access this.	Elizbar's written request to read the medical records was acknowledged and he was sent a copy.
Inaccurate information must be corrected as soon as you realise there is an error.	Aba was upset to see 'father unknown' recorded in her notes because in fact he had died before she was born.

Case study

It's Friday night and the staff from Long Acre nursery have met up at the pub as usual. It's nice to relax together, but Mickey is annoyed about one of the mums complaining about the nursery requesting money for the summer outing. 'She said we're always scrounging off parents!' he exclaimed. 'She's got a cheek, when she's claiming benefits. Who's the bigger scrounger?' Natalie remarks that he shouldn't worry. To distract him, she does an impersonation of three-year-old Benji, tongue hanging out, trying in vain to use scissors. Everyone falls about laughing.

1. In what ways has confidentiality been breached?
2. What could the potential consequences be?
3. What would be a more acceptable way for Mickey to discuss his upset?

Disclosing confidential information

There are some situations when confidentiality needs to be breached to report information to a higher authority. The **disclosure** of private and personal information should only take place when:

▶ withholding the information is likely to threaten the safety and wellbeing of others

▶ a crime has been, or is likely to be, committed.

How to disclose confidential information

It is your responsibility to check the policy and procedure at your place of work about disclosure of confidential information, in order to be clear about how to act and who to contact should the need arise.

Speak to a senior person within or outside your work setting who is able to act on the information appropriately.

It is a mistake to think this is only a matter for senior care staff, because it is common for children and young people to prefer to confide in a junior member of staff whom they feel they can relate to more closely.

Never promise confidentiality to an individual, but reassure the person you would only share the information if necessary and that you will inform them if you need to do so.

Whistle-blowing

Whistle-blowing is a term used to describe the disclosure of wrong-doing within an organisation to a higher authority or the media. This might be about unsafe or illegal working practices or abuse within the system. The Public Interest Disclosure Act 1998 protects whistle-blowers but requires firm evidence, including evidence that it would not have been possible to use the internal system for complaints within the company.

Your assessment criteria:

4.3 Describe the potential tension between maintaining an individual's confidentiality and disclosing concerns

Key terms

Disclosure: the breaching of a confidence in order to report information that may threaten the wellbeing of an individual

Whistle-blower: a person who reveals wrongdoing within an organisation to the public, via the media, or to a higher authority

Over to you!

You may hear colleagues talk about sharing confidential information on a 'need to know' basis only. What do you think is meant by this term? Does your place of work ask parents' permission to collect and store certain information about the children or young people in your care?

Case study

Fifteen-year-old Dena is furious with youth worker Latif. Right in front of everyone else at the club she screams at him that he's ruined her life and she's reporting him to the police for breaching her human right to privacy. Latif is shaken by this outburst and is concerned that he may have made a mistake by informing Dena's social worker of her plan to meet a friend she'd made over the internet. He tells another youth worker that he tried to warn Dena of the danger she might be putting herself in, but she wouldn't listen.

1. Was Latif right to disclose this confidential information?

2. How would you have handled the situation?

Practical Assessment Task

4.3

When you work with children and young people you will get to know confidential information concerning their personal situation. It is also likely there will be occasions when information must be disclosed to maintain a person's safety or wellbeing. To complete this assessment task you need to follow these steps.

1. Identify a situation where a potential tension between maintaining or breaking confidentiality may occur.

2. Complete a table like the one here by describing reasons why information relating to the situation should remain confidential and alternative reasons why this information should be disclosed.

Confidentiality situation	Reasons why information should remain confidential	Reasons for disclosing confidential information

Your evidence for this task must be based on your practice in a real work environment and must be in a format that is acceptable to your assessor.

All personal information, such as height and weight, must be kept confidential

Are you ready for assessment?

AC	What do you know now?	Assessment task	✓
1.1	The different reasons why people communicate	Page 5	
1.2	How communication affects relationships in the work setting	Page 9	

Your tutor or assessor may need to observe your competence in your placement or work setting.

AC	What can you do now?	Assessment task	✓
2.1	Demonstrate how to establish the communication and language needs, wishes and preferences of individuals	Page 19	
2.2	Describe the factors to consider when promoting effective communication	Page 19	
2.3	Demonstrate a range of communication methods and styles to meet individual needs	Page 19	
2.4	Demonstrate how to respond to an individual's reactions when communicating	Page 19	
3.1	Explain how people from different backgrounds may use and/or interpret communication methods in different ways	Page 21	
3.2	Identify barriers to effective communication	Page 23	
3.3	Demonstrate ways to overcome barriers to communication	Page 23	
3.4	Demonstrate strategies that can be used to clarify misunderstandings	Page 25	
3.5	Explain how to access extra support or services to enable individuals to communicate effectively	Page 29	
4.1	Explain the meaning of the term confidentiality	Page 31	
4.2	Demonstrate ways to maintain confidentiality in day-to-day communication	Page 33	
4.3	Describe the potential tension between maintaining an individual's confidentiality and disclosing concerns	Page 37	

2 | Engage in personal development in health, social care, or children's and young people's settings (SHC 32)

Assessment of this unit

The focus of this unit is on developing your own practice when working with children and young people and their families. You will look in detail at the duties and responsibilities of your work role and see how these relate to the laws and standards required of you in the workplace. It will provide you with tools to help you reflect on your practice, evaluate your progress and create your own personal development plan.

To complete this unit successfully you will need to produce evidence of your knowledge, as shown in the 'What you need to know' chart opposite. You also need to produce evidence of your practical ability, as shown in the 'What you need to do' chart. The 'What you need to do' criteria must be assessed in a real work environment by a vocationally competent assessor. Your tutor or assessor will help you to prepare for your assessment and the tasks suggested in this chapter will help you to create the evidence you need.

CHAPTER 2

AC What you need to know

1.1	The duties and responsibilities of your own work role
1.2	Expectations about your own work role as expressed in relevant standards

AC What you need to do

2.1	Explain the importance of reflective practice in continuously improving the quality of service provided
2.2	Demonstrate the ability to reflect on practice
2.3	Describe how own values, belief systems and experiences may affect working practice
3.1	Evaluate own knowledge, performance and understanding against relevant standards
3.2	Demonstrate use of feedback to evaluate own performance and inform development
4.1	Identify sources of support for planning and reviewing own development
4.2	Demonstrate how to work with others to review and prioritise own learning needs, professional interests and development opportunities
4.3	Demonstrate how to work with others to agree own personal development plan
5.1	Evaluate how learning activities have affected practice
5.2	Demonstrate how reflective practice has led to improved ways of working
5.3	Show how to record progress in relation to personal development

This unit is designed to develop your working practice, which is relevant to every chapter of this book, but has particular links to other mandatory units:

CYP 3.2	Promote child and young person development
EYMP 2	Promote learning and development in the early years
EYMP 4	Professional practice in early years settings

Some of your learning will be repeated in these units and will give you the chance to review your knowledge and understanding.

Understand what is required for competence in your own work role

Your assessment criteria:

1.1 Describe the duties and responsibilities of your own work role

Key terms

Collaborate: work together with others to achieve a shared goal

Duty: something a person is expected or required to do

Job description: a written outline of the duties and responsibilities of a work role

Person specification: a written outline of the qualifications, experience and qualities needed to perform a particular work role

Responsibility: what a person is expected to do

What are the duties and responsibilities of your own work role?

To be an effective children and young people's practitioner and to be successful in gaining your diploma qualification, you need to identify and understand the specific requirements of your own work role.

Job descriptions

Job descriptions differ from job to job, but many ask for similar basic requirements. Most job descriptions include the following information:

▶ **duties:** the roles and tasks you are expected to carry out at work

▶ **responsibilities:** the obligations you hold, particularly towards the children and young people in your care and their families, but also to the colleagues within your team, any visiting practitioners and your employer

▶ **person specification:** the qualifications, experience and qualities or abilities that a person requires for a particular job. If you are a student on placement your school or college and the placement organisation should **collaborate** to produce guidelines relating to your role.

Qualities and skills

Figure 2.1 and the text on page 43 describe the qualities and skills you will need to show when carrying out your work role.

▶ *Knowledge:* this will be reflected in the way you perform your duties and apply your learning and understanding to your role.

▶ *Skills:* these are demonstrated through the competence and confidence with which you carry out your work tasks.

▶ *Functional skills:* these are the literacy, numeracy and ICT skills required to carry out duties and responsibilities.

▶ *Appropriate attitude:* this refers to your manner and approach at work as you respond to a range of different people and situations.

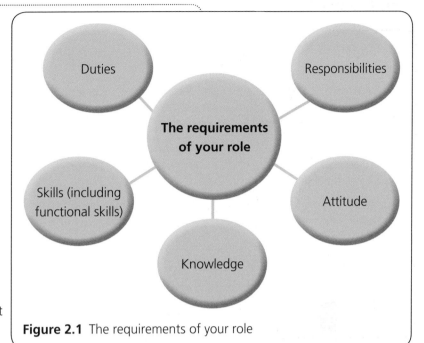

Figure 2.1 The requirements of your role

Functional skills

Functional skills are the underlying skills required in terms of literacy, numeracy and ICT (information and computer technology) to enable you to carry out your duties. Here are some examples.

▶ 'Observe and document children's behaviour during play' requires a level of competence in reading and writing English.

▶ 'Reporting to and liaising with parents and carers' requires a level of fluency in speaking English.

▶ 'Monitoring statistics related to children's attendance at playgroup' requires a level of mathematical ability.

▶ 'Keeping computerised records' requires the ability to use ICT equipment.

Over to you!

▶ *What does your job description say about the duties and responsibilities associated with your work role?*

▶ *Ask your employer for a copy of your job description, if you don't have one. If you are a student on placement, check your placement guidelines to identify the duties and responsibilities associated with your work role.*

Roles and responsibilities

Job descriptions indicate what your employer expects for your work role.

▶ 'Experienced' and 'qualified' mean previous experience, or a certain level of expertise is required. Most job descriptions will specify whether a skill is needed or just desired.

▶ 'Willing to be trained' or to 'undergo further study' means that previous experience is not necessarily needed, but personal and professional development is expected.

▶ 'Assist with' and 'help out' indicate that your role supports a more senior role.

▶ 'Organise' and 'operate' suggest you will be expected to take the initiative and perhaps lead others in carrying out a duty.

Read figures 2.2 and 2.3, which show example elements of job descriptions.

Your assessment criteria:

1.1 Describe the duties and responsibilities of your own work role

Nursery worker

Duty: plan and provide a weekly menu of nutritious snacks for the children in your nursery group.

Responsibilities: provide nutritious food that is suitable for and attractive to three-year-olds and helps them to broaden their experience.

Knowledge: basic nutrition and its relationship to health; child development and psychology; potential hazards (choking, allergy).

Skills: safe food handling and preparation (hand washing; food hygiene); basic paediatric first aid (for anaphylaxis, choking); communication (persuading child to taste and try; rewarding with praise); observation and reporting about how children manage and enjoy their snack, interact with others.

Attitude: calm, reassuring, positive and encouraging manner.

Figure 2.2 Example of elements of job description for a nursery worker

Youth club volunteer

Duty: plan a weekly outdoor activity.

Responsibilities: provide interesting and challenging activities with regard for safety from accidents, injury and other harm.

Knowledge: health and safety; development and psychology of adolescence.

Skills: risk assessment and management; communication skills (persuading young people to participate; acknowledging achievement).

Attitude: encouraging and empowering manner; reliable and clear-thinking.

Figure 2.3 Example of elements of job description for a youth club volunteer

Starting a new job

Clear guidance is needed for anyone who starts a new job. Your manager should ensure that you have an **induction** that covers:

▶ practical issues such as the layout of the work setting and the normal routines

▶ any special ideas and values that underpin the work of the setting

▶ the **policies** and **procedures** used in the setting, especially in relation to health and safety

▶ an introduction to your colleagues and other support workers

▶ an introduction to the children and parents who use the setting.

It is professional to make use of the greater experience and assistance of your supervisor and work colleagues by asking questions. They will expect you to clarify issues, and this avoids mistakes being made. This process will help you take on board all the new information that you need to succeed in the job.

Knowledge Assessment Task   1.1

Think about your role in your placement or work setting as a child or young person's worker or volunteer (or, if you are not yet in post, think about any contact you have had with children or young people lately). Create a job description to cover the various aspects of your role, using the headings below. If possible, compare this to your actual job description, so that you can see if you (or your employer!) has overlooked anything.

▶ **Duties**
▶ **Responsibilities**
▶ **Attitude**
▶ **Knowledge**
▶ **Skills**

You should keep the written work that you produce for this activity as evidence towards your assessment.

Over to you!

Think about a recent interaction you have had with a child or young person at work.

▶ *What duties and responsibilities were required of you during this interaction?*

▶ *What particular qualities were needed by you, in terms of knowledge, skills and attitude?*

Ask these two questions on a regular basis to help you analyse your work role.

You could carry out this exercise with a colleague, because sharing ideas can increase your understanding.

Key terms

Induction: a period of basic training

Policies: written documents that set out an organisation's approach towards a particular issue

Procedures: documents that set out in detail how a particular issue should be dealt with or how particular tasks should be carried out

How do expectations for your work role correspond to relevant standards?

Your assessment criteria:

1.2 Explain expectations about your own work role as expressed in relevant standards

When you work with children and young people you are obliged to work in ways that:

▶ fulfil legal obligations

▶ meet the requirements of your profession

▶ conform to any underlying ideals and **ethos** of your service.

Together these are referred to as **standards**, which you must keep to and which must be reflected in the way you carry out your work.

Types of standards

Standards can be analysed in terms of:

▶ legislation ▶ professional guidelines ▶ underlying principles.

Legislation – laws and legal regulations

Standards related to legislation concerning children and young people cover two major aspects of care (see Figures 2.4 and 2.5):

▶ protection – preventing problems occurring and enabling intervention when things go wrong

▶ provision – creating the best possible environment within which children and young people can learn, thrive and develop.

Key terms

Ethos: the philosophy or ideals that underpin and guide the way a service is provided

Standards: may include legislation, codes of practice, regulations, minimum standards, national occupational standards, as well as any underlying ethos that informs the way a service is provided

Figure 2.4 Legislation for the protection of children and young people

Country	Act	Reason for law
England and Wales	Children Act 1989 and 2004	The need to work in ways that safeguard children and young people, protecting them from harm and ensuring their rights are upheld.
Scotland	The Children Act 1995 and 2003 Children Hearings Act 2011	
Northern Ireland	Protection of Children and Vulnerable Adults Order 2003; Safeguarding of Vulnerable Groups Order 2007)	

Figure 2.5 Provision for the best possible environment for children and young people

Country	Act	Reason for law
England and Wales	Every Child Matters (ECM), 2003; Children Act, 2004 and 2006	The need to provide care that promotes health and happiness, offers challenge and a sense of achievement and enables children and young people to develop into fulfilled and contributing citizens.
Scotland	Children Act 1995	
Northern Ireland	Children Act 2001	

Professional guidelines

Standards linked to a profession differ according to the area of childcare and whether you work in England, Northern Ireland, Scotland or Wales. Standards also sometimes link to a system of registration for which you must provide evidence that your working practice fulfils them. Figure 2.6 gives examples, but check which relate to your role.

Figure 2.6 Examples of professional standards

Area of UK	Standard	Who it concerns
England and Wales; NI	Every Child Matters (0–19 yrs), five outcomes	All child and young people's care workers
Scotland	Getting it Right for Every Child, 2011	All child and young people's care workers
England 0–5 yrs	Early Years Foundation Stage	Early years workers, such as nursery and primary teachers and staff
Northern Ireland 0–6 years	Early Years Strategy	
Scotland 0–8 years	Curriculum for Excellence	
Wales 0–3 years 3–7 years	Flying Start Foundation Phase	
England	Child Register requirements	Child minders and home-carers
Scotland	National Care Standards for Early Education and Childcare up to the age of 16	Child minders; homecarers; playgroups; out-of-school clubs; nurseries and schools
England	National Minimum Standards 2010	Care workers for children's homes and adoption and foster care; boarding schools
England; Wales; NI	National Occupational Standards (NOS) for supporting teaching and learning	Teaching assistants, learning support assistants and any other staff who provide support to children and young people in schools
Scotland	Scottish Social Services Council Codes of Practice	Social Services workers
UK	The UK Scouting Association 'Young People First' code of practice	For all volunteers with Beavers, Cubs, Scouts, Rainbows, Brownies and Guides

Some professions check whether standards are upheld, for example, the Office for Standards in Education (Ofsted) inspects nurseries and schools to make sure EYFS is being implemented adequately. Self-evaluation is part of some inspection processes, for example for child minders. The reliability of self-assessment is checked during the subsequent inspection process.

Key terms

Self-evaluation: a process carried out (usually online) by the care worker who assesses their own progress in providing care that fulfils standards

Case study

Justyna started working as a child minder six months ago and is hoping to take on more children and build her career. She has been given an inspection date and is keen to receive a high rating so the parents using her service feel confident and recommend her to others. She has been advised she must fill in a self-assessment evaluation online and decides there is nothing to stop her from exaggerating her performance so as to appear more impressive.

1. Is this a good idea of Justyna's? Explain why you take this viewpoint.
2. What are some of the laws and standards Justyna will need to demonstrate as an early years practitioner?
3. Who will be carrying out Justyna's inspection and what standards will they be applying?

Your assessment criteria:

1.2 Explain expectations about your own work role as expressed in relevant standards

Your own work role and the standards

You need to uphold the standards in your area of childcare and be aware of the expectations that are relevant to your position. Some key areas are summarised below.

▶ *Internal policies and procedures:* your employer should make you aware of the relevant standards as part of the internal policies and procedures, and many settings offer induction and training sessions where you have the opportunity to learn more.

▶ *The Health and Safety at Work Act (1974)* requires that employers are responsible for providing a safe and secure work environment, safe equipment, and information and training about health, safety and security. To meet the legal responsibilities, employers must carry out health and safety risk assessments, develop procedures such as fire evacuation, provide equipment such as fire extinguishers, ensure that the workplace has built-in safety features such as smoke alarms, provide information such as warning signs for fire exits, and train their employees so that they understand the requirements. As an employee, you would have a responsibility to work safely within the care setting, monitor the work environment for health and safety and report any risks.

▶ *Legislation*, such as The Children Act (2004) in England and Wales, places a legal duty on local authorities to ensure practitioners uphold and reflect the law in their working practice.

▶ *Professional standards* apply for your area of work and for the region of the UK in which you work. For example, EYFS in England requires early years practitioners to satisfy the five wellbeing requirements: safeguarding and promoting children's welfare; suitable people; suitable premises; environment and equipment; organisation and documentation.

▶ *The National Occupational Standards* (NOS) are used to develop care qualifications such as this one, and courses that seek to improve practice in the sector. Employees and students are responsible for working to the NOS. Your employer should provide ongoing support and training opportunities and you have a duty to make the most of these.

Underlying principles

Some organisations operate according to a particular ethos or philosophy that underlies the service being provided. Underlying principles may reflect the origins of a service, such as a charity that promised when it was started that 'no child will ever be turned away'. Or it may reflect its reputation that has been built up over many years of service. Some organisations have developed according to a particular philosophy, such as Steiner schools where the emphasis is on the importance of experiential and child-led learning.

Many organisations will have a 'mission statement' that explains the aims and objectives of its underlying principles and this will provide a useful indication of the ways in which you would be expected to work. Before you apply to work for an organisation it is a good idea to find out about its underlying principles – the ideals and ethos that underpin it – so that you can understand the basis for its standards and the expectations for your role.

Over to you!

▶ *Do you know where you would find a copy of the policies and procedures at work if you wanted to check something today?*

▶ *The website of the Children's Workforce Development Council (www.cwdcouncil.org.uk) provides a range of information on standards that apply to work with children and young people, along with copies of the National Occupational Standards.*

Knowledge Assessment Task

1.2

As a children and young people's workforce practitioner you must show that your work meets the standards expected by your profession and your workplace. For example, when Livvy, a playgroup leader, takes the children to a local play park she must demonstrate the requirement to keep children safe within the Early Years Foundation Stage statutory framework.

This task requires you to show how your work relates to standards.

1. Identify two key standards, codes of practice or regulations which you are expected to keep to at work.

2. Give examples of scenarios, explaining how these show some of the ways in which you fulfil these standards in your role.

You should keep the written work that you produce for this activity as evidence towards your assessment.

Your assessment criteria:

2.1 Explain the importance of reflective practice in continuously improving the quality of service provided

Key terms

Mindful: being in touch with and fully aware of the present moment, rather than operating in an automatic, routine manner

Reflective practice: a process for analysing personal work, in order to develop personal working practice and improve overall quality of service

Self-aware: taking careful note of your inner experience, especially your thoughts and feelings, and recognising the way these might impact on others

How does reflective practice improve the quality of service provided?

Reflective practice is a process to help evaluate your work. It provides opportunities to learn from your experience and develop your working practice. It is both a tool to help you analyse specific interactions or incidents that have occurred at work and a method of working in the moment that is mindful and self-aware.

The function of reflective practice

Reflective practice offers a range of opportunities to develop the way in which you work. Through the regular practice of reflecting on your work your powers of observation will improve, allowing you greater insights into those responses and interventions that bring the most positive results. By incorporating these insights into your working practice you will be able to improve your performance at work. If you work with others who are equally committed to the reflective practice process it can transform team working and thereby improve the overall quality of the service provided. Have a look at Figure 2.7, which shows the functions of reflective practice.

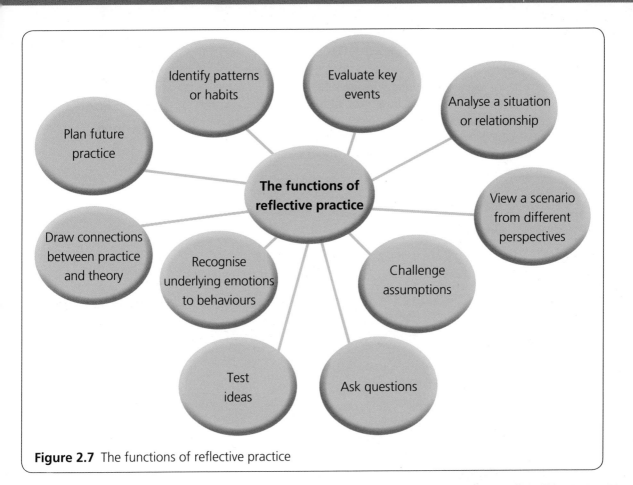

Figure 2.7 The functions of reflective practice

Sharpening observation and insights

Working with children and young people is unpredictable. This is because each person is a unique individual with different needs and preferences, which may change from day to day and even hour to hour. This means that no one approach (even to similar situations) can be guaranteed to work for every person all the time. You must be adaptable and responsive to each child or young person and every unique situation that arises. Reflective practice is a method of working that sharpens observation and offers insights during this potentially complex process.

Over to you!

Native American Indian folklore recommends that before you make a judgement about a person you should walk a mile in their moccasins.

▶ *How would you express this in your own words?*

▶ *How does the Native American Indian folklore relate to reflective practice?*

Case study

When Xavier stopped to think carefully about how things were going at the after-school club he runs, he realised that the children who attend have fewer accidents and incidents on those days when they are given a short physical activity as soon as they arrive, followed by a drink and a snack.

1. What tool is Xavier using to think about his work?
2. How does it help his working practice?
3. If you were Xavier, how would you follow up this process?

How do you carry out reflective practice?

Your assessment criteria:

2.2 Demonstrate the ability to reflect on your practice

Reflective practice brings the most benefit when you take time to carry it out on a regular, preferably daily basis. You also need to make it a priority, rather than considering it an occasional luxury that you only manage if time allows. In the long term reflective practice is a process that will save you time and which helps you use the time you have productively.

Reflective practice methods

Reflective practice is carried out in two main ways.

▶ *Reflecting-in-action*: taking place in the moment, while an issue arises or an event takes place.

▶ *Reflecting-on-action*: considering afterwards what worked well and how things could have been managed differently.

It is carried out using different methods.

▶ *Thinking*: bringing your self-awareness to a situation and considering it from all points of view.

▶ *Writing*: through a reflective journal, setting down your experiences and observations on a day-by-day basis; using writing exercises to explore a specific event or occurrence; writing what happened from another person's point of view to bring fresh understanding.

▶ *Discussion*: sharing experiences and exploring possibilities with colleagues and other practitioners at work.

▶ *Role play*: acting out a scenario, to understand better what occurs between individuals, perhaps to do with emotions and relationships, brings insights.

The reflective practice process

Here is an explanation for each step of the reflective practice process, also shown in Figure 2.8.

▶ *Time and place*: if you are reflecting-in-action, this takes place on the spot while you are interacting. If you are reflecting-on-action, set aside time and find a quiet place where you won't be distracted or get interrupted. You might need to let those around you know so they make a point not to disturb you.

▶ *Self-awareness*: identify and, as far as possible, set aside your own defences and prejudices. These influence the way you see things and how you judge others. Try to apply a more objective view and see things from different perspectives.

▶ *Honesty*: remember that this process is all about seeing what is happening as clearly as possible. This is an exploratory process and there are usually no right or wrong answers.

▶ *Pose questions*: it is useful to ask yourself a number of searching questions.

- What did I do, say and feel during this scenario?

- What were the reasons behind my words and actions?

- How do I feel about the situation?

- Is there evidence to back up the way I am feeling?

- What was the response of each individual involved and the outcome for each?

- What was it that I wanted to achieve through my words and actions?

- What else could I have tried?

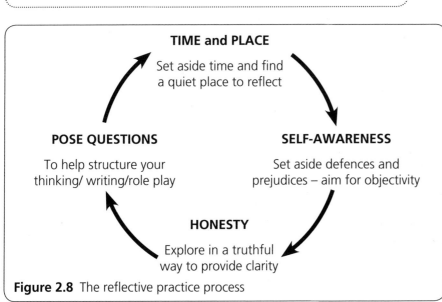

Figure 2.8 The reflective practice process

TIME and PLACE
Set aside time and find a quiet place to reflect

SELF-AWARENESS
Set aside defences and prejudices – aim for objectivity

HONESTY
Explore in a truthful way to provide clarity

POSE QUESTIONS
To help structure your thinking/ writing/role play

Case study

Valentyn is a childminder who looks after a boy of 16 months, a girl of three years and another of four years. Things are pretty chaotic as the children are at different stages of development and their needs are very different. Sometimes this leads to conflict, such as when the girls want to do art and craft activities, but the toddler tends to wreck their efforts, or the girls get involved in noisy imaginative play just as the little boy is trying to have a nap. Valentyn always means to take them out to the park or to feed the ducks at the pond, but they often run out of time or forget, which upsets all the children.

1. In what ways might reflective practice help Valentyn in her work?
2. What questions could she ask herself to help this process?
3. What methods of reflective practice would you recommend to Valentyn and why?

What is the potential impact on working practice of personal values and experience?

Every individual, from early childhood, is influenced and shaped by their unique experience of life. This will include the values they have been brought up with, perhaps passed on by significant people, such as parents and teachers. It also includes beliefs, such as a religious faith or a political ideology, which guide the way you behave. Values, beliefs and experiences influence the way you look at life and make it impossible to maintain objectivity, which is the ability to be unaffected by personal bias and prejudices. This is not necessarily a bad situation, because who you are and how you think and behave makes up the unique person you are, but it is important to be aware of these influences and to recognise that other people's influences and experiences will be different from your own.

Influences to consider

There will have been many influences in your life – here are just a few to consider.

► *Family background:* the make-up of your immediate and extended family and their impact; whether you were an only child or there were many children; sibling rivalry; a mix of genders; the history of your family; whether there was harsh discipline or a permissive attitude, and so on.

► *Environment:* the house/flat/caravan you grew up in and its location, within town or rural setting, within a certain geographical area, or a different country.

► *Finances:* whether you were wealthy or struggled to have your basic needs met.

► *Education:* the ethos of your school; whether single or mixed sex; boarding or day school; inspirational teachers; whether you succeeded academically or not; whether you were bullied; whether you developed special interests.

► *Religious or spiritual belief system:* including whether you embraced or rejected this.

► *Moral influences:* values passed on to you as being of central importance to the way you live your life.

Your assessment criteria:

2.3 Describe how your own values, belief systems and experiences may affect working practice

Key terms

Objectivity: the ability to view or describe something without being influenced by your own feelings and prejudices

Over to you!

Think about the different influences on your life.

► *Can you see the specific ways in which these may have an impact on the way you view life?*

► *Choose an area of your work, for example, the discipline of children and consider how your experiences as a child might affect the way you view this issue now.*

Practical Assessment Task

2.1 **2.2** **2.3**

Reflection is an important part of practice in work with children and young people. Use the stages set out below to demonstrate your use of reflective practice to improve your work performance and the quality of the service provided. Show how you maintain an awareness of the ways values, belief systems and personal experience might be having an influence on this. Record your reflections, using an appropriate method such as a written or audio diary or journal.

► Select a scenario that has occurred recently in your workplace. This might be an occasion you were involved with, or something you witnessed happening.

► Give a brief description of what happened, making sure you do not use real names so as to protect the confidentiality of the individuals involved.

► Complete the reflective practice process diagram (see Figure 2.8, page 53).

► Make a note of any values, beliefs and personal experiences which might be influencing your reflective process findings.

► Describe your insights gained from using the reflective practice process.

► Show the ways these have improved both your individual work performance and the quality of the service provided.

Your evidence for this task must be based on your practice in a real work environment and must be witnessed by or be presented in a format that is acceptable to your assessor.

Be able to evaluate your own performance

How do you evaluate your performance and use feedback to develop working practice?

When you have identified and understood the expectations of your work role and become familiar with the process of reflecting on your working practice, the next step is to evaluate your progress. In a similar way to the reflection process, evaluation of your performance needs to be carried out in an ongoing way. As well as your own evaluation it is useful to consider the **feedback** of others, who will be able to view your performance from a different perspective.

Evaluation

Evaluation is the process of examining and questioning something to assess it against an agreed standard. There may be a range of standards against which to evaluate your knowledge, performance and understanding at work. The requirements of your job description will be one standard, combined with the expectations of your manager and the satisfaction of the children and young people and adults for whom you provide a service. If you work within a particular profession there may be additional codes of practice to adhere to and these are commonly linked to your registration within that organisation. Also, an element of following a course of study, such as this one, is the requirement to evaluate whether you have reached the necessary standard for the qualification.

Knowledge, performance and understanding are broad terms which can be reflected in the particular skills and areas of expertise relevant to your role. To evaluate your performance you will need to ask yourself questions for each relevant area of your work.

Key terms

Evaluation: a process of close examination and questioning to assess and judge performance, usually against an agreed standard

Feedback: written or spoken information about your performance from another person's perspective

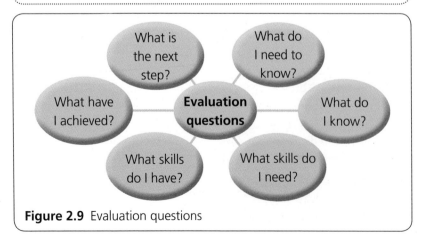

Figure 2.9 Evaluation questions

Producing evidence of achievement

By creating a chart in which to record the answers to your evaluation questions and by gradually adding to this as your working practice develops, you can create your own personal evaluation tool. This provides a useful reference which, if you complete it regularly, will map your progress over time.

Have a look at the beginnings of an evaluation chart Figure 2.10, which a nursery teacher is using to evidence her achievement.

In order to fulfil Ofsted requirements the nursery teacher is required to use the Early Years Foundation Stage (EYFS) framework as a key standard against which to evaluate her performance. Another standard concerns the Little Red Hen Nursery philosophy, where most of the play and learning must take place outdoors. In addition she must remain aware of the individual needs of the particular children who attend and the wishes of their parents.

Figure 2.10 Example evaluation chart to show evidence of achievement

Relevant standards for evaluation: Focus on one of the four principles of *EYFS – A Unique Child* and look at Child Development; Inclusive Practice; Keeping Safe; Health and Wellbeing.

Nursery philosophy: The majority of learning takes place out of doors. Be risk aware and not risk averse. If we remove all challenges children lose the ability to self risk-assess.

Knowledge, performance, understanding	Evidence	Development
Have read EYFS 'principles into practice' cards via Department for Education website, looking especially at Keeping Safe 1.3. Also have re-read nursery ethos about allowing children to explore their physical limits in the outdoors and learn to take risks as safely as possible.	• Spent circle time encouraging my group of children to think about the ways we keep ourselves and each other safe when climbing trees: • G said, 'I get scared climbing up a tiny bit, but D doesn't.' We agreed we are all different; that it is good to have different strengths; that it is sensible to notice if we are scared, because this protects us; that no-one should feel they have to climb as high as another person. • Z said, 'I feel braver when a grown up is standing next to the tree.' We agreed it is good to ask for help; we recognised that support helps us do more than we thought possible. • C remembered how, 'T got sand in his eye from D's boots when he climbed up behind him.' We agreed we need to leave space between us, or take turns climbing the same tree to avoid accidents.	• Think about how we can record these insights, perhaps by producing the children's own risk assessments, maybe picture rules. • Think about how we can keep parents informed, perhaps by the children putting on a play about safety when climbing trees. • Need to record these developments to inform health and safety policy and as evidence for inspection documentation.

Evaluation areas to consider

When you evaluate your knowledge, understanding and performance it helps to focus on specific areas of your working practice. For example, think about health and safety (risk assessment, safeguarding, first aid), planning and running activities, observation and communication skills, encouraging positive behaviour, leadership and management skills, confidentiality and data protection, multi-agency working, record-keeping and so on.

Feedback

Feedback can be gained from formal and informal sources at work.

Formal sources provide a structured system for feedback.

▸ **Appraisal** every six months or year when performance is reviewed.

▸ **Supervision** sessions with a manager or senior colleague. Supervision can be squeezed out when work pressures are high, but these are the times when feedback can be most valuable, so remind your manager or tutor that you are due for a supervision session.

▸ Study courses provide feedback from trainers and assessors which helps to link theory with practice.

▸ Surveys and questionnaires are used increasingly to gather feedback about service-users' levels of satisfaction. These can be completed by the respondent at home, or used to interview a child or parent. If you are making up a questionnaire try to ask **open questions** that encourage a fuller response, rather than a 'yes' or 'no' answer.

Informal sources provide feedback through everyday encounters.

▸ Discussions with colleagues or fellow learners.

▸ Casual conversations with children, young people and their families can provide useful insights.

▸ Non-verbal responses, which are picked up from the **body language** of those you work with, including children and young people and their parents.

Responding positively to feedback

Hearing another person's evaluation of your knowledge, performance and understanding will help you to recognise how others perceive you. This can be affirming and encouraging when feedback is positive, but if the person has something critical to say it can feel uncomfortable. Try to keep an open mind and not be defensive, but concentrate on using the feedback to improve your performance. If you feel the person has overlooked or misinterpreted something, ask if you may speak with them about it. It may not be possible to do this in the moment, but make a note of the points you wish to make and wait for a convenient time, such as during supervision.

Your assessment criteria:

3.1 Evaluate your own knowledge, performance and understanding against standards

3.2 Demonstrate use of feedback to evaluate own performance and inform development

Key terms

Appraisal: an expert or official evaluation of your work and progress, undertaken every six months to a year

Body language: non-verbal communication involving gestures, posture and facial expressions that reveal a person's feelings

Open questions: questions that are worded so they cannot be answered with a simple yes or no, but require a more developed answer

Supervision: regular supportive sessions by a senior staff member overseeing the performance and progress of a more junior colleague

Over to you!

▶ When was the last time you received formal or informal feedback about your work?

▶ How did it feel? Do you think the person's observations and assessment were accurate?

▶ Was it helpful and in what ways were you able to use it to develop your work practice?

Practical Assessment Task

3.1 **3.2**

It is important to be able to link your knowledge and learning, as well as the way you perform your duties to the standards expected of you at work. This process is enabled by feedback from others, both formal and informal, and contributes to your professional and personal development.

1. Identify the standards expected of you at work, for example, the Playwork Principles or the Early Years Foundation Stage (EYFS) statutory framework.

2. Focus on a specific aspect of your work role that relates to these standards (such as communication with very young children, or internet safety for young people).

3. Evaluate your performance and write it up, providing evidence for your evaluation.

4. Make a note to demonstrate how you have used feedback in this process.

5. Describe your insights gained from using the evaluative process and feedback. Show the ways these have improved both your individual work performance and the quality of the service provided.

6. Remember to respect confidentiality, for example, by using initials for any names you may need to mention in the evidence for your evaluation.

Your evidence for this task must be based on your practice in a real work environment and must be witnessed by or be presented in a format that is acceptable to your assessor.

Be able to agree a personal development plan

What sources of support are available to plan and review your personal development at work?

A **personal development plan** is, above all, personal. There is no set format to follow, but it is helpful to find a structure that helps to give an overview of your work, shows the progress of your working practice and your aims for the future. You will find that the tools you have been developing through this diploma course, such as reflective practice and methods to evaluate your work, will help you to plan and review your personal development. This is not something that happens overnight, but it is an ongoing process.

Reviewing looks back at where you have come from and planning builds on this to meet future aims.

The reasons for support

Personal development reviewing and planning is greatly helped by using the resources and support of others.

You will be asking yourself such questions as these.

▶ How am I doing?

▶ What am I looking for in my work?

▶ What do I need to do to reach the next level?

▶ What are my goals and ambitions?

▶ Am I making the right decisions to take me where I want to be?

To answer these questions you will need:

▶ the right information to make informed choices

▶ supportive people around who know the area you work in and whom you can trust

▶ opportunities to experiment and test your abilities and limits

▶ opportunities to extend your knowledge and skills

▶ experts and specialists to guide you.

Sources and methods of support

There is a range of support available to you as you plan and review your personal development. Some of the ways you can gain support are:

▶ formal support within or outside the organisation (with a specific person at an appointed time)

Your assessment criteria:

4.1 Identify sources of support for planning and reviewing your own development

Key terms

Personal development plan: a structure to help you reflect on and appraise your learning and work performance, record your findings and plan how to develop in stages towards future goals; it is also known as an individual development plan or a personal enterprise plan

▶ informal support (perhaps seizing an opportunity or having a quick word)

▶ supervision (regular planned session for feedback)

▶ appraisal (reviewing progress, for example, every six months)

▶ shadowing (working alongside a senior colleague to understand their way of working)

▶ peer support (sharing ideas between colleagues at a similar level).

Figure 2.11 shows individuals to whom you can turn for personal development support.

Over to you!

Take a moment to think about the support available to you:

▶ *Note down the names of relevant individuals, or organisations.*

▶ *Include the sort of support each is likely to be able to offer.*

▶ *Consider whether there are any gaps and ways to fill these.*

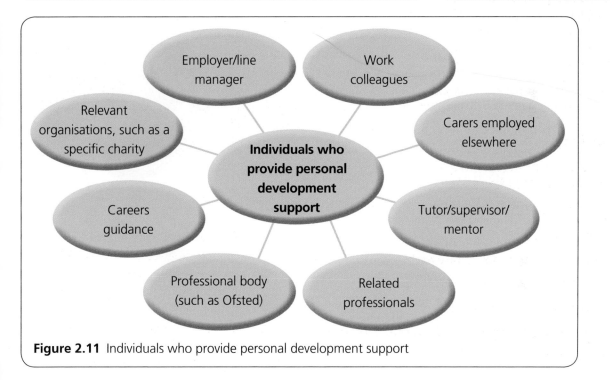

Figure 2.11 Individuals who provide personal development support

Reviewing your learning needs

The process of creating your personal development plan comes out of reviewing your learning needs, professional interests and development opportunities. It is greatly aided by having one particular person to help work on it with you – perhaps a senior colleague or tutor.

Learning needs will become clear through identifying areas of competence in which your skills are established, and the knowledge that informs these. You will then be able to recognise where there are gaps in skills or knowledge. Some skills will be specific to an area of work, such as changing a baby's nappy, and others will be transferable, such as being able to carry out a risk assessment. Try using a structure such as a table to list your skills and corresponding knowledge in all areas related to childcare.

Reviewing your learning needs *continued*

You might want to think about these areas:

- ▶ experience of working with children or young people
- ▶ aspects of physical care (e.g. changing nappies, toileting, feeding)
- ▶ including all children equally
- ▶ encouraging play in and outdoors
- ▶ planning and leading small and large group activities
- ▶ communication (with different age groups)
- ▶ observing and recording children's progress
- ▶ making sure children are enjoying following a healthy diet
- ▶ keeping children safe from harm
- ▶ building positive relationships with children
- ▶ supporting children with special needs
- ▶ partnership with parents
- ▶ managing a budget.

Each skill area will relate to a knowledge base. For example:

- ▶ the skill of carrying out a risk assessment relates to knowledge about safeguarding and health and safety
- ▶ the skill of changing nappies relates to knowledge about infection control, maintaining healthy skin and making sure a baby or young child is comfortable.

Carrying out this exercise will take quite a while, but it is useful to do so in a thorough manner over a period of time.

Professional interests and development opportunities

Professional interests and development opportunities will present themselves as you become keen to discover more about a particular area and this may relate closely to the way you wish your career to develop.

There are a number of ways in which you can pursue professional interests.

- ▶ *Newspaper articles and professional journals* keep you up to date about what is current in your area of work.
- ▶ *Books* provide an established foundation on a subject, but do be aware of when they were written as they can go out of date.
- ▶ *Training sessions and courses* offer a focus on a particular area of your work.
- ▶ *Self-study materials* such as DVDs and CDs allow you to study in your own time and at your own pace.

Your assessment criteria:

4.2 Demonstrate how to work with others to review and prioritise your own learning needs, professional interests and development opportunities

4.3 Demonstrate how to work with others to agree your own personal development plan

▶ *Conferences* provide an opportunity to hear the current thinking on a topic with the added stimulation of being able to meet and talk with fellow practitioners.

▶ *Workshops* are usually practice based and allow you to try new ways of working and sharing with colleagues.

▶ *Shadowing another practitioner*, such as a speech and language therapist, to understand their role better and to see how it relates to your own.

Prioritising your needs

You cannot do everything at once and will need to prioritise your learning needs, professional interests and development opportunities into a hierarchy. Priority might be determined by:

▶ relevance to your work

▶ availability of courses or materials or funding

▶ opportunities arising of which you can take advantage

▶ practicability in terms of whether you have the time to spare and the money to spend.

Using the input of others

People are a useful resource for planning your learning needs and reviewing your progress. Different individuals at different times will be able to give you encouragement and support, make suggestions, offer expert opinions, be willing to listen and help you to reflect. Think about colleagues who have specialist knowledge, experience and an understanding of your work setting, as well as tutors and assessors who know about the academic area related to your work. Consider, too, practitioners from other professions who can provide another viewpoint from a different specialism.

Over to you!

Think about the ways you work best.

▶ *Are you self-disciplined or do you need someone to keep you focused?*

▶ *Do you get on with things, or do you waste energy finding reasons not to get on with tasks?*

Practical Assessment Task

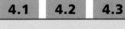

Prioritising and planning your learning needs and reviewing your development are greatly helped by seeking support and collaborating with others.

1. Make a list of the sources of support available to you.

2. Show the specific ways in which each source can provide help with the process of reviewing and prioritising your learning needs, professional interests and development opportunities.

3. Show exactly the ways in which you can work with others to agree your own personal development plan.

Your evidence for this task must be based on your practice in a real work environment and must be in a format that is acceptable to your assessor.

You need to demonstrate to your assessor and provide evidence on how you review and prioritise your own learning needs, professional interests and development opportunities, and work with others to agree your own personal development plan.

How can you evaluate how learning activities and reflective practice have affected your working practice?

Learning activities and reflective practice offer opportunities to develop your working practice. By recording your progress you will produce a useful document that shows how far you have come and helps to plan the way ahead.

Evaluating learning activities

Learning activities should stimulate your interest, broaden your knowledge, extend your skills and deepen your understanding. Study days and training courses are valuable, but are even more so if you apply what you learn in practice. Remember that self-directed learning, such as reading a relevant article or book, also extends your learning. Take advantage, too, of less formal opportunities, such as observing colleagues as they carry out tasks or take part in interactions.

Reflecting on learning activities

Reflective practice helps you draw together the different aspects of your learning experiences and apply them to your work. You might want to reflect on:

- ▶ knowledge and learning
- ▶ your relationships with the children and young people in your care
- ▶ how well you work in a team
- ▶ your communication with other practitioners from different professions
- ▶ the interventions you make and the activities you run.

Your assessment criteria:

5.1 Evaluate how learning activities have affected practice

5.2 Demonstrate how reflective practice has led to improved ways of working

5.3 Show how to record progress in relation to personal development

Case study

Charlie works in a nursery. His interest in safeguarding is stimulated after he has close dealings with a child who is in temporary foster care as her mother is in prison for drugs offences. An article he reads, about duty of care and safeguarding, prompts him to ask his supervisor for more information about laws and standards on safeguarding in EYFS. This increases his awareness of how certain procedures in the nursery reflect laws and standards. The designated child protection officer notices his interest and suggests that he works at building a relationship with this child, who has become more withdrawn since being fostered. Increasingly, Charlie recognises how important skilled communication is when interacting with a

continued...

child who has experienced trauma and gradually, as his ability to listen actively improves he feels he is gaining the child's trust.

1. What different learning activities has Charlie been involved with?

2. How has reflective practice contributed to his working practice?

3. What suggestions do you have to further Charlie's knowledge, understanding and skills in this area?

Over to you!

Think about the last training course or study day you attended.

▶ *Do you recall what you learnt about?*

▶ *Were there specific ways you put this into practice?*

Recording professional development progress

Recording your professional development progress helps to:

▶ *gather information for easy reference* – in a box or ring-binder file, in one place at home or at work, collect materials from training courses (including certificates), personal study and conference attendance

▶ *provide a document of evidence* – to demonstrate that you are up to date in your practice to prospective employers; for college or university courses

▶ *demonstrate to you how far you have come* and remind you of the steps along the way.

You should keep your professional development records, at home or at work, where you can easily access and add to them.

Agreeing a personal development plan

When you have agreed your personal development plan, set it out as an action plan, with targets. The SMART method is a useful tool:

Specific – with clear and well defined targets

Measurable – itemising your achievements

Achievable – manageable, given your resources, ability and time

Relevant – with identified goals related to your practice

Time-limited – with realistic times and deadlines for achievement.

Practical Assessment Task | 5.1 | 5.2 | 5.3

Evaluating how learning activities and reflective practice have improved your working practice contributes to your personal development. By keeping a record of this you provide clear evidence of your progress.

To complete this task, create a personal development file and gather material to go in it.

▶ Identify a learning activity you have undertaken and show how you have applied your knowledge to your working practice.

▶ Demonstrate how reflective practice has led to the development of your working practice.

▶ Record your development in a way that shows the process of your progress (for example, by using the SMART approach).

Your evidence for this task must be based on your practice in a real work environment and must be in a format that is acceptable to your assessor.

Are you ready for assessment?

AC	What do you know now?	Assessment task	✓
1.1	Describe the duties and responsibilities of your own work role	Page 45	
1.2	Explain expectations about your own work role as expressed in relevant standards	Page 49	

Your tutor or assessor may need to observe your competence in your placement or work setting.

AC	What can you do now?	Assessment task	✓
2.1	Explain the importance of reflective practice in continuously improving the quality of service provided	Page 55	
2.2	Demonstrate the ability to reflect on practice	Page 55	
2.3	Describe how own values, belief systems and experiences may affect working practice	Page 55	
3.1	Evaluate own knowledge, performance and understanding against relevant standards	Page 59	
3.2	Demonstrate use of feedback to evaluate own performance and inform development	Page 59	
4.1	Identify sources of support for planning and reviewing personal development at work	Page 63	
4.2	Demonstrate how to work with others to review and prioritise own learning needs, professional interests and development opportunities	Page 63	
4.3	Demonstrate how to work with others to agree own personal development plan	Page 63	
5.1	Evaluate how learning activities have affected practice	Page 65	
5.2	Demonstrate how reflective practice has led to improved ways of working	Page 65	
5.3	Show how to record progress in relation to personal development	Page 65	

3 | Promote equality and inclusion in health, social care or children's and young people's settings (SHC 33)

Assessment of this unit

This unit focuses on ways of working with children and young people that ensure all individuals are treated equally and included fairly, in a manner that accepts, celebrates and promotes difference and diversity.

You will develop an understanding of key words or terms and ideas relating to equality and inclusion and learn about forms of discrimination that can occur in children's and young people's settings, as well as the legal aspects of dealing with inequality and discrimination. You will develop your knowledge about ways of working with people in an inclusive, anti-discriminatory way and learn how to model and support diversity, equality and in your working practice that challenge discrimination and promote change.

To complete this unit successfully you will need to produce evidence of your knowledge of concepts, practices and the law relating to equality and inclusion, as shown in the 'What you need to know' chart opposite. You also need to produce evidence of your practical ability to promote equality and work in an inclusive way in your workplace, as shown in the 'What you need to do' chart. The 'What you need to do' criteria must be assessed in a real work environment by a vocationally competent assessor. Your tutor or assessor will help you to prepare for your assessment and the tasks suggested in this chapter will help you to create the evidence that you need.

CHAPTER 3

AC What you need to know

1.1	What is meant by diversity, equality and inclusion
1.2	The potential effects of discrimination
1.3	How inclusive practice promotes equality and supports diversity

AC What you need to do

2.1	Explain how legislation and codes of practice about diversity, equality and inclusion apply to your own work role
2.2	Show interaction with individuals that respects their beliefs, culture, values and preferences
3.1	Demonstrate actions that model inclusive practice
3.2	Demonstrate how to support others to promote equality and rights
3.3	Describe how to challenge discrimination in a way that promotes change

Assessment criteria 2.1–3.3 must be assessed in the workplace or in conditions resembling the workplace.

This unit also links to some of the other mandatory units:

CYP 3.1	Understand child and young person development
CYP 3.3	Understand how to safeguard the wellbeing of children and young people
CYP 3.7	Understand how to support positive outcomes for children and young people
EYMP 4	Professional practice in early years settings

Some of your learning will be repeated in these units and will give you the chance to review your knowledge and understanding.

What is meant by diversity, equality and inclusion?

It is important to understand the meaning of the terms 'diversity', 'equality' and 'inclusion' in order to recognise how they fit together as a principle to guide the care you give to children and young people and their families.

Diversity

As a practitioner you will work with children and young people and their families, colleagues and other practitioners from a wide range of social, cultural, language and ethnic backgrounds. You will work with men, women, girls, boys, people with different types of ability and disability, individuals who speak different languages and who have different cultural traditions, as well as people who could be described as middle class, working class, as 'black', 'white' or of mixed heritage. You should value and treat each person fairly and equally.

The **diversity** in the United Kingdom population is vast; if you think about the local area where you live, you can probably identify a number of different sub-groups within the community. This means that the population consists of individuals with a huge range of different characteristics.

These differences impact on people's needs. As a result, you have a responsibility to value difference as a way of meeting the individual needs of children, young people and their families.

Equality

You will probably know from your own experience of service users, and perhaps from being a service user yourself, that children, young people and their families want to be treated equally and fairly.

Equality means showing that you value each individual and that you provide **equality of opportunity** for all. It *does not* mean that, in order to be fair, you treat everyone exactly the same, because that fails to take people's different needs, wishes and preferences into account. It *does* mean acting in ways that demonstrate that each person is no more or less important than another. Each person should be given appropriate opportunities to make choices and reach decisions to the best of their ability and in line with their own interests.

Your role as a practitioner will involve informing and supporting each individual so that they benefit from the support, care, services and facilities that are best suited to their particular needs.

Your assessment criteria:

1.1 Explain what is meant by diversity, equality and inclusion

Key terms

Diversity: the range of differences (age, gender, social, cultural, language, ethnic) within a population

Equality: treating a person fairly or in a way that ensures they are not disadvantaged

Equality of opportunity: a situation in which everyone has an equal chance

Over to you!

In what ways do you think young carers who look after parents who are disabled or unwell experience inequality and unfairness in their lives?

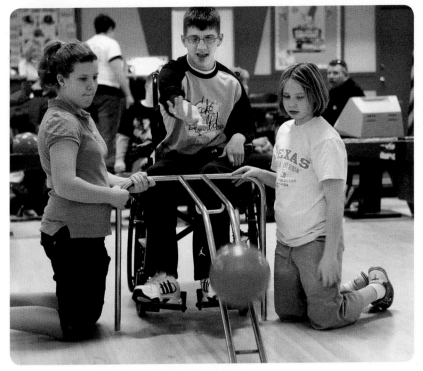

A young wheelchair user being enabled to join in with ten-pin bowling

Inclusion

A children's and young people's service must promote social inclusion, which means no individual is excluded because of differences such as who they are, what they look like, where they are from, what they think or believe, or what they can or cannot do. The aim is to provide equality of opportunity to all by:

► identifying and removing barriers to access and participation

► enabling people to use the full range of services and facilities

► welcoming, valuing and supporting everyone who uses the care setting.

Inclusion doesn't happen by chance. The people who work in children's and young people's settings have to:

► be honest and reflective about how their workplace operates

► be critical in a constructive way, so that positive changes can be made

► work at identifying *actual* barriers to access and participation

► remain alert to *potential* barriers that may exclude some people

► act in practical ways to remove actual and potential barriers

► place the individuals who need care at the centre of planning and support-giving processes.

Key terms

Social inclusion: the process of ensuring that all members of society have access to available services and activities

Over to you!

► *Using library or internet sources, find out what you can about social exclusion, especially in relation to children and young people.*

► *Ask at your workplace whether there are policies in place to prevent social exclusion in your children's and young people's setting.*

Diversity, leading to inequality and exclusion

The ways in which individuals are different are too numerous to itemise. Look at Figure 3.1 to examine those differences that most commonly lead to individuals and groups being treated unfairly and excluded. You have a responsibility to ensure that each person is valued equally and is included as a unique individual in your children's and young people's care setting. This concept goes further than mere tolerance of difference – it embraces diversity and explores its potential.

Your assessment criteria:

1.1 Explain what is meant by diversity, equality and inclusion

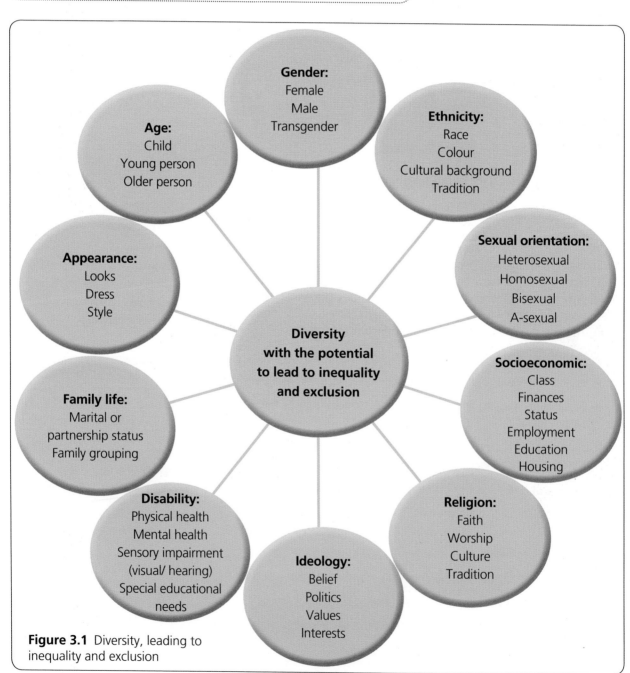

Figure 3.1 Diversity, leading to inequality and exclusion

Situations where inequality and exclusion might occur

Here are some examples that show how differences can mark out an individual or group in ways that have the potential for inequality and unfairness to occur:

▶ a family living in poverty

▶ a woman who is living as a man before undergoing a sex-change operation

▶ a small community of Muslims in a predominantly Christian area

▶ a child at a state school who is gifted in mathematics

▶ a toddler with Downs syndrome whose family live in a small village

▶ a homosexual couple who want to become adoptive parents

▶ a family from Somalia seeking asylum

▶ a community of travellers that includes a number of children who have recently arrived in a small town.

Over to you!

Think about your friends, family and colleagues and the ways in which you differ from and are similar to one another.

▶ *Do you think your differences ever lead to inequalities and to individuals being excluded?*

▶ *Is there anything you can say or do to make individuals you know feel more included?*

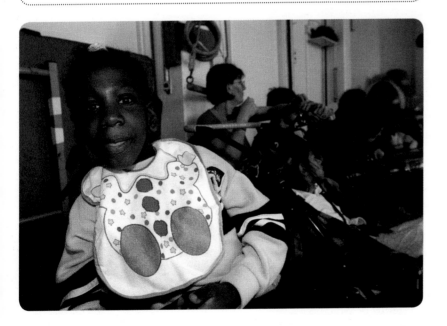

What are the potential effects of discrimination?

Your assessment criteria:

1.2 Describe the potential effects of discrimination

Diversity is not welcomed or celebrated by everyone, despite the fact that the UK has been a multicultural society for many years. Diversity and difference frightens some people, leading to a view of people as either 'them' or 'us'. This can result in unfair treatment or **discrimination** against those who are different from the majority.

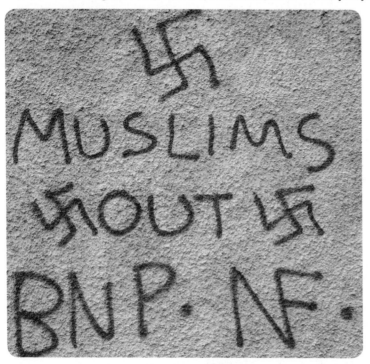

Racist graffiti spray-painted on a wall

What is discrimination?

Two forms of discrimination are recognised under UK law.

▶ Discrimination that is obvious and deliberate and which results in intentionally unfair treatment is known as **direct discrimination**; for example, if a child minder refuses to look after black children on grounds of their race and colour.

▶ Discrimination that happens inadvertently or which is carried out in a secretive, hidden way is known as **indirect discrimination**. Normal procedures or rules can result in the exclusion of certain individuals or groups who are not able to comply with these. For example, if a youth group is held in a hall that has steps leading up to it, a young person with disabilities cannot gain access.

The youth group doesn't state, 'no young people in wheelchairs allowed', but practical reasons prevent their attendance.

Key terms

Direct discrimination: obvious and deliberate unfair treatment

Discrimination: unfair or less favourable treatment of a person or group of people in comparison to others

Indirect discrimination: unfair treatment that occurs inadvertently

How prejudice leads to discrimination

Prejudice is at the root of discrimination. A prejudice is an opinion, feeling or attitude of dislike directed towards another individual or group of people. Prejudices are typically based on inaccurate information or unreasonable judgements. A person acting on a prejudice becomes involved in discrimination. People are not born with prejudices – these have to be learnt. However, children can be quick to pick up these views if they hear others talking in a prejudiced way. Acknowledging diversity, challenging prejudices and tackling all forms of discrimination are important elements of anti-discriminatory practice in work with children and young people.

Prejudice: a judgement or opinion, positive or negative, formed without genuine factual basis; generally an irrational hostile attitude, often towards a particular group, race or religion

How prejudice is expressed

Prejudice is revealed and expressed through the things people say and the way they behave towards individuals or groups who are different in some way.

Prejudice:

▶ is often expressed through derogatory name-calling and by drawing attention to any physical differences, such as skin colour, facial and bodily features and behaviours

▶ thrives where there is uncertainty, anxiety and fear about an individual, or group who are different, or unfamiliar in some way

▶ asserts that people are less intelligent, less able or abnormal because of their differences

▶ claims that a person is inferior – less valuable, less worthy of attention and less deserving – because of their differences

▶ states that a person is wrong and unnatural, rather than just different.

The expression of prejudice can range from petty insults to extreme violence towards individuals, or groups who are different in some way. It can be expressed through unfair or unkind treatment, or by isolating and excluding a person or group. You have a responsibility to recognise discrimination and prejudice in a children's and young people's setting, and to encourage understanding and provide an inclusive setting where each individual is valued (see the photos on the right).

By embracing diversity it is possible to focus on shared experiences

75

The negative effects of discrimination

Deliberate discrimination within children's and young people's settings is relatively unusual. Where discrimination does occur it usually happens inadvertently or by accident. It is useful to be familiar with a number of terms that help you to identify and tackle prejudice and discrimination in children's and young people's settings.

Bias

Bias is a tendency to favour one side, or be influenced in a particular direction when making a judgement, rather than remaining impartial. An example of bias is a teacher who consistently praises and rewards the girls in the class much more often than the boys.

Bigotry

Bigotry is the practice of remaining firmly persuaded by a prejudiced opinion and behaving with aggressive intolerance towards the object of that prejudice. An example of a bigot is a young person who starts fights with Asian people, because he thinks they are taking jobs that should be available, by right, to white people.

Labelling

Labelling means using usually derogatory terms to identify a type of person, or behaviour that then influences the way the person continues to be viewed and treated. An example is of a child who steals a classmate's pencil and is ever after labelled a thief by the other pupils.

Stereotype

A stereotype is a generalisation that characterises a type of person or group of people in an oversimplified way, which fails to recognise individual differences. Stereotypes can be positive, such as all people with glasses are intelligent, or negative, such as all girls are cry-babies. Some stereotypes include elements of truth that make them recognisable, but they never provide a fair or complete picture.

Stigma

Stigma is something that identifies a person (to some people) as being less deserving, or causes others to avoid or reject them. For example, the stigma of having head lice means the other children don't want to sit next to the child who was infested, even though he or she has been treated and is clear of head lice.

Your assessment criteria:

1.2 Describe the potential effects of discrimination

Key terms

Bias: tendency to a 'one-sided' perspective, favouring one side over the other

Bigotry: strong partiality to one's own group or belief, and intolerant of those who differ

Labelling: derogatory terms used to identify a type of person or behaviour

Stereotype: set and often ill-informed generalised ideas, for example, about the way people from certain backgrounds behave or feel

Stigma: a quality, such as behaviour, race or reputation, that makes a person disapproved of socially, causing others to avoid or reject them

Over to you!

Think about common stereotypes that might particularly affect children and young people, such as:

- *'Young lads are hoodies.'*
- *'Gypsy kids are dirty.'*
- *'Girls are cry babies.'*

Describe some ways to challenge these and other stereotypes when you come across them.

The effects on individuals of discrimination

Discrimination has a negative impact on the targeted individual or group and often ripples out to impact on their family and friends as well. It can spread more widely to affect organisations and then society as a whole. There is also a negative impact for those who inflict discrimination – the perpetrators – because they fail to experience the benefits of diversity, equality and inclusion and the consequent broadening of their horizons.

Look at the spider diagram in Figure 3.2 for the specific ways in which discrimination impacts negatively on individuals.

Over to you!

Find out about the work of the Children's Society, particularly in relation to discrimination. You could write to them for information (The Children's Society, Edward Rudolf House, Margery Street, London WC1X 0JL) or visit the website (www.childrenssociety.org).

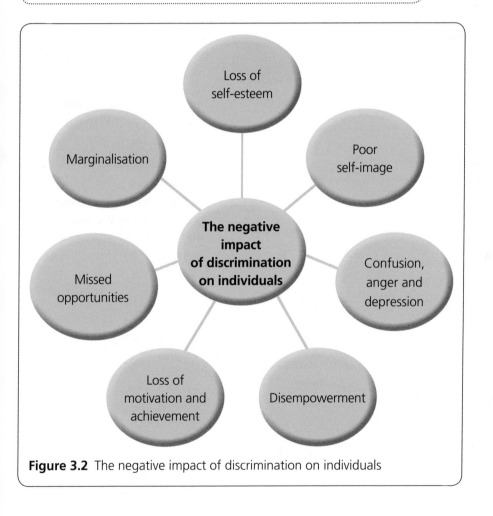

Figure 3.2 The negative impact of discrimination on individuals

Children forced to live alone on the streets, due to the loss of family ties and resultant poverty

The cycle of disadvantage

One negative effect of discrimination can impact on another, having a snowball effect. This is sometimes referred to as a **cycle of disadvantage**. For example, if a child who comes from a Romany gypsy community is teased for living in a caravan and moving from place to place, the child will probably find it harder to make friends and feel accepted when at school. This may affect school work and lead to poor academic success and perhaps cause the child to truant from school, which in turn has a negative impact on future employment potential. The impact of discrimination can be so debilitating that ultimately a person's potential for good health, sound education, work opportunities and personal fulfilment is severely reduced.

Impact on family and friends

Those who are close to a person who is a victim of discrimination can also be negatively affected, even though they don't experience discrimination directly. For example, a parent with a child with disabilities might find certain holidays or recreational activities are not open to them, because of access issues or issues to do with care needs for their child. Not only is the child with the disability discriminated against because they are unable to participate, but their parents and other siblings who don't have disabilities miss out as well.

Key terms

Cycle of disadvantage: a chain reaction of disadvantages that occurs as a result of the negative impact of a child or young person being the victim of discrimination, so that the process is repeated

Case study

A project providing supportive housing for six young people leaving care at the age of 16 has been set up. Two live-in workers will ensure that the house and garden are maintained, as well as assisting the young people to find and keep employment and learn skills towards independence such as cooking, cleaning, laundry and managing finances. A large house in a residential area has been purchased and planning permission sought for a change in usage, but neighbours have begun a campaign against the project. They claim that:

▶ there will be unacceptable levels of noise from music, shouting and swearing

▶ delinquent acts and petty crime will increase

▶ there will be problems with alcohol and drugs

▶ fights will break out

▶ the place will attract drug pushers and even prostitution

▶ their children and older members of the community will be placed in unacceptable danger by this project.

1. List all the prejudices the neighbours have against young people who have been in care.

2. Describe how you would feel if you were one of the young people selected to be part of this project.

3. Describe how you would feel if you were a worried neighbour concerned for the wellbeing of your family.

Over to you!

Sometimes children with disabilities, such as autistic spectrum disorder or Down's syndrome, receive good support when they are very young but find there is less available as they grow older.

▶ Focusing on a particular condition with which you have a professional connection, or that particularly interests you, and using library or internet resources, try to find out about care provision and support for young people in their teens in your local area.

Institutional discrimination

Institutional discrimination describes the unequal treatment of a particular group within an organisation, where discrimination has become so established it is almost written into the systems that operate within the company. It does not rely on the prejudice of individuals to continue the discrimination, but rather on the majority of people just going along with it in an unthinking way. An example might be an organisation that was not originally set up with women in mind and consequently does not provide proper toilet facilities for women, only employs women for particular low status jobs, pays women on a reduced pay scale and does not provide opportunities for the promotion of women. This could be described as institutionalised sexism, which discriminates against women. Another example might be a nursery or pre-school setting that does not embrace a multicultural approach.

Discrimination within society

Discrimination can occur within certain sections of society where particular groups become associated with disadvantage and are less likely to prosper and advance. The word 'ghetto' is used to describe impoverished and neglected residential areas within cities that might be associated with a particular ethnic group, or socioeconomic class and characterised by higher levels of unemployment and crime. The term 'ghettoised' can also be used in a broader way to refer to any group that is disadvantaged and socially excluded, for example, children or young people from Roma, gypsy or traveller backgrounds.

Impact on the perpetrator of discrimination

There is also a negative impact on the person who inflicts discrimination on others, in that they fail to experience the stimulus of diversity and the benefits of variety. Their narrow view remains and unless challenged may become more deeply entrenched. An example might be a youth leader who shows discrimination against girls.

Your assessment criteria:

1.2 Describe the potential effects of discrimination

Key terms

Institutional discrimination: a collective failure within an organisation to provide for all individuals equally, due to discrimination through prejudice, stereotyping, ignorance and thoughtlessness, which disadvantages a minority group

Case study

Acorn is 12 years old and lives with her parents and three brothers on a double-decker bus in a traveller community. They mostly stay in the local area, which means that the children go to the same school, but spend the summer travelling around the country. Acorn experiences unkind teasing about her name and feels ignored by the girls in her class because she's not really into make-up and clothes like they are and she can't be on facebook, because her family don't have a computer. She says, "They call me names like

continued...

'gypo' and 'pikey'. They make it sound horrible. Mum says we call ourselves travellers because our home travels with us. The kids at school also say I'm a 'tea-leaf', meaning thief, because they reckon people like us steal stuff.

1. Why is it important to Acorn that others refer to her by the term 'traveller', with which she feels comfortable?

2. What damaging effect do you think the stereotype of a traveller being a thief could have on Acorn?

3. If you were able to talk with the girls who are unpleasant to Acorn, what might you say or do to help them understand Acorn's way of life better?

Over to you!

▶ *Think about children or young people who you know or work with who experience discrimination, for whatever reason.*

▶ *Consider how this impacts on them, their families and their friends.*

▶ *Is it possible to identify a spreading effect of discrimination rippling out from the individual?*

Some examples of discrimination

If you think about the individual children and young people you work with, you can probably identify several differences to do with their circumstances and experiences. Some of these differences could lead to discrimination. Here are two different scenarios to illustrate this.

1. A child carer

Palomar's mum has physical disabilities, which mean she is a wheelchair user. Palomar, who is 11 years old and in her final year at primary school, provides some care for her mum before and after school, as well as shopping for the family, helping with younger siblings and running other errands. There is a three-day school trip coming up to an outdoor adventure centre. It is organised for all the local primary schools so that they can meet other children who will be moving on to the same secondary school. Palomar would love to go too, but she doesn't even tell her mum, because she knows there's no way she can leave her for that long.

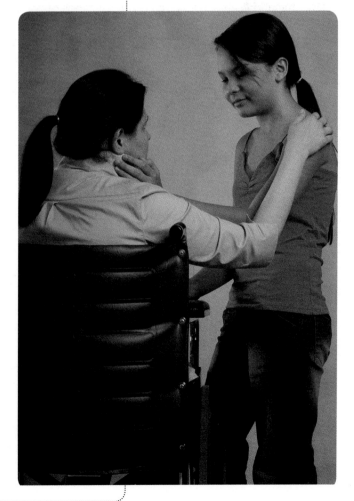

2. A boy in an all-female household

Colin is eight and the only boy in a family of five children. He has two older and two younger sisters. His dad left home when his mum was pregnant with his youngest sister and he has barely seen him since. He is teased at school because some of his handed-down clothes are a bit 'girly' and he's never had the opportunity to take part in activities that other boys in his class have, such as going to football matches. His mum doesn't have much money and these activities don't interest his sisters.

How does inclusive practice promote equality and diversity?

Seeing each child, young person or colleague with whom you work as an individual, with unique qualities and particular needs, is an important way of avoiding prejudice, discrimination and barriers so that individuals are accepted and involved equally.

It is vital that those who work in care settings for children and young people behave inclusively because, as well as helping to reduce and remove the negative potential of prejudice, it will provide more positive outcomes for all.

What is inclusive practice?

Inclusive practice is behaviour that is based on a number of principles (truths that inform actions).

The principles of inclusion are that each child and young person is to:

▶ be valued as a unique individual

▶ feel confident about their self-identity

▶ have their individual needs recognised and met

▶ feel safe and know they belong

▶ be given the opportunity to communicate in the way they prefer

▶ be able to participate equally in activities

▶ have an equal chance to learn and develop.

The positive outcome of inclusive behaviour

There are immediate benefits to inclusive behaviour, but there are also ongoing and wide-reaching benefits. The way in which gender, ethnicity, culture and social background are portrayed in a person's early years has an impact on the expectations they develop about their future.

All children and families should be encouraged and supported to believe that everyone can:

▶ take an active role in society

▶ achieve success in a variety of ways

▶ aspire to valued, responsible and influential positions in life.

Your assessment criteria:

1.3 Explain how inclusive practice promotes equality and supports diversity

Key terms

Inclusive practice: behaviour that ensures individuals are accepted and included equally

How can you promote equality and inclusion?

You can encourage children and young people to embrace difference, rather than rejecting it just because it isn't familiar, by promoting the following behaviours.

- **Reducing fear and anxiety.** Fear of the unknown is often at the root of discriminatory behaviour and being supported to ignore or overcome this can help to provide positive outcomes, which go on to reduce anxiety generally. Children and young people will find they had nothing to be afraid of and much to welcome by including people who are in some way different from themselves.

- **Broadening experience.** Inclusive behaviour opens up opportunities to share more widely with others from different backgrounds and experiences. Aspects of the different cultures and traditions of others are made available to them, providing new interests and revealing new possibilities.

- **Increasing understanding.** Including those who come from a diverse range of backgrounds provides different perspectives on issues and allows new insights into an individual or group point of view. This develops understanding between different people.

- **Encouraging collaboration.** Sharing thoughts and ideas with a wide range of individuals encourages the generation of new ideas and brings fresh creativity.

Over to you!

- *Think about specific ways in which your life has been enriched by diversity within your friendship circles and with colleagues.*

- *Are there people in your life now, perhaps colleagues or acquaintances, who are different in some way and have different life experiences, who you might like to know better?*

Knowledge Assessment Task

1.1 **1.2** **1.3**

The Children and Families team from your local authority are running an inclusion campaign that aims to raise awareness of issues relating to equality and diversity in children's and young people's settings. Your supervisor has asked you to produce a poster or leaflet that could be used as part of this campaign. Your leaflet or poster should:

- explain, using examples relevant to your practice, what is meant by the concepts of diversity, equality and inclusion
- describe the potential effects of discrimination on children and young people and their parents
- explain how an inclusive approach to practice promotes equality and supports diversity.

You should keep the written work that you produce as evidence for your assessment.

Your assessment criteria:

2.1 Explain how legislation and codes of practice relating to equality, diversity and discrimination apply to own work role

How do legislation and codes of practice about diversity, equality and inclusion relate to your work role?

Diversity, equality and inclusion are such important issues that they are protected by laws and promoted through codes of practice.

What is the legal framework for a children's and young people's practice?

Children's and young people's practitioners have to work within a framework of legislation, codes of practice, policies and procedures that are designed to promote equality and inclusion and prevent discrimination.

The children's and young people's legal framework promotes diversity and protects the rights of individuals (service users, families and practitioners) in care settings.

You need to be able to explain how legislation, codes of practice and policies and procedures relating to equality, diversity and discrimination affect your role. You should also be able to explain the legal responsibilities that children's and young people's care employers and employees have for promoting diversity and rights.

In children's and young people's settings, the main statutes promoting diversity and equality and protecting people from discrimination are outlined in the table in Figure 3.3.

Key terms

Code of practice: a document setting out standards for practice

Legislation: another term for written laws, such as Acts of Parliament

Policies: plans of action

Procedures: documents that specify ways of doing something or dealing with a specific issue or problem

Figure 3.3 The legal framework for children's and young people's settings

UK law	About the law	How it affects you
The Human Rights Act 1998	Inspires and forms the basis of a lot of legislation and guidance to do with diversity, equality and inclusion.	You must work in ways that acknowledge the human rights of both adults and children.
The Equality Act 2010	Brings together and simplifies all previous legislation associated with discrimination concerning age, disability, gender reassignment, marriage and civil partnership, pregnancy and maternity, race, religion and belief, sex and sexual orientation.	You must treat all people fairly and equally with dignity and respect, regardless of their differences.
The United Nations Convention on the Rights of the Child 1989	The Convention is a universally agreed set of standards and obligations to be respected by governments. It includes a number of statements regarding equality for all children, regardless of race, culture, religion, disability, educational needs and other differences.	You must work in ways that recognise and respond to the human rights of all children.
The Children Act (2004) (England)	This Act strengthened the child's legal position, to give children equal rights, acknowledging feelings and wishes, and ensuring that children are consulted and kept informed.	You need to work in ways that make the child's – rather than the adult's – needs, opinions, feelings and wishes central to decisions.
Every Child Matters (ECM) 2003	ECM set out the Government's vision for children and young people, which concentrates attention on provision more than protection. It identifies what must be provided for all children and young people to develop healthy, happy and meaningful lives.	You must be familiar with ECM and work in ways that allow equality of opportunity for all the children and young people to achieve the five outcomes.
The Childcare Act (2004) (England and Wales)	Provided the legal framework for ECM.	See above.
The Childcare Act 2006	Concerning child care in the 'Early Years', it offers a framework (e.g. Sure Start centres) for reducing inequalities in the five outcomes of ECM for pre-school children.	Those working with babies and children from birth to five years must understand the relevance of this Act for their role.

Check with your manager or tutor to make sure you know the laws about equality that are relevant to the area of the UK in which you work.

Codes of practice

Codes of practice provide guidelines on implementing the often complicated legislation that affects children's and young people's practice. By working within codes of practice you will remain within the law. For example, The Special Educational Needs (SEN) Code of Practice 2006 was designed to be considered alongside the 2006 Equality Act. It provides guidance about policy and procedure to enable teaching staff and other care workers to ensure that pupils with special needs fulfil their potential.

Codes of practice provide guidance and rules on ways of implementing legislation and policy, as well as guidance on professional standards of behaviour and standards of practice. They identify what children's and young people's practitioners should do in specific situations.

Government charters identify entitlement to services and define national standards of care that people can expect to receive. Policies produced by individual care organisations also incorporate the legal framework of children's and young people's care and should be used in practice by all employees.

Over to you!

▶ If a child complained to you that height restrictions on an amusement park ride are unfair because it means they can't experience the ride, when their older brother can, what might you say to justify this seeming inequality?

▶ Can you think of other examples where discrimination can be justified?

Over to you!

▶ Discuss and identify each religious or cultural celebration in the four photographs opposite.

▶ Which, if any, of these celebrations have you experienced at your placement or work setting?

▶ What is the code of practice about religious and cultural celebrations at your placement or work setting?

▶ Discuss whether or not you agree with this. If you do not agree, how would you change it?

Practical Assessment Task

2.1

How do legislation and codes of practice relating to equality, diversity and discrimination affect the way that you carry out your work role? Talk to colleagues and look at the policies in your placement or work setting that relate to inclusive practice. Produce a table, poster or leaflet that explains the links between relevant examples of legislation and codes of practice and the ways in which you work with children or young people.

Your evidence for this task must be based on your practice in a real work environment and must be presented in a format that is acceptable to your assessor.

Children and young people involved in religious and cultural celebrations

How can you show respect in your interactions?

Interacting with service users and their families in ways that clearly demonstrate respect is a very important part of inclusive practice in children's and young people's settings. Everybody who uses your setting should be valued and respected for who they are, whatever their physical characteristics or their social or cultural background. People feel respected when you:

▶ treat them as an equal while recognising their individual needs, wishes and preferences

▶ acknowledge and recognise that their beliefs, culture and traditions are an important part of who they are

▶ use inclusive, non-discriminatory language that avoids stereotypes, labelling, prejudices, slang and **stigmatised** or derogatory terms

▶ are open-minded and prepared to discuss their needs, issues and concerns in a way that recognises the unique qualities of each person, as well as the characteristics they share with others

▶ show interest in their cultural and religious traditions and take part in an appropriate way in celebrating festivals and events that are significant for them and their community.

Your assessment criteria:

2.2 Show interaction with individuals that respects their beliefs, culture, values and preferences

Key terms

Stigmatised: socially disapproved of

Communicating and working together helps to break down cultural barriers

Practical Assessment Task 2.2

How do you use your interactions with children and families to show respect for their beliefs, culture, values and preferences? Complete a reflective diary or record over the next week, recording examples of instances where your approach and behaviour showed respect towards a child, young person or family's:

▶ beliefs and culture
▶ values
▶ preferences.

You should use examples that were witnessed by a senior colleague, your workplace assessor or the manager of your workplace and ask the person to confirm that you did show respect during the interactions you describe.

Your evidence for this task must be based on your practice in a real work environment and must be witnessed by or be in a format that is acceptable to your assessor.

Over to you!

Think about the ways in which you show respect in your interactions with individuals who are different in some way.

How do you balance the need to meet different needs while treating people equally?

Case study

Yalda and Rahim are third generation British Pakistanis. They have come with their daughters to live in a small, typically English village. She and her husband were fed up with the pace of city life and wanted their girls to be educated at a small school, with beautiful countryside as their playground. Initially a few of the villagers asked if they were going to open a corner shop or Indian restaurant and were disappointed this wasn't the plan! The girls also experienced curiosity from other children. Some attention was drawn by their skin colour and the fact that they had pierced ears. Yalda and Rahim were prepared for this, as an Asian family moving to a totally white environment. Yalda joined the parent volunteers at the school and was approached by the head teacher to help the senior pupils prepare an assembly about diversity.

1. Why do you think the village residents and their children made remarks about the family?

2. What do you understand by the term 'third generation British Pakistani'? Can you think of a more appropriate term?

3. Is it racist to ask Yalda to help with the assembly and in what ways do you think Yalda could contribute?

How can you model inclusive practice in a care setting?

Your assessment criteria:

3.1 Demonstrate actions that model inclusive practice

Inclusive practice begins with the individual. It does not matter what your position is within the hierarchy of your care setting, because everyone has a crucial role to play in promoting diversity, equality and inclusion.

Reflective practice

Reflective practice is an important element of your working practice. It requires you to re-play in your mind the various situations you have encountered during the day and the conversations you have been involved with at work.

You need to apply self-awareness to this process, such that you can lay aside the influence of your own beliefs, justifications and prejudices and identify occasions where you missed an opportunity to behave more inclusively.

Make sure you also notice the positive aspects of your working practice and make a point of continuing to develop these.

Reflective practice is a valuable tool that brings the most benefits when you take time to practice it on a daily basis. There is more about this in Chapter 2.

Being a role model

When you work in a care setting for children and young people you are a role model, whether you know it or not, or like it or not! The ways in which you work and respond to those around you will be seen and experienced by the children and young people you work with, by their families, by your colleagues and by other practitioners who visit your place of work. Children will look up to you, and do as you do, and their parents may at times take their lead from you as well, especially if they see you as a practitioner with expertise about children and young people.

Colleagues who are less experienced may also follow your example. This is your chance to be a positive role model for inclusive behaviour and make a difference where you work.

Key terms

Reflective practice: being mindful and giving yourself time to think carefully about the ways in which you work

Promote opportunities for inclusion for younger children

Most children and young people tend not to be set in their ways and are open to new ideas and experiences. This means you can introduce the principles of inclusion as part of daily activities and in this way limit the likelihood of prejudice developing. Emphasise the positive aspects of inclusion and the opportunities that diversity and equality offer in giving people new experiences that enrich life. Here are some ideas.

► Use multi-ethnic dolls, globes and maps, musical instruments to illustrate differences between countries and traditions.

► Use images that embrace diversity, such as images of children with disabilities, from different countries, both boys and girls.

► Find stories that explore and celebrate differences and similarities between people.

► Talk about the ways in which people look and sound different and come from different sorts of family group.

► Introduce food that is related to different ethnic groups and have feast days when children try out different flavours and textures associated with the traditional cuisine of various ethnic groups and traditions.

► If Makaton or other sign language is used, let other children also learn elements of this to help them communicate with specific children.

► Provide dressing-up clothes that can be used to create clothing of different ethnic backgrounds, such as saris and turbans.

► Celebrate special days associated with a range of faiths and religions.

Promote opportunities for inclusion for older children

- ▶ Facilitate discussions about subjects such as racism, sexism and homophobia.

- ▶ Invite speakers from different nationalities, backgrounds and traditions to give talks and encourage discussion.

- ▶ Arrange visits to places of worship for different religions.

- ▶ Have ethnic cookery sessions where the young people are able to experiment with recipes from around the world.

- ▶ Set a challenge, such as learning sign language or making your way around town in a wheelchair, to experience the hurdles that face some young people with physical disabilities.

- ▶ Form a volunteering group to help and support a local group with particular needs.

- ▶ Fundraise for a charity that supports individuals and groups who are in a minority group.

Case study

Mervyn has cerebral palsy and is a wheelchair user. He has a carer, Thandi, who provides support in various ways and the two of them are a common sight around town and at the library and health centre. One day Mervyn is at the bottom of the steps of a local fast-food restaurant waiting for Thandi who is inside purchasing

continued...

lunch for them both. A passer-by, finding the wheelchair in his way, shouts through the door to Thandi, 'Mate, you need to move this please – normal residents can't get by.'

1. In what different ways is Mervyn discriminated against by the whole incident?

2. If you were Thandi, what would you say to the passer-by to address his discriminatory behaviour in a way that promotes positive change?

3. How can respect be shown to those with disabilities in a local community?

Model different approaches

As you will by now be aware, diversity, equality and inclusion are not about treating everybody in exactly the same way in order to be fair. Children and young people must all be treated with equal concern and valued alike, but their differences mean they have individual needs. You will need to alter your approach and manner accordingly and it is necessary to consider differences such as:

▶ age and stage of development

▶ personality traits and characteristics

▶ confidence and competence

▶ preferences (likes and dislikes)

▶ cultural background and influences.

Over to you!

Think about the ways in which you provide opportunities for all children and young people in your care to be included equally.

▶ *Do you know how others in your position approach this?*

▶ *Is there more you could do?*

Young people with disabilities can be included in many activities

How can you support others to promote equality and rights?

As well as working in ways that promote equality and rights for the children and young people you work with, you are also in a position to support their families, and your colleagues to do the same. There are a number of ways in which you can do this, as Figure 3.4 shows.

Identify areas of concern

If you work according to the principle that each individual has the right to be treated fairly, regardless of their differences, you will become more alert to any potential discrimination taking place around you. This might come from family members of the children and young people you work with, or from less-aware or inexperienced colleagues. Recognising and identifying discrimination is the first step to tackling it. In order to work out the best way to manage this it is advisable first to seek advice from individuals whose judgement you trust. In most care settings there will be a forum, such as a staff meeting where you can discuss with colleagues, in general terms any concerns you may have.

Figure 3.4 Ways of supporting others to promote equality and human rights

Provide information

There is usually a great deal of information available about a range of issues relevant to a care setting. You can make sure that the available literature about equality and rights has a high profile and bring this to the attention of those you have identified as particularly needing this information. Make sure you know the policies to do with equality and rights at your workplace and talk about these with the adults you come into contact with at work. Policies should be displayed prominently for all to see and read, so if this is not the case do bring it to the attention of your manager. You could also suggest holding an information-giving session about equality and rights that explains how your place of work is ensuring that these are implemented. You could take this on as a project and produce a leaflet about the specific ways in which equality and rights are promoted at your place of work.

Over to you!

▶ Are there aspects of your work that invite unfairness and infringe rights?

▶ What part could you play in supporting others to improve this situation?

Make links with outside agencies

There are a number of outside agencies that are particularly concerned with equality and rights. The Equality and Human Rights Commission (www.equalityhumanrights.com) is a good source for general information and provides links to other groups concerned with a particular aspect of rights and equality, such as disability or race relations.

Invite consultation and feedback

If there are families using your services that are part of a minority group, suggest to your manager that they be invited to share their experiences and contribute to a consultation on equality and rights. Check with these individuals that their needs are being met satisfactorily and explain to other staff why you are doing so. By making a point of including those who may feel on the fringes you prevent them from being overlooked and their needs ignored.

Be an advocate

Keep your awareness raised to the possibility of discrimination where you work. **Advocacy** is the process of standing up for those who are overlooked or put down because of their differences. You can be an advocate where you work by supporting individuals who are vulnerable to discrimination because of their differences. Speak up in your support of all voices being heard equally and every person being treated fairly. It may be necessary to contact advocacy services to represent families you work with who have particular needs.

Over to you!

Think about the links you or your placement or work setting have with other outside agencies.

- ▶ *What part do you play in maintaining communication with these?*
- ▶ *Is there anything you could do to strengthen or increase links?*

Key terms

Advocacy: speaking on behalf of another person, giving them active support, especially in protecting them from injustice or in a legal context

Practical Assessment Task   3.1   3.2

Imagine that you are about to take part in a performance and development review with the manager of your early years setting. The review will focus on your ability to promote equality, diversity and inclusion.

1. In preparation for the review you have been asked to work with a group of children or young people in a way that demonstrates your ability to use inclusive practice and to support others to promote equality and rights. Ideally you should organise, support or assist with activities that can be witnessed by your manager or assessor.

2. Following the activity you should reflect on your performance and write some brief notes on:
   - ▶ how your actions modelled or demonstrated inclusive practice
   - ▶ how you supported others to promote equality and rights during the activity.

Keep your written work as evidence towards your assessment. Your assessor may want to observe and question you about your performance. The evidence for this activity should be assessed in the workplace.

How can you challenge discrimination and promote positive change?

Occasions may arise when you witness or are made aware of discrimination taking place. It is not acceptable to ignore or make excuses for this. You must act, but it is more productive to intervene in ways that lead to positive change in those you challenge, rather than in ways that may lead to negative resentment and misunderstanding.

Understand why discrimination occurs

It is useful to understand something of the psychology behind discriminatory behaviour. Figure 3.5 gives some examples of why discrimination occurs.

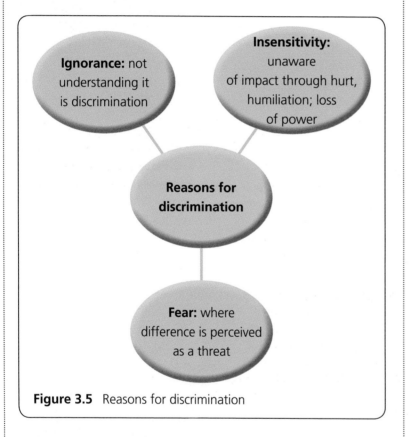

Ignorance: not understanding it is discrimination

Insensitivity: unaware of impact through hurt, humiliation; loss of power

Reasons for discrimination

Fear: where difference is perceived as a threat

Figure 3.5 Reasons for discrimination

Positive methods of challenging discrimination

When challenging discrimination, your approach should take into consideration whether the perpetrator is a child or an adult, a member of staff or a parent. It is always advisable to talk over the best approach for challenging discrimination with someone whose opinions you respect, such as your tutor or manager.

Over to you!

- ▶ *What different ways have you witnessed or used to challenge discrimination?*
- ▶ *How successful were these interactions?*
- ▶ *What made them work or fail?*

There are a number of positive methods to challenge discrimination.

▶ *Direct confrontation*: This is an immediate response that gives a clear message of non-toleration. At times this approach is appropriate. Children especially may need to be told in a straightforward manner why discriminatory behaviour is unacceptable and won't be tolerated. For example, it is not acceptable to name-call or leave a person out because of some actual or perceived difference. However, it is important to maintain a calm manner and offer information that guides behaviour, rather than making the perpetrator feel uncomfortable or upset. Be aware that the child may be unwittingly repeating prejudiced ideas learnt at home and this might need to be followed up later with the parents.

Encouraging inclusion discourages discrimination

▶ *Initiate discussion*: In some circumstances direct confrontation leads to angry arguments, which could cause the perpetrator to act defensively and perhaps become even more entrenched in their discriminatory behaviour. Respectfully sharing your thoughts with the perpetrator is more likely to help the person engage with and explore the issues and – hopefully – reach a new understanding.

▶ *Support those who are discriminated against*: If you say nothing in the face of discrimination this could be interpreted as being in agreement with it. It is never OK to condone (go along with) discrimination. Without being confrontational it is possible to act assertively and refuse to get involved in discriminatory behaviour. Standing beside those who have been on the receiving end of discrimination is a supportive action in itself, but it also gives a message to others that you will always challenge discrimination.

▶ *Reporting discrimination*: Ultimately it is illegal to act in ways that discriminate against individuals and groups and the law provides one of the major methods positively to challenge discrimination. Most organisations will have a reporting system and complaints procedure, which can be used to record the incidence of discrimination and ensure that a situation is followed up.

Over to you!

▶ *Are you aware of the proper channels for reporting discrimination in your placement or work setting?*

▶ *In what ways do you think positive change can come out of making a formal complaint?*

Using positive discrimination to promote change

Positive discrimination and affirmative action are terms to describe the favouring of groups who are discriminated against through being marginalised and disadvantaged, in order to even the power balance. This is a direct method of challenging discrimination, but it is controversial.

Through positive discrimination groups who are disadvantaged are promoted in some way to compensate for the inequalities they experience. An example is those organisations that are obliged to have a certain percentage of people with disabilities represented among their employees and therefore favour candidates with disabilities when interviewing, in order to meet the quota. Another example concerns the debate regularly held in Parliament as to whether women, who are grossly unrepresented in the House of Commons should have a quota of protected positions, so that men are not permitted to compete for the same seat.

Those in favour of positive discrimination state that discrimination has created such deep-rooted disadvantage within society that it cannot be equalised without affirmative action. Those who are against positive discrimination state that it is patronising and dilutes the innate strength and power of these groups when they are shown partial treatment.

Key terms

Affirmative action: action that favours those who are, or who are perceived to be, victims of discrimination

Positive discrimination: discrimination in favour of those who are disadvantaged

Case study

Mary-Ann has just started a six-week placement in a crèche. It seems a happy environment and she has enjoyed her first few days. However, she has begun to notice something going on that makes her feel less comfortable. The manager's own child and one of the other workers' children also attend the crèche and Mary-Ann notices that often when the children need help, for example, when putting on coats for outside play, or washing hands for lunch these members of staff attend to their own children first. Mary-Ann thinks that some of the other children notice this and perhaps don't feel as 'special' as the crèche workers' children. One day Mary-Ann observes the manager's daughter grab a toy roughly from a little boy, who begins to cry and grabs the toy back, causing the manager's daughter to cry as well. The manager didn't witness the whole incident but, on hearing her daughter crying, walks briskly across to tell the boy to give back the toy and picks up her daughter to give her a cuddle. Mary-Ann feels very uneasy about this incident and doesn't know how to respond.

1. In what way is this an example of discrimination?

2. Who is being affected by the discrimination and how?

3. If you were Mary-Ann, what would you do?

Over to you!

► What do you think about positive discrimination?

► Are you aware of it being practised at your place of work?

Practical Assessment Task

3.3

Children and young people may discriminate against each other during play or learning activities for various reasons. Where this occurs, practitioners have a responsibility to respond in a way that challenges the discrimination but which also promotes change. In this activity you are required to reflect on your own experiences of practice and to:

▶ describe an example of direct or indirect discrimination that you have witnessed in the work setting (remember to protect confidentiality)

▶ describe how you challenged, or could have challenged, the discrimination in a way that promoted change.

This activity must be assessed in the work setting and should draw on your own practice. Keep any notes or written work that you produce as this may be used for your assessment. Your assessor may also want to ask questions about your experience or about ways of challenging discrimination more generally.

Are you ready for assessment?

AC	What do you know now?	Assessment task	✓
1.1	What is meant by diversity, equality and inclusion	Page 83	
1.2	The potential effects of discrimination	Page 83	
1.3	How inclusive practice promotes equality and supports diversity	Page 83	

Your tutor or assessor may need to observe your competence in your placement or work setting.

AC	What can you do now?	Assessment task	✓
2.1	Explain how legislation and codes of practice about diversity, equality and inclusion apply to your own work role	Page 87	
2.2	Show interaction with individuals that respects their beliefs, culture, values and preferences	Page 89	
3.1	Demonstrate actions that model inclusive practice	Page 95	
3.2	Demonstrate how you support others to promote equality and rights		
3.3	Describe how to challenge discrimination in a way that promotes change	Page 99	

4 | Principles for implementing duty of care in health, social care or children's and young people's settings (SHC 34)

Assessment of this unit

The focus of this unit is the meaning of the term 'duty of care' and how this obligation relates to your work role with children and young people. It addresses the potential tension between maintaining a duty of care and upholding a child's rights and it sets out appropriate ways to deal with potential conflicts or complaints that might arise as a consequence.

The assessment of this unit is all knowledge based and you will need to produce evidence of your knowledge as shown in the 'What you need to know' chart opposite. Your tutor or assessor will help you to prepare for your assessment and the tasks suggested in this chapter will help you to create the evidence you need.

AC   What you need to know

1.1	What it means to have a duty of care in your own work role
1.2	How duty of care contributes to the safeguarding or protection of individuals
2.1	The potential conflicts or dilemmas that may arise between the duty of care and an individual's rights.
2.2	How to manage risks associated with conflicts or dilemmas between an individual's rights and the duty of care
2.3	Where to get additional support and advice about conflicts and dilemmas
3.1	How to respond to complaints
3.2	The main points of agreed procedures for handling complaints

There is no practical assessment for this unit, but your tutor or assessor may question you about some of the following points.

What you need to do

Apply your knowledge about the duty of care to your practical work in your placement or work setting

This unit is designed to develop your working practice, which is relevant to every chapter of this book, but has particular links to other mandatory units:

CYP 3.2	Promote child and young person development
CYP 3.3	Understand how to safeguard the wellbeing of children and young people
CYP 3.4	Support children and young people's health and safety
CYP 3.7	Understand how to support positive outcomes for children and young people
EYMP 3	Promote children's welfare and wellbeing in the early years
EYMP 4	Professional practice in early years settings

Some of your learning will be repeated in these units and will give you the chance to review your knowledge and understanding.

What does having a 'duty of care' mean?

A **duty of care** is a legal term referring to the obligation of all adults to be aware of the wellbeing of others and take reasonable steps to ensure that no one comes to harm, as a result of any action or inaction. According to UK law a duty of care applies to all people you come into contact with, but it is of particular significance where children and young people are concerned, because they are too young to meet their own needs or be aware of potential dangers.

How a duty of care relates to your work role

When you work with children and young people, having a duty of care brings specific responsibilities to:

- ▶ uphold their rights
- ▶ promote their interests
- ▶ ensure **safe practice**
- ▶ protect their health, safety and wellbeing.

Figure 4.1 shows those people to whom you owe a duty of care.

Your employer also has a duty of care towards you as an employee and must, as far as possible, protect your health, safety and welfare while you are at work. Risk assessments must include assessing the risk of harm to employees and taking measures to limit risks to an acceptable level.

Duty of care and the law

Laws are in place to protect everyone – you and your colleagues, the children and young people you work with and their relatives. Fulfilling your duty of care means you must always work within the law. This means only carrying out tasks that you are trained and competent to do and making decisions within your work remit.

Duty of care and safe practice

Part of a duty of care is to maintain safe working practices. To achieve this you need to be aware of:

- ▶ the laws relating to your area of work
- ▶ the standards you are expected to meet
- ▶ the policies and procedures operating in your workplace.

Your assessment criteria:

1.1 Explain what it means to have a duty of care in your own work role

Key terms

Duty of care: the legal obligation to act toward others with careful attention and reasonable caution to protect their wellbeing and prevent harm occurring

Safe practice: working in ways that uphold laws and standards, prevent harm and protect and promote the safety and wellbeing of others

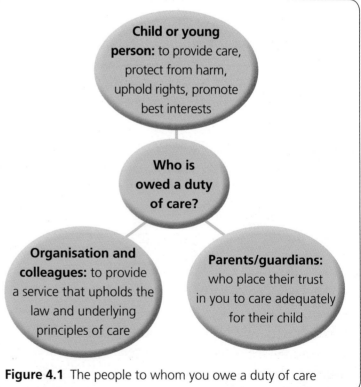

Figure 4.1 The people to whom you owe a duty of care

As well as this, your practice must keep up to date with any changes and you must attend any necessary training.

If you are concerned about any aspect of your duty of care it is your responsibility to talk to your manager. Do not allow colleagues to put you under pressure to undertake a task you are not trained for or to cut corners in the care you give.

The consequences of failing in a duty of care

Duty of care is often considered only after an incident has occurred, when it is possible to view the consequences of an action with the benefit of hindsight. Even when no harm has occurred it is possible to lose employment or be removed from a professional register if you are found to have failed in your duty of care.

Over to you!

▶ Can you think of occasions at home or in your placement or work setting when you need to be particularly aware of having a duty of care towards others?

▶ Think about situations of potential negligence where something you do, or fail to do could result in harm to another person.

Case study

Mr Phelps is a biology teacher who is taking a group of 12 and 13-year-old pupils on a field trip to study seaside habitat. He is known for his exciting and interactive lessons and his easy-going manner makes him a popular member of staff with the children. When the young people on the trip discover Mr Phelps having a cigarette behind the sand dunes he decides to turn this potentially embarrassing situation into a learning opportunity. He explains in graphic detail the negative physical effects of smoking and finishes by offering a cigarette to whoever wants to try one. His theory is that this will put them off smoking, hopefully for life.

1. Has Mr Phelps fulfilled his duty of care to these pupils?
2. What might be the potential consequences of Mr Phelp's behaviour?
3. If you were Mr Phelps, how would you have handled being discovered smoking?

Over to you!

Duty of care includes working in ways that demonstrate safe practice.

▶ In what specific ways does your placement or work setting reflect safe practice?

▶ Think about laws, regulations, standards, codes of practice and policies to do with health and safety, safeguarding and upholding rights.

Knowledge Assessment Task   1.1

All practitioners working with children and young people must show a duty of care by being aware of the wellbeing of others and taking reasonable steps to ensure that no one comes to harm, as a result of any action or inaction.

Look at the four headings below and give an example for each that explains the ways in which you fulfil your duty of care to the children and young people you are responsible for at work.

▶ Uphold children and young people's rights
▶ Promote their interests
▶ Ensure safe practice
▶ Protect them from harm.

Keep your written work as evidence towards your assessment.

In what ways does a duty of care safeguard children and young people?

Babies and very young children are completely vulnerable and depend on their parents or other carers to fulfil their basic needs for nutrition, warmth and shelter, as well as meeting psychological and emotional needs to be loved and nurtured. Moving from childhood to adulthood means learning to meet your own needs and gradually becoming more independent, but older children and young people still require guidance, supervision and support. Young people are not always aware of risks and dangers, or the potential consequences of their actions. **Safeguarding** describes this vigilant and nurturing care and it is an important element of a duty of care.

The safeguarding aspects of a duty of care

The main safeguarding aspects of a duty of care when working with children and young people are reflected in the actions set out in Figure 4.2.

Your assessment criteria:

1.2 Explain how duty of care contributes to the safeguarding or protection of individuals

Key terms

Safeguarding: the process of looking after children and young people in ways that protect them from illness, injury and abuse, promote their interests, and value and uphold their rights

Knowledge Assessment Task 1.2

Safeguarding is an important element of a duty of care when you work with children and young people. Look at each statement and explain how having a duty of care contributes to the safeguarding of individuals.

1. Brad will not allow the lads in his group, who are all 14, to watch a certificate 18 film, despite them trying to persuade him that he would be acknowledging their maturity, that it would be a boost to their self-esteem and that most of them have seen certificate 18 films before.

2. Fran ensures that she has emergency contact details for each child before their outing to SeaWorld.

3. Mustaphe sends information to all parents at the nursery to request that no nut products are included in children's snackboxes, because a little boy at the nursery has a severe nut allergy.

4. Although nursery worker Juan has been told by baby Violet's parents that she settles to sleep better on her front, he knows that at four months old she is vulnerable to cot death and follows paediatric advice by laying her on her back for a nap.

5. Child minder Gemma does not allow Freddie and Dean to jump off the swings or hang upside down from the frame of the slide, even though they say their mum lets them.

Keep the written work you produce for this task as evidence for your assessment.

Figure 4.2 The main safeguarding aspects of a duty of care when working with children and young people

Principle of safeguarding	Duty of care action
Recognise and meet physical, emotional and psychological needs	• Knowledge about what is required for healthy child development • Observe and record **developmental milestones** that indicate a child is progressing according to expectations • Be aware of health, safety and welfare issues at all times • Liaison with parents and practitioners • Show empathy, support and caring
Anticipate danger and manage risks	• Carry out risk assessments • Take precautions to avoid hazards and prevent illness, accidents and injury • Discuss risk with children and young people
Intervene and support in the event of illness or injury	• Intervene with appropriate first aid • Seek appropriate treatment or support • Liaise with practitioners and parents • Report to appropriate authority
Be alert to the potential of exploitation, abuse and neglect	• Knowledge and observation of the signs of abuse and neglect • Follow child protection procedures • Report to appropriate authority
Provide guidance and supervision of play and activity	• Set clear expectations and appropriate boundaries • Use strategies to manage challenging behaviour • Support creativity and exploration
Uphold and value rights	• Knowledge about the rights of the child • Treat as unique individuals with equality and fairness • Protect from discrimination • Communicate with others in support of their best interests

Key terms

Developmental milestones: specific abilities that most children are able perform within a certain age range, such as walking, talking, being toilet trained and so on

How do you recognise the problems that arise when a duty of care conflicts with an individual's rights?

All people, including children and young people, have **rights** which are protected by law. Parents have rights, but they also have responsibilities towards their children. When you work with children and young people, situations will sometimes arise in which a duty of care appears to clash with the principle of respecting a child's and their parent's rights, causing a **dilemma** or **conflict**. You need to be aware of the potential for this to happen in your work setting and to have an understanding of these issues:

▶ children's and young people's rights

▶ parental rights and responsibilities

▶ balancing **risks** and rights.

The rights of children and young people

Children's rights are set out in the United Nations Convention of Children's Rights, 1989. The Convention applies to all children everywhere, whatever their background or family circumstances. When you have responsibility for children and young people, either as parents or working with them, you must help them to understand their rights, directing and guiding them according to their age and level of understanding. See also Chapter 15, page 388.

Your assessment criteria:

2.1 Describe potential conflicts or dilemmas that may arise between the duty of care and an individual's rights

Key terms

Conflict: disharmony between two incompatible positions, people, ideas, or interests

Dilemma: a difficult situation arising because of a clash between two opposite positions, where no one answer will satisfy both parties

Rights: entitlements that are protected by law and agreed upon by society as being fair and just expectations

Risk: the possibility of suffering harm, damage or loss together with an indication of how serious the harm could be

The convention details the minimum standards that are acceptable for the care of children, some of which include the right to:

▶ life, survival and development

▶ be listened to and have opinions respected and taken into account

▶ be protected from harm

▶ freedom of expression, and access to information concerning them

▶ health and health care, social welfare the right to education, leisure, culture and the arts

▶ live in a family environment and not be separated from their parents, except when this is necessary in the interests of the wellbeing of the child.

The best interests of the child or young person must be your central concern in making decisions that may affect them.

Parental rights and responsibilities

Parents have a legal right to look after their children in ways they feel are appropriate, without the interference of the authorities. This right includes such matters as:

▶ deciding where and how they will live

▶ selecting how they will be educated

▶ disciplining their child or children

▶ overseeing their health

▶ deciding what religion, if any, they practice.

As a practitioner working with children and young people, you must be respectful of the way parents wish to raise their children. When a child is in your care you should look after them, as far as possible, in the way parents approve. For example, if you look after a child who is being brought up as a vegetarian, you must make sure that no meat products are included in the meals offered while the child is with you, even if the child is too young to understand whether they are eating meat or not.

It is part of your job to find out about a parent's wishes for their child, to respect these wishes and to reflect them in the way you work with their child.

Over to you!

▶ *Do you take time to consider fully the rights of the children you look after?*

▶ *In what ways does your work reflect your understanding of a child's right to be listened to and have his or her opinions taken into account?*

The responsibilities of parents

The Children Act of 1989 changed the emphasis of parental rights to **parental responsibility**. It introduced the idea that:

▶ a parent's rights are balanced by their responsibility to ensure the welfare of their child

▶ the child's rights can overrule those of the parents, especially if they fail to provide adequate care.

In most circumstances:

▶ the mother automatically has parental responsibility for her child

▶ this responsibility is often shared by the father, but not always

▶ the law recognises different family circumstances, where a divorced parent usually continues to have parental responsibility if they no longer live with the child and where other adults may acquire parental responsibility in addition to the parents.

Note that the legal regulations concerning parental responsibility differ slightly between England and Wales and Scotland and Northern Ireland.

Although you have a duty of care to the children and young people you work with, the person with parental responsibility maintains overall responsibility, even when their child is away from them and in your care. That is why it is necessary for childcare workers to obtain permission from parents to enable children and young people to take part in various activities, or to allow photos or film to be taken of them.

You cannot assume who has parental responsibility for each child or young person you work with, so it is important that you are aware of their individual circumstances and don't make assumptions. This is especially relevant when it comes to ensuring that the adult collecting a child from your work setting is authorised to do so.

Your assessment criteria:

2.1 Describe potential conflicts or dilemmas that may arise between the duty of care and an individual's rights

Key terms

Parental responsibility: a legal term to indicate the person or people (usually the parents) with legal responsibility of caring for and raising a child

Case study

Vanita is a child minder who looks after baby Nicky, who is two months old, and two three-year-old girls, Jessie and Steph. Nicky's parents are quite anxious and do not want their son to be taken anywhere by car when he is in Vanita's care. She respects this and is often to be seen around town pushing Nicky in the pram, with Jessie and Steph on either side as they go to the park and the library and the Little Tots music group. However, when the girls start nursery Vanita finds they are so tired when she picks them up after a morning's activities that the journey home can be very slow and difficult. She decides it is in the girls' best interests to use the car, just for this one journey and that Nicky's parents need never find out, because they both work out of town.

1. Do you think Vanita is showing a duty of care to the children in her care?

2. How can Vanita look after the best interests of Jessie and Steph while upholding the rights of Nicky's parents?

3. How would you handle this situation?

Balancing risks and rights

Your assessment criteria:

2.1 Describe potential conflicts or dilemmas that may arise between the duty of care and an individual's rights

You have a duty of care to keep the children and young people in your care safe, but this needs to be balanced with their rights and their need to explore and have new experiences.

The two main areas where conflict is most likely to arise between maintaining a duty of care and upholding rights are:

▶ risk taking

▶ maintaining confidentiality.

Positive and negative aspects of taking risks

Risk is a part of everyday life and, to some extent, it is unavoidable. Risk is not necessarily negative either, because taking risks can extend a child's or young person's abilities, especially to manage their life, boost their self-belief and teach them about their limitations. Young people need to understand the difference between danger and risk. By assessing the risks involved in a dangerous activity, they can make informed choices about their actions.

Some activities that children take part in involve physical risk, such as running, climbing and jumping. Stopping them from joining in might prevent an accident, but it also restricts their freedom and may hold back their confidence and sense of self-esteem. Other activities hold different sorts of risk for children and young people, to do with learning about the adult world. For example, parents have different ideas about how soon children should learn about sex and substances such as alcohol and drugs.

Parental concern about risk

Conflict can arise if parents hold different ideas about risk from those of practitioners Parents might be:

▶ risk averse, where fear for the safety of their child leads them to restrict the child's freedom and avoid risk

▶ risk permissive, where the child is encouraged to do whatever they please, regardless of risk.

Both extremes can create conflict for you as a children's and young person's practitioner trying to fulfil your duty of care.

Duty of care and confidentiality

Children and young people and members of their families are likely to confide in care practitioners, where sharing is often a sign of trust. Your duty of care means, on the one hand, that you must keep personal information confidential. However, at the same time, it can mean doing the very opposite and sharing information with other practitioners or higher authorities in order to keep a child or young person safe. For example, a child may disclose an incident of abuse, but beg a care worker not to tell anyone. The care practitioner would be failing in their duty of care if they did not pass on this information and the child remained at risk of further abuse.

On other occasions you may witness something that you must report to keep people safe. For example, a care practitioner may tell his colleague he still feels intoxicated after a heavy drinking session the night before, but is sure he's fine to drive children in his care to a football match in the club minibus. It would be negligent for the person he confided in to keep the information to herself when the children would be put at risk of being involved in an accident due to his alcohol levels.

There is more about confidentiality in Chapter 7 (page 180).

Case study

Laurie is a helper at a holiday club where children of different ages arrive each day for activities. Max, her colleague, asks Laurie to see to Gregor, a new boy, aged 11, who is furious with his parents for 'dumping me in a kids' club. Mark suggests that she lets him join quad-biking, the most exciting group on the programme, even though, strictly speaking, he's a bit under age. Laurie asks for Gregor's parental consent form, but Max says to keep quiet about that and sort it out later. At the same time, Laurie is trying to give attention to 13-year-old Arti, who has been plucking up courage to try out the quad bikes all week. Arti's mum is worried because she thinks her daughter is not a physical person, so is more likely to have an accident. Her father has given his consent, but teases Arti about her nervousness, rather unkindly saying that it proves it's not really an activity for girls. Arti really wants to succeed and prove herself to her parents.

1. What aspects of this scenario require a duty of care to be demonstrated?

2. What conflicts or dilemmas to do with risk and confidentiality are apparent?

3. If you were Laurie what would you do to demonstrate your duty of care?

Over to you!

Can you think of occasions when you have been concerned enough about the safety of a child in your care that you have restricted their play?

▶ *What were your concerns?*

▶ *Do you think you were justified in your actions?*

How do you manage risks and find support and advice when responsibilities conflict with rights?

When confidentiality issues or dilemmas and conflict arise between fulfilling your duty of care and risk taking, you need to be able to manage the situation. At times there will not be one right answer to enable you fully to reconcile the dilemma between maintaining a duty of care and upholding individuals' rights. A difficult decision may need to be made to give one a higher priority over the other. This requires careful thought and assessment, a process that is enhanced by seeking support and advice.

Ways to manage risk

The way you go about managing risks is probably as important as the decision you finally make. A number of steps, as shown in Figure 4.3, can help you make decisions.

Positive risk taking

Positive risk taking (PRT) is an approach that views risk as an important learning opportunity, rather than a situation to fear, ignore or avoid. PRT is increasingly been promoted in settings for children and young persons because it is recognised that learning how to deal with risk enables children and young people to:

► learn the difference between breaking rules and taking risks

► understand that actions have consequences

► recognise and assess levels of danger

► use resources to remove or reduce risk, including seeking advice from adults.

At the end of this process there may still be a risk that remains, but the child or young person is by this stage able to make an informed choice and taking a risk has become a deliberate and planned strategy to manage conflict or dilemma.

There is more about risk assessment and management in Chapter 8, page 210.

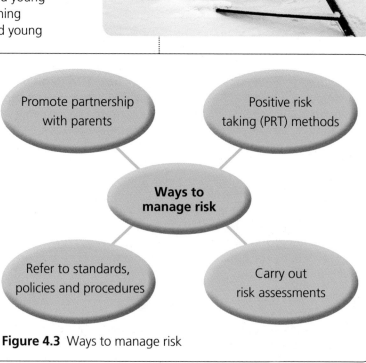

Figure 4.3 Ways to manage risk

Carry out risk assessments

The process of carrying out a formal risk assessment helps to identify the risks in a clear way and points to steps that can be taken to minimise risk to an acceptable level. It also provides evidence of the reasoning behind your decision, which may be useful if this is later questioned. Your argument is much stronger if you record the process and can produce written evidence that is clearly dated. PRT alongside your own risk assessment provides a strong combination. On occasion the decisions reached by a child or young person through PRT and your formal risk assessment may differ. As the adult, you may need to take the decision to overrule their decision. Try to continue a dialogue and acknowledge their feelings of disappointment and anger.

Promote partnership with parents

By working closely together in **partnership with parents** of the children to whom you have a duty of care, a trusting relationship will build between you. Take time to recognise and understand what is important to the parents about bringing up their child. At the same time explain your role and how at times it may be necessary to reach a compromise in order to resolve dilemmas. It may be appropriate to include older children and young people in discussions, in order to help them understand why decisions are made.

Refer to standards, policies and procedures

You might find it useful to look at standards, such as the Early Years Foundation Stage (EYFS) Statutory Framework, where you can check whether your decision fulfils the guidance given. Similarly, have a look at policies such as the confidentiality policy and safeguarding policy that set out the principles you should follow in your workplace.

Over to you!

Find out if your colleagues and manager in your placement or work setting have heard of the concept of positive risk taking.

- ▶ *If so, find out how this is put into practice in your work setting.*
- ▶ *If not, take opportunities to explain what this means and the benefits it can bring.*

Key terms

Partnership with parents: working together with a child's parents to understand their priorities and point of view and explain your responsibilities towards their child

Sources of advice and support

Your assessment criteria:

2.3 Explain where to get additional support and advice about conflicts and dilemmas

Seeking support and advice is a crucial part of any decision-making process. Figure 4.4 suggests useful sources.

Liaise with others

Initially you could speak to a colleague whose opinion and judgement you trust. Sometimes just talking about a dilemma with someone else helps you to organise your thoughts and brings clarity. Discussing difficult situations with others may bring a fresh angle to the dilemma or they might have past experiences to draw on. However, make sure you do not breach confidentiality during discussions. Sometimes it is best to go straight to a senior colleague or supervisor who has more authority to support you. Specific practitioners will have specialist information or expertise to guide you. Union representatives can be a valuable source for legal information to do with employment law and can provide free advice and support.

Approach organisations

There are several organisations that may be a rich source of advice. These are available through their websites or by telephone. These

Figure 4.4 Sources of advice and support

might be in the public or the voluntary sector and many produce literature in the form of leaflets, which can be very informative. Such organisations include:

▶ professional bodies, such as Ofsted

▶ service providers, such as the police or children and family services departments

▶ advisory centres, such as the Citizens Advice Bureau

▶ charities, such as the NSPCC and Childline

▶ supportive organisations, such as a union, who are particularly qualified to provide legal information related to particular employment.

Consult documents

There is a range of relevant documents which, between them, can provide information or evidence or support for your position. Think about your job description and contract of employment. Also, there may be information about laws, standards and codes of practice relevant to your area of working practice. Workplace policies and procedures offer step-by-step guidance covering issues such as confidentiality, whistle-blowing, safeguarding and health and safety.

When you gather together all your information from people, organisations and documents, before using it to make decisions, check that it is:

▶ up to date

▶ relevant

▶ reliable

▶ complete.

Over to you!

▶ *What sources of advice and support are available to you in your placement or work setting?*

▶ *Who might you speak to you if you are faced with a dilemma between your duty of care and a child's rights or a parent's responsibility?*

Knowledge Assessment Task | 2.1 | 2.2 | 2.3

Sometimes conflicts and dilemmas arise between a duty of care and an individual's rights, making it necessary to make a decision based on relevant support and advice. Read the scenario below and respond to the questions that follow.

It is a beautiful, clear day and an 8 cm covering of snow lies in the primary school playground. Most of the children are excited about playing out in the snow, but others are worried because they don't have boots, gloves and hats. One concerned parent phones, anxious about accidents resulting from slipping, but another threatens to take her children out of school if they are not allowed out to experience play in the snow before it melts. The teacher on playground duty fears that carelessly thrown snowballs could cause accidental damage, injury and upset feelings. The school caretaker fears people will slip inside on floors that are wet from children's shoes. One teacher has already announced to his class that they will do some experiments with snow, looking at the properties of water and the art teacher had decided they will study and draw snowflakes.

1. Describe each aspect of the dilemma and conflict the staff team faces between exercising a duty of care and upholding the rights of children and parents.
2. Describe how you would manage the risks associated with the conflict or dilemma between the staff members' duty of care and the children's and parents' rights.
3. Explain where you might look for additional support and advice to deal with each aspect of the dilemma or conflict.

Keep your responses as evidence for your assessment.

Your assessment criteria:

3.1 Describe how to respond to complaints

3.2 Explain the main points of agreed procedures for handling complaints

How should you respond to complaints, using proper procedures?

It is inevitable that from time to time a **complaint** will arise within a service for children and young people. Commonly these will concern the tension between maintaining a duty of care and upholding the rights of an individual. Perhaps a parent perceives that their child has not been looked after with sufficient care, or that a right due to the child has been overlooked. How the complaint is handled is very important for finding a satisfactory resolution, as well as to enable learning from the experience.

Dealing positively with complaints

It is important to acknowledge that people have a right to complain and to listen to such complaints with an open mind. Although it can feel uncomfortable to receive what feels like negative criticism, try to view complaints as useful opportunities to receive feedback that can help you improve the service you provide.

Sometimes a complaint can be handled with a quick conversation, almost in passing, which can clear up a misunderstanding or give information that had been overlooked. At other times it is a more serious situation that needs to be handled by a formal complaints procedure. Always ask for help from a colleague if you are unsure how to deal with someone wishing to make a complaint.

Figure 4.5 highlights some suggestions for handling a complaint in a professional way.

Key terms

Complaint: an expression of concern, dissatisfaction or disappointment in a situation or service

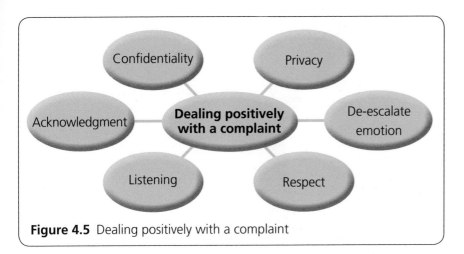

Figure 4.5 Dealing positively with a complaint

Privacy

It is best to find a place to talk where the complaint can be discussed in private, away from the work area and the presence of children and other parents. During your conversation avoid answering the phone or dealing with any other interruption.

De-escalate emotion

If the person is angry and upset, speaking calmly and quietly in response may help them settle. Suggest that you sit comfortably and offer refreshment to help the person relax and let go of intense emotions.

Respect

Respect is shown by the way you respond to the person. Be aware of your **body language**, such as facial expression, tone of voice, proximity and gestures. For example, allow some space between you and the person, do not defensively cross your arms in front of your body and have frequent eye contact, but avoid staring.

Listen

The most important response is to listen carefully, giving your full attention and clarifying their words when necessary to make sure you understand their point correctly.

Acknowledgment

Emphasise the person's right to complain and show them you are taking their complaint seriously. If you try to ignore a complaint it is unlikely to go away and could escalate to a more serious level.

Confidentiality

The parent should be reassured that the matter will be held in confidence and only shared by those who need to know about it.

Key terms

Body language: the non-verbal messages communicated through facial expression, tone of voice, proximity and gestures

Over to you!

Has anyone ever complained to you or about you, or your work?

▶ *How did it make you feel?*
▶ *How did you respond?*

Complaints procedures

Complaints at work should always be dealt with according to a **complaints procedure** that is set down in a complaints policy. This ensures that the rights of the parents are supported in a proper way, while also protecting the practitioner. For example, while it is right that you should listen to a complaint, you are not expected to tolerate aggression or verbal abuse from the complainant.

The policy must be available for parents to see at any time and should include information about who to take their complaint to if they are not satisfied with the way it is being handled. Contact details, such as a name, address and telephone number must appear in the complaints policy and are often also displayed on a notice board.

Complaints procedures set out each stage of the process, including a timescale, so the complainant knows what to expect.

1. A verbal response should be forthcoming, within a certain timeframe.

2. A meeting should be arranged at a mutually agreed time and place.

3. There should be a written response following the meeting.

4. If this does not resolve the matter the complaint needs to be put in writing to a higher authority.

Key terms

Complaints procedure: an official process to deal with a complaint, where specific steps are taken to ensure that it is thoroughly investigated with fairness shown to all parties

Over to you!

► *Have you read the complaints procedure in operation at your placement or work setting? List the procedure.*

► *Do you know who you should go to for support and advice if a complaint is made about you or your work?*

Knowledge Assessment Task   3.1   3.2

Responding to complaints in a positive way and following a formal complaints procedure correctly are both important for finding satisfactory resolutions to problems. Read the scenario below and respond to the questions that follow.

Scenario

Reno is a primary school lunch-time assistant and supervises the children going into meals and eating their lunch. He is frequently approached by a parent, Mrs Bane, who constantly grumbles to him about school meals not being nutritious enough; too high in fat; vegetables overcooked. She says it puts her daughter off eating at school. Reno usually finds some cheerful reply such as, 'It's better than starving Mrs B,' or joking, 'I eat them and I'm still here!' but she seems to be getting more annoyed as the weeks go by.

1. Why do you think Reno's approach isn't working?

2. Can you describe a better way for Reno to respond to Mrs Bane's complaints?

Find a copy of the complaints procedure at your placement or work setting and answer the question below with reference to this.

3. If Mrs Bane were to take her complaint further, how would you explain the main points of the correct procedure for doing this?

Keep your responses as evidence for your assessment.

Are you ready for assessment?

AC	What do you know now?	Assessment task	✓
1.1	What it means to have a duty of care in your own work role	Page 105	
1.2	How duty of care contributes to the safeguarding or protection of individuals	Page 106	
2.1	The potential conflicts or dilemmas that may arise between the duty of care and an individual's rights.	Page 117	
2.2	How to manage risks associated with conflicts or dilemmas between an individual's rights and the duty of care	Page 117	
2.3	Where to get additional support and advice about conflicts and dilemmas	Page 117	
3.1	How to respond to complaints	Page 121	
3.2	The main points of agreed procedures for handling complaints	Page 121	

There is no practical assessment for this unit, but your tutor or assessor may question you about the following points.

What can you do now? ✓

Can you apply your knowledge about the duty of care to your practical work in your placement or work setting? Could you discuss this with your assessor?

5 | Understand child and young person development (CYP 3.1)

Assessment of this unit

This unit is about the development of children and young people, from birth to 19 years old. It covers some of the theories that underpin our understanding of child development, the expected pattern of development and some of the factors that can influence this, including transitions. The unit also covers the monitoring of children and young people's development and the importance of early intervention, if development does not follow the expected pattern.

The assessment of this unit is all knowledge based (things that you need to know about) but it is also very important to be able to apply your knowledge practically, in the real work environment or in your placement.

To complete this unit successfully, you will need to produce evidence of your knowledge. The following chart explains what you need to know, alongside the relevant assessment criteria.

Your tutor or assessor will help you to prepare for your assessment, and the tasks suggested in this chapter will help you to create the evidence you need.

AC	What you need to know
1.1	The sequence and rate of each aspect of development from birth to 19 years
1.2	The difference between sequence of development and rate of development and why the difference is important
2.1 2.2	How children and young people's development is influenced by a range of personal factors and external factors
2.3	How theories of development and frameworks to support development influence current practice
3.1	How to monitor children and young people's development using different methods
3.2	The reasons why children and young people's development may not follow the expected pattern
3.3	How disability may affect development
3.4	How different types of interventions can promote positive outcomes for children and young people where development is not following the expected pattern

4.1	The importance of early identification of speech, language and communication delays and disorders and the potential risks of late recognition
4.2	How multi-agency teams work together to support speech, language and communication
4.3	How play and activities are used to support the development of speech, language and communication
5.1	How different types of transitions can affect children and young people's development
5.2	The effect on children and young people of having positive relationships during periods of transition

There is no practical assessment for this unit, but your tutor or assessor may question you about some of the following points.

What you need to do

Apply your knowledge about the development of children and young people to your practice in the real work environment.

Apply your knowledge about early intervention and monitoring the development of children and young people to your practice in the real work environment.

Apply your knowledge about the effects of transitions on the development of children and young people in the real work environment.

This unit links with some of the other mandatory units:

SHC 31	Promote communication in health, social care or children and young people's settings
CYP 3.2	Promote child and young person development
CYP 3.7	Understand how to support positive outcomes for children and young people
EYMP 5	Support children's speech, language and communication

Some of your learning will be repeated in these units and will give you the chance to review your knowledge and understanding.

Understand the expected pattern of development for children and young people from birth to 19 years

Your assessment criteria:

1.1 Explain the sequence and rate of each aspect of development from birth to 19 years

1.2 Explain the difference between sequence of development and rate of development and why the difference is important

What is development?

Development is a continuous process, which begins at **conception** and continues throughout life into old age. It is not about physical growth but refers to the process of maturing and developing skills and abilities.

The **sequence** of development in children and young people will always be the same, for example, children will always learn to walk before they can run, hop or skip. However, the **rate** of development varies a great deal in different children, for example, some will begin to walk at a very early age and learn to talk much later.

Equally, some young people will experience puberty at an earlier age than others.

Young children often concentrate on one area of development at a time, for example, learning to walk, and this can mean that other areas of development, such as talking or potty training, seem to lag behind.

Children's development is usually monitored by examining **milestones** or development norms. Milestones provide an average guide for assessing a child's progress, but it is important to remember that there is a very wide range of normal and every child or young person will progress in their own individual way.

Key terms

Conception: the start of life, when the ovum is fertilised by the sperm

Milestones: important features or stages in development

Rate: the relative speed of progress or change

Sequence: pattern or order

Over to you!

Can you remember (or have you been told) at what age you first:

▶ *learnt to walk*

▶ *said your first word (Do you know what it was?)*

▶ *learnt to ride a bike (with or without stabilisers)*

▶ *learnt to swim?*

Compare your experiences with those of others in the group. What differences do you notice?

Aspects of development

This unit will examine the development of children and young people in the following different areas.

Physical

The development of the body and physical skills such as balance, body co-ordination, gross motor skills such as climbing, skipping and kicking a ball, and fine motor skills such as threading, fastening buttons and using a pencil.

Intellectual (cognitive)

The development of thinking skills, including imagination and creativity, memory and concentration, problem-solving skills and understanding concepts such as size, shape, space and time.

Communication

The development of speech, language and non-verbal communication, including learning to talk and speak in sentences and developing listening skills.

Social, emotional and behavioural

The development of confidence and independence, including learning how to manage feelings and behaviour, understanding how to get along with others and developing self-esteem.

Moral

The development of values and beliefs and an understanding of what is right and wrong.

All areas of development are linked and influence each other and it is important to view this in a holistic way.

Key terms

Fine motor skills: the use of hand and finger movements

Gross motor skills: the use of large body movements

Holistic: emphasising the importance of the whole child

Over to you!

Make a list of all the different areas of development (physical, communication, intellectual, social, emotional, behavioural and moral) for the children involved in the following activities.

- *A seven-month-old baby, sitting with a familiar adult and playing 'peep-bo'*
- *A five-year-old using a computer*
- *An eight-year-old playing football in a team*

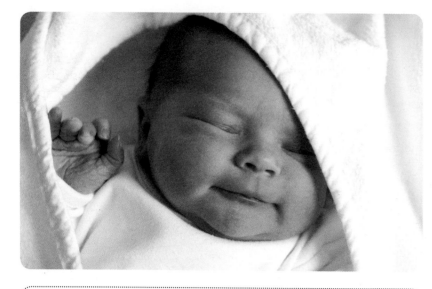

Development from birth to three years

Children's development progresses extremely rapidly in the first three years of life.

Physically, their bodies become stronger and they learn to co-ordinate their movements with both gross and fine motor skills. In the first year of life, most babies will gain control of their neck and back muscles, which helps them to support their own head and sit up.

As they gradually develop more strength, they learn to stand and eventually to walk.

Most 18-month-olds can walk by themselves, although they will often be quite unsteady.

Muscle strength, balance and body co-ordination continue to develop and, by the age of three, most children can run, jump and pedal a tricycle.

At around four months of age, most babies will start to reach out and grasp toys. They start by using their whole hand (**palmer grasp**), but this soon progresses to a **pincer grasp** (using the thumb and index finger) at about 10 months. Toddlers become more skilled in using their hands as their **manipulative skills** and **hand–eye co-ordination** develop. Most two-year-olds can scribble with a chunky crayon and by the age of three years, most children can thread large beads and build a tower with eight blocks.

Intellectually, children progress rapidly in their thinking skills. Babies rely on their senses to provide them with information about their world. For example, they learn to recognise their parents by sight, the sound of their voices and their smell. Gradually they learn to make sense of this information and start to piece it together as their thinking skills develop. Most toddlers will use simple problem-solving skills, such as **cause and effect**, as they

Key terms

Cause and effect: associating actions with their results

Hand–eye co-ordination: the ability to make the hands work together with what the eyes can see

Manipulative skills: ability to use the hands to complete precise, detailed tasks

Palmer grasp: using the whole hand to hold an object

Pincer grasp: using the thumb and index finger to hold an object

learn what they can do and how things work. For example, they will learn that 'If I push this knob, then the Jack-in-the-Box will pop up.' Most two-year-olds can complete a simple inset puzzle; by the age of three years, children can usually understand basic **concepts** such as size, shape and colour.

Communication development progresses at an amazing rate during this time.

Young babies communicate by crying but, with encouragement, they soon learn to babble and form their first words. Most toddlers can understand far more than they can actually say and often make themselves understood by using lots of gestures, such as pointing. As young children gain more experience, for example, at pre-school groups, their language skills develop rapidly, their vocabulary expands and they learn to communicate in different situations. Most three-year-olds have a vocabulary of approximately 200 words and can use simple sentences to communicate.

Emotionally, socially and behaviourally, children make a lot of progress in the first three years of life. Babies are totally dependent on adults for all their care but, by the age of three years, most children are confident and independent individuals.

Learning to get along with others can be quite challenging for young children. In the first three years of life, children are very **egocentric**, which means that their viewpoint is very centred on themselves. Social skills, such as sharing, turn-taking and co-operating, have to be learnt and don't always come easily! Very young children do not have the level of understanding or the language skills to express their feelings and this can lead to a lot of frustration.

Moral development is starting to emerge at this age and children are learning about acceptable and unacceptable behaviour. They can usually follow simple rules but need consistent guidance from caring adults to help them with this process.

Key terms

Concepts: ideas that form the building bocks of our ideas and understanding

Egocentric: self-centred, concerned only about your own needs

Your assessment criteria:

1.1 Explain the sequence and rate of each aspect of development from birth to 19 years

Over to you!

Think about children in your placement, work setting or others that you know, aged from three to five years. Make a list of the skills and abilities you have observed in their holistic development. Remember to include:

▶ *physical skills (both gross and fine motor)*

▶ *intellectual (cognitive) skills*

▶ *communication skills*

▶ *emotional, social and behavioural*

▶ *moral development.*

Development from three to five years

Between the ages of three and five, children make great strides in their development.

They become physically stronger, their language skills progress very rapidly and they become increasingly independent and capable.

Physically, children develop more body co-ordination with their gross motor skills and learn to control their movements more skilfully. Fine motor skills are also developing as children learn how to use their manipulative skills to complete more complex tasks. By the age of five, many children can hop and skip and most five-year-olds will use a dominant hand (being either right-handed or left-handed).

Intellectually, children are starting to understand more difficult concepts (such as time) and will use problem-solving skills to work out things for themselves (see Figure 5.1). By the age of five, most children are learning to read and write.

Communication skills also progress very rapidly during this period, as the child's vocabulary expands and they constantly ask questions! Talking with children, and listening and responding to them carefully, will help them learn to communicate more confidently. Most five-year-olds have a wide vocabulary and can communicate using complex sentences that are mostly grammatically correct.

Emotionally, socially and behaviourally, children undergo many changes between the ages of three and five years. For many children, this will be the stage at which they start nursery and then move on to school. Being in different situations encourages children to learn about managing their feelings and behaviour, but they will still need help in learning to share and co-operate in social situations. By the age of five, most children can separate more easily from their parents and are able to do things for themselves, for example, they may go to the toilet independently.

Moral development is also progressing and children are generally more thoughtful towards others. They also understand the difference between right and wrong.

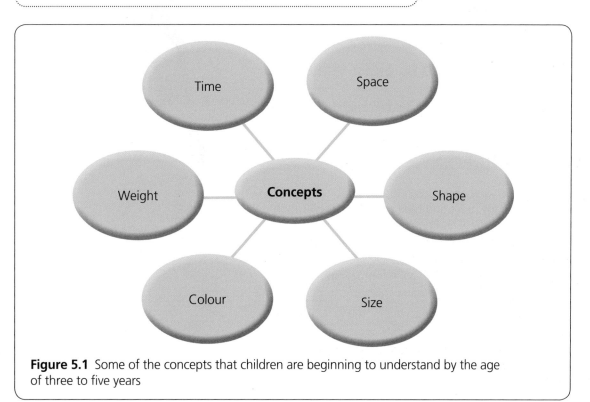

Figure 5.1 Some of the concepts that children are beginning to understand by the age of three to five years

Your assessment criteria:

1.1 Explain the sequence and rate of each aspect of development from birth to 19 years

Over to you!

▶ *Make a list of games and activities that would encourage the development of gross motor skills with children at the ages of six to eight years.*

▶ *Share your list with others in the group.*

Development from five to eight years

Between the ages of five and eight, children are becoming much more independent and capable.

Physically, children develop more stamina and improved body co-ordination.

Team games such as football are very popular with children at this age. They will enjoy practising their physical skills through exercise and outdoor play. Children also become more skilful with their manipulative abilities as they learn more challenging tasks. Some activities, such as tying shoe laces, require more practice but most six-year-olds can kick and control a football and have legible handwriting. By the age of eight, many children can ride a bicycle without stabilisers and create quite detailed drawings.

Intellectually, a great deal of children's learning will now take place in school. Children will develop their skills in literacy (reading, writing, speaking and listening), their understanding of problem solving and mathematical skills such as counting, calculating and estimating. At six years old, most children can do simple calculations and, by the age of eight, children will usually be able to tell the time.

Communication skills also develop a great deal as children learn about descriptive language and the rules of grammar. Bilingual children may be learning two systems of communication: one that they use for their learning in school and a different one for communicating at home. Most six-year-olds will enjoy chatting and, by the age of eight, most children can engage in more complex conversations and will enjoy telling jokes.

Emotionally, socially and behaviourally, children are becoming much more mature and independent. Friendships are very important at this stage and most children will have a 'best friend', usually of the same gender. With their improved language skills, children are much more capable of expressing their feelings and managing their behaviour. By the age of eight, most children will have stable friendships and enjoy being part of a group.

Morally, children at this age are very concerned about rules and the difference between 'fair' and 'unfair'. They will often remind others about the rules and tell when rules have been broken.

Case study

Anya is a healthy six-year-old girl. She lives with her mum, dad and three-year-old brother and attends the local primary school. She enjoys ballet and gymnastics and is learning to swim. At school, Anya is an enthusiastic pupil and has a close group of friends. She is confident in most situations and enjoys reading aloud and group singing sessions.

1. Describe **two** aspects of Anya's physical, intellectual, communication, social, emotional, behavioural and moral development that you would expect at this age.
2. Summarise the developmental progress, in all areas, that you would expect Anya to make over the next two years.

Over to you!

▶ *Make a list of all the children's games you can think of that have rules, for example, about taking turns, who goes first or how the winner is decided.*

▶ *Share your list with others in the group.*

Development from eight to 12 years

This period in children's development includes some major transitions.

Physically, the first signs of puberty can start in girls from around the age of nine; some girls may even start to menstruate at around the age of 10 or 11. Puberty usually starts later in boys, often when they are around 13 or 14 years old.

Intellectually, children's thinking skills are maturing and most 10-year-olds can now understand **abstract** ideas, such as feelings. Their reasoning and problem-solving skills are becoming more developed. Most 10-year-olds can complete quite complicated calculations, interpret graphs and solve equations involving algebra, fractions or decimals. Reading and writing skills are also more developed and most 10-year-olds can read more challenging texts and write complex stories.

Communication skills develop in a range of different directions. Children at this stage will enjoy chatting in friendship groups and many will develop their own slang words, which can be very specific to particular groups or cultures. Children may also start using other methods to communicate, such as texts and emails.

Emotionally, socially and behaviourally, this can be a very challenging time for children. The transition to secondary school can be extremely demanding and some children will experience intense anxiety and real fear. It can also be a stage in children's lives when they feel a great deal of pressure to be like their friends. It is now that they may start to rebel against their parents or carers.

Key terms

Abstract: a theoretical idea that does not have a concrete existence

Morally, children are much more aware of the consequences of their own behaviour (for example, the effects on the environment) and have more understanding of the need for rules in society.

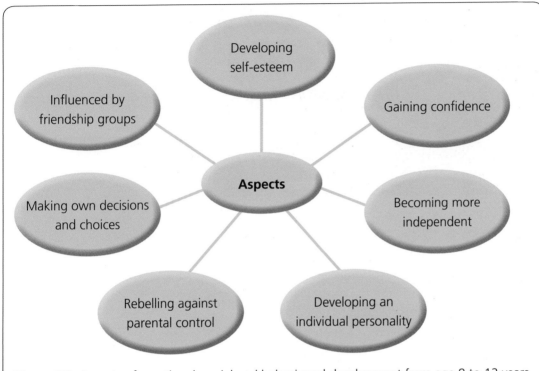

Figure 5.2 Aspects of emotional, social and behavioural development from age 8 to 12 years

Children can now read more challenging texts

135

Development from 12 to 19 years

During this period of development, young people are maturing into adults. They start to become independent from their parents or carers and are developing their own ideas and individuality.

Physically, most girls will complete the process of puberty by the age of 15 or 16 years.

Their body shape will change as their breasts and hips develop and menstruation becomes established. For most boys, puberty starts at around the age of 14 years. Their voices become deeper, they grow facial and body hair and develop a more muscular body shape. Some boys can grow very rapidly at this stage, which can lead to some degree of clumsiness and poor spatial awareness.

Intellectually, young people will be faced with challenges in school as they prepare for examinations and start to think about their future. This can be a very stressful time for young people, as the pressure to achieve and succeed is a powerful force. Young people are required to stay in some form of education or training until the age of 18. For some this will mean staying on at school but, for others, it may involve moving on to college or some other further education facility. Beyond the age of 18, many young people will be going on to higher education in university or entering employment.

Communication skills become more diverse as many young people become increasingly involved with electronic communication such as social networking. Further and higher education will make different demands on the communication skills of young people in expressing themselves, discussing ideas and analysing information.

Over to you!

Write a personal statement to describe yourself. Include what you are good at and what you like to do. Your statement should describe your skills and abilities, interests and strengths and your hopes for the future.

Key terms

Spatial awareness: well-considered awareness of things in the immediate environment

Emotionally, socially and behaviourally, this is a time when young people are experimenting with ideas, feelings and behaviour. Many young people will experience their first romantic relationship at this stage and this can lead to some complicated emotions that are difficult for young people to manage. Boys as well as girls at this stage can become overly concerned about their appearance, weight or body image. In some cases, this can lead to eating disorders, low self-esteem or depression.

Morally, young people are generally showing more interest in moral issues. Some may experiment with cigarettes, alcohol or other drugs at this stage and it is important that young people have access to reliable information, in order to make informed choices about their behaviour.

Knowledge Assessment Task   1.1   1.2

Create a series of information pages for a parenting website that includes the following information:

1. Explain the difference between the sequence and rate of development and why this difference is important.

2. Summarise the sequence of development in children and young people from 0 to 19 years of age.

You can illustrate your pages with suitable images. Remember to include aspects of physical, intellectual, communication, social, emotional, behavioural and moral development.

Keep your notes as evidence towards your assessment.

What are the factors that can influence development?

There are many different influences, both positive and negative, that can affect the development of a child or young person at various stages in their life. Some of these influences will be as a result of personal factors, such as health or disability, and some will be because of external factors such as family background or environment. Poverty and deprivation can have a long-lasting negative effect on children's development. (See also Chapter 11, page 286.) However, a supportive environment, with caring adults who provide opportunities for play and education, will have a positive influence.

A child's health is another major factor that can have an influence on development. For example, if a child suffers from a chronic illness such as **asthma**, a physical disability or learning difficulties, their development can also be affected. Many factors that influence development occur before birth, for example, **genetic** conditions such as **cystic fibrosis**. Other factors will have an influence during pregnancy, for example, if a pregnant woman smokes or becomes infected with the rubella virus (German measles), the child's development can be affected. Equally, if the baby is born **prematurely** then development can be delayed.

Some of the major influences on the development of children and young people are summarised in Figure 5.3.

Key terms

Asthma: a non-infectious condition that can be triggered by allergic reactions and causes respiratory difficulties

Cystic fibrosis: a hereditary condition affecting the child's pancreas and lungs, which causes respiratory and digestive problems

Genetic: hereditary condition occurring among members of a family

Prematurely: born before the 37th week of pregnancy

Figure 5.3 Some of the major influences on the development of children and young people

Personal factors	Example
Health	Chronic conditions such as asthma can cause children to have time off school; infections such as **meningitis** can cause developmental delay
Disability	**Cerebral palsy** can result in brain damage and cause problems with mobility
Sensory impairment	Hearing difficulties are one of the most common causes of language delay and speech problems in young children
Learning difficulties	**Down's syndrome** can result in developmental delay, learning difficulties and health problems

External factors	Example
Family background	Family values, culture and the way a child is encouraged and cared for can all affect a child's development and progress
The environment	Housing conditions, safety and opportunities for play and education can all influence how a child develops
Poverty and deprivation	Lack of money can lead to poor nutrition, lack of opportunities and lower expectations
Looked-after children (children in care)	Children and young people in the care system are more vulnerable, often due to a lack of stability and **attachment disorder** – this can affect their emotional, social and academic development
Personal choices	Choices young people make, for example, about drug use or sexual behaviour, can influence their development and life chances

Key terms

Attachment disorder: the failure to form a secure attachment relationship and an inability to develop significant emotional connections with other people

Cerebral palsy: a group of conditions caused by brain damage before or during birth, which can result in problems with speech, muscle tone and movement

Down's syndrome: a chromosomal disorder caused by the presence of all or part of an extra 21st chromosome

Meningitis: inflammation of the protective membranes around the brain and spinal cord, known collectively as the *meninges*

A hearing impairment can affect speech and language development

How do theories about child development influence current practice?

Some theories about child development were formulated many years ago and it is sometimes easy to discount them as being 'old fashioned' and no longer relevant in our modern world. However, it is important to remember that current practice is based on years of knowledge and experience, which helps us to understand children's learning, development and behaviour.

Research into different aspects of child development is an ongoing process and new information is emerging all the time. It is therefore important for anyone who works with children and young people to keep up to date with new developments as they arise and to incorporate new ideas into their professional practice.

Many of the principles of our current early years' frameworks are based on sound theories about child development. The approach known as social pedagogy seeks to bring together theories and concepts from psychology, sociology and education to create a holistic way of working with children and young people.

Theories about children's cognitive development and learning

Piaget (1896–1980)

Jean Piaget was a Swiss theorist who claimed that children learn actively through their play. He suggested that children build up (or construct) their knowledge and understanding, based on their experiences of the world around them. Piaget used the term schema to define a child's mental structures and suggested that children's learning progresses in distinct stages, as outlined in Figure 5.4.

Your assessment criteria:

2.3 Explain how theories of development and frameworks to support development influence current practice

Key terms

Schema: a mental structure which the child can generalise and use in a variety of different situations

Social pedagogy: a framework for the holistic education and care of children and young people

Figure 5.4 Piaget's stages of cognitive development

Stage and approximate age	Characteristics	Example
Sensori-motor (0–2 years)	Learning about self and the environment through senses and movements	Babies learn to recognise their main carer through sight, smell and the sound of their voice Learning that their movements can cause things to happen (e.g. shaking a rattle makes a sound)
Pre-operational (2–7 years)	Applying the new knowledge of language to represent thoughts and objects; thinking is very concrete and egocentric	Children use language to ask questions, name objects and express themselves; thinking is dominated by their own perspectives
Concrete operational (7–11 years)	Ability to think logically and use reasoning	Can solve problems and work things out based on the ability to conserve
Formal operational (11–15 years)	Ability to think in the abstract (without using concrete representations)	Can fully understand abstract concepts such as feelings; can perform mental calculations and organise ideas in their minds

Key terms

Conserve: the ability to problem solve using logical thinking and reasoning, irrespective of apparent visual evidence

Over to you!

▶ Investigate Piaget's theory about schema.
▶ Make a list of some of the schemas he described (for example, rotational) and the characteristics of different schemas that can sometimes be observed in children's play behaviour.

Vygotsky (1896–1934)

Lev Vygotsky was a Russian theorist who claimed that children learn predominantly through their interactions with adults and the environment. He suggested that children are born sociable and that adults play an extremely important role in extending children's learning and helping them to achieve their full potential (their **zone of proximal development**).

Adults provide a framework to support children's learning through the process of scaffolding

Bruner (born 1915)

Jerome Bruner is an American psychologist who developed ideas about children's thinking and problem-solving skills. He emphasised the role of adults in **scaffolding** children's learning, by providing a framework to support their thinking. This theory underpins the concept of 'sustained, shared thinking' in early years practice. (See Chapter 13, page 332.)

Your assessment criteria:

2.3 Explain how theories of development and frameworks to support development influence current practice

Key terms

Scaffolding: the process of adults providing a framework of support to encourage children's learning

Zone of proximal development: the difference between what a child can do without adult help and what they can do with adult help

Over to you!

Although classical conditioning is not used in modern-day practice with children and young people, think about the influence and importance of this theory in situations such as:

▶ *children and young people responding instinctively to the sound of the fire alarm in a setting*

▶ *children and young people learning to respond to a bell as a signal for the end of a class, time to line up in the playground or home time*

▶ *babies anticipating a meal time by waving their arms or banging their spoons*

▶ *children and young people learning to overcome a phobia, for example, of dogs, needles or the dark.*

Can you think of any other examples?

Pavlov (1849–1936)

Ivan Pavlov was a Russian physiologist who developed the theory of classical conditioning. His work was based on studying the responses of dogs when they were being fed. He noticed that the dogs always salivated just before their food arrived. He concluded that the dogs were making an association between the arrival of food and other factors (such as the sound of footsteps) and this was causing them to salivate. He confirmed this by ringing a bell every time the dogs were fed and, eventually, the dogs salivated just at the sound of a bell, without any food being produced at all. Pavlov called this a **conditioned response** and suggested that it forms an important part of the learning process. John B. Watson (1878–1958) was an American psychologist who further developed Pavlov's theories in his work on helping children to deal with **phobias**.

Pavlov (on the right) developed the theory of classical conditioning

Skinner (1904–1990)

Burrhus Frederic Skinner was an American psychologist who developed the theory of **operant conditioning.** His work was based on the study of rats in a specially constructed box, which was designed to train the rats to behave in a particular way. If the rats travelled the right way through the box, they were rewarded with food (positive reinforcers), but if they travelled the wrong way, they received a mild electric shock. Skinner discovered that the rats learnt to travel the correct way because they were encouraged by **positive reinforcement** (food). He also found that by maintaining the positive reinforcement, the rats continued to repeat the 'correct' behaviour.

This theory has a direct influence on the way we understand children's behaviour today through the use of praise and encouragement, stickers and other rewards to encourage appropriate behaviour.

Bandura (born 1925)

Albert Bandura is a Canadian psychologist who developed the social learning theory. His work suggests that children learn by observing and imitating others and that adults have an extremely important responsibility to be good role models for children and young people.

Key terms

Conditioned response: a type of learned response that occurs through association with a specific stimulus

Operant conditioning: basic process by which an individual's behaviour is shaped by reinforcement or by punishment

Phobia: irrational fear of simple things or social situations

Positive reinforcement: giving encouragement to a particular behaviour with the result that it is more likely to be repeated

Over to you!

► In your placement or work setting, think about situations in which you have observed children imitating adult behaviour, for example, in the role-play area. Share your experiences with others in the group.

► Do you set a good example for children and young people through your own language and behaviour?

Theories about children's social and emotional development

Bowlby (1907–1990)

John Bowlby was a British psychologist who developed **attachment theory**. His work emphasised the importance of young children developing a strong attachment relationship (emotional connection) with their main carer and the significance of this attachment for children's security, self-esteem and emotional development. This attachment relationship is particularly important in the first year of life. Building on this firm foundation, most young children are able to develop confidence, become more independent and learn to get along with others. Attachment theory underpins the development of the key-person approach in many settings and helps us to understand children's reactions to being separated from their main carers.

Maslow (1908–1970)

Abraham Maslow was an American psychologist who developed theories about motivation and personality, based on his hierarchy of needs. His work highlighted the importance of meeting fundamental, individual needs in order for people to reach their full potential ('self-actualisation'). This theory reminds us about the importance of meeting children's basic needs (such as food, warmth and sleep) in order for them to develop and learn. (See also Chapter 11, page 286.)

Freud (1856–1939)

Sigmund Freud was an Austrian psychoanalyst, who is best known for his theories about the unconscious mind. His theories about psychosexual development have been widely criticised. However, his work has given rise to many terms in common usage today, for example, the oral stage (describing the way that infants use their mouths to explore objects).

Erikson (1902–1994)

Erik Erikson was a German-American psychologist who is best known for his theories about the stages of psychosocial development. He described a series of life stages and challenges that must be overcome by all children and young people on their journey to adult maturity. He argued that each stage must be understood and accepted as an integral part of personality development.

Your assessment criteria:

2.1 Explain how children and young people's development is influenced by a range of personal factors

2.2 Explain how children and young people's development is influenced by a range of external factors

2.3 Explain how theories of development and frameworks to support development influence current practice

Key terms

Attachment theory: a theory concerning the formation of an emotional bond between children and their significant carers

Influences on current practice

Although most of these theories were originally developed many years ago, it is important to remember that research into child development is an ongoing process. Work with children and young people is constantly influenced by new ideas, which are based on established theory.

Some of the major influences on current practice are summarised in Figure 5.5.

Figure 5.5 Some of the major influences on current practice

Theory	Theorists	Influences on current practice
Constructivist	Piaget	The importance of 'hands on' experience, play and active learning
	Vygotsky	The importance of adults scaffolding children's learning and asking open-ended questions
	Bruner	
Behaviourist	Pavlov	The importance of praise, encouragement and positive reinforcement for encouraging acceptable behaviour
	Watson	
	Skinner	
Social learning	Bandura	The importance of being a good role model for children
Psychoanalytical	Freud	Understanding how the unconscious mind can influence children's behaviour, for example, fears and phobias
	Erikson	
Humanist	Maslow	The importance of satisfying children's basic needs in order for them to develop and learn
Attachment	Bowlby	The importance of a strong attachment relationship and the key person system

Knowledge Assessment Task 2.1 2.2 2.3

Prepare a presentation that could be shown to students who are studying child development. Your presentation should explain how:

▶ the development of children and young people can be influenced by both personal and external factors

▶ theories of development influence current practice

▶ frameworks to support development influence current practice.

You can use ICT or other resources to illustrate your presentation.

Keep your presentation and notes as evidence towards your assessment.

Over to you!

Look again at Maslow's hierarchy of needs (Figure 11.2, page 290). Think about your placement or work setting and make a list of the different ways that you meet children's basic needs for:

▶ *food*

▶ *security*

▶ *friendship*

▶ *self-esteem*

▶ *achievement.*

Your assessment criteria:

3.1 Explain how to monitor children and young people's development using different methods

Why is it important to monitor children's and young people's development?

All children and young people will develop in their own way and at their own rate, but not all children will follow the expected pattern and this can sometimes be a cause for concern. It is important for everyone who works with children and young people to be able to recognise when development is not following the expected pattern and to know how to respond.

Monitoring children and young people's development is very important in supporting their wellbeing and measuring their progress. Routine observation can often highlight problems or concerns with development and is often the starting point for **early intervention**. Recognising and responding to concerns about development can sometimes prevent further problems occurring. For example, if a child's language skills are not developing, they will not be able to communicate or make themselves understood. This will influence both their social and emotional development, as it will be difficult for them to make friendships and they will become frustrated at not being able to express themselves. If this is not recognised and responded to, the child will start to lose confidence and may develop a negative attitude and behaviour pattern.

Key terms

Early intervention: diagnosing and treating problems early in their development

Over to you!

In your placement or work setting, think about the different ways that children's development is monitored.

▶ *How do you use observations to monitor children's progress?*

▶ *How do you gain information from parents or carers about children's progress and how is this recorded?*

▶ *Do you use any standardised testing of children or young people?*

Share your experiences with others in the group.

Methods of monitoring children and young people's development

The development of children and young people is monitored in many different ways, by a variety of different professionals. For example, young children's developmental progress may be monitored by a health visitor, whereas the progress of a child's learning in school is monitored through standardised testing. Many different methods are used to monitor the development of children and young people, including observation and standardised assessment.

Regular observation is an extremely effective way to monitor development, as it provides a process for watching and recording what a child can do. There are many different ways to carry out observations of children and young people. Specific observation methods are discussed in Chapter 6, page 158.

Assessment frameworks also provide a method for monitoring children's development. For example, the Early Years Foundation Stage Framework (EYFSF) monitors the progress of children from birth to age five years and assesses their achievement against the Early Learning Goals. The **Common Assessment Framework (CAF)** provides a means of monitoring concerns about children or young people, including issues about their development, and creates a way for professionals to share information and work together.

Standard measurements are used in a variety of different ways and enable professionals to assess a child's progress relative to others in the same age group. For example, standard measurements include height and weight and results of vision and hearing tests, IQ tests or Standard Assessment Tests (SATs) in schools.

Information from parents and carers is also very important in monitoring the development of children and young people. Parents have a unique insight into their own children and will often be the first to notice problems with development or other difficulties. Practitioners need to make sure that parents are fully involved with the monitoring of children and young people's development.

Key terms

Common Assessment Framework (CAF): a nationally standardised approach to conducting an assessment of the needs of a child or young person and deciding how they should be met

What if development does not follow the expected pattern?

There are many reasons why development may not follow the expected pattern. It is important to be aware of the variations in order to provide support for the child and their family. Development can be influenced by many different factors, including health, disability, environment and family background. These have been outlined in Figure 5.3 on page 139 in this chapter.

Your assessment criteria:

3.2 Explain the reasons why children and young people's development may not follow the expected pattern

3.3 Explain how disability may affect development

Case study

Aisha is six years old and she lives with her large, extended traveller family in a caravan. The family move around a lot and Aisha's attendance at school is very erratic. She has attended three different primary schools so far and the family are about to move on again. They usually stay on established caravan sites but sometimes park on waste ground or on the roadside. Aisha has three brothers and sisters and they all share the same sleeping space in the caravan. Her brother, who is three years old, wets the bed at night. Both of Aisha's parents smoke cigarettes and Aisha suffers with asthma and uses an inhaler regularly.

1. Explain, with reasons, why Aisha's development may not follow the expected pattern.

2. Describe the possible impact of Aisha's lifestyle on her physical, intellectual, communication, emotional, social, behavioural and moral development.

You may want to refer to Figure 5.3 on page 139 to help you.

The effect of disability

Disability can affect the development of children and young people in a variety of different ways. Some examples are listed below.

Physical development may be affected by limited mobility if a child uses a wheelchair.

Intellectual development may be affected by a learning difficulty, for example, in a child who has Down's syndrome.

Communication may be affected by conditions such as cerebral palsy.

Emotional, social and behavioural development may be affected by conditions such as **autistic spectrum disorder (ASD)**.

Attitudes towards disability are discussed in Chapter 11, page 286.

It is extremely important for anyone who works with children or young people to focus on the individual, rather than on their disability. Terms such as 'the Down's syndrome child' or 'the special needs child' are disrespectful and can have a very negative affect on the emotional and social development of children and young people with disabilities.

It can also be very easy to make assumptions about the developmental needs of children with disabilities. For example, if a child has a physical disability and uses a wheelchair, it should never be assumed that they also have learning difficulties or that they can't hear or understand you. This can lead to stereotypical attitudes and discrimination; it is the responsibility of all practitioners to meet the individual needs of children or young people with disabilities to ensure that opportunities for learning and development are maximised.

Key terms

Autistic spectrum disorder (ASD): a neuro-developmental disorder of varying degrees, characterised by inflexibility of thought and imagination, impaired social interaction and difficulties with communication

Over to you!

▶ *Can you think of any situations where you have witnessed discrimination towards someone with a disability?*

▶ *Share your experiences with others in the group.*

Types of intervention

If the development of children or young people is not following the expected pattern, it is important not only to recognise this, but also to implement early intervention to maximise development and promote positive outcomes. Different types of intervention might include help from professional specialists, specific adaptations or assistive technology and equipment. Some interventions are highlighted in Figure 5.6.

Figure 5.6 Types of intervention

Professional intervention	Role
Physiotherapist	Specialises in mobility and maximising the body's movement and function; may help a child with muscle weakness, stiffness or difficulty in controlling their movements, e.g. cerebral palsy
Speech and language therapist	Provides support for children and young people with speech, language and communication difficulties
Special educational needs co-ordinator (SENCO), or inclusion co-ordinator	Organises support services in schools and nurseries for children with special educational needs
Educational psychologist	Provides support for children and young people with behavioural and educational difficulties, e.g. attention deficit hyperactivity disorder (ADHD)

Equipment and technology	Purpose
Sensory room	Stimulation for all the senses, e.g. through lights, sounds and textures, for children with sensory impairment, autistic spectrum disorder (ASD) and other disabilities
Hydrotherapy pool	Provides the opportunity for water-based exercise and stimulation for children with mobility difficulties, e.g. cerebral palsy
Voice-activated computer programs (used instead of a mouse or keyboard)	Provides assistance for children or young people with fine-motor skill or co-ordination problems
Specialised stands, chairs and frames	Enable children and young people with mobility problems to access resources, move around in the setting or participate in play activities

Your assessment criteria:

3.1 Explain how to monitor children and young people's development, using different methods

3.2 Explain the reasons why children and young people's development may not follow the expected pattern

3.3 Explain how disability may affect development

3.4 Explain how different types of interventions can promote positive outcomes for children and young people where development is not following the expected pattern.

Knowledge Assessment Task 3.1 3.2 3.3 3.4

Tom is four years old and has Down's syndrome. He attends a mainstream nursery every morning and a special playgroup on three afternoons every week. He is a very sociable boy, who enjoys music and dancing and active play. He participates enthusiastically in most nursery activities, including singing, story time and group time with other children.

Tom can pedal a tricycle, kick a football and catch a large ball, although he has difficulty with some fine motor skills such as using scissors. He can communicate his needs, using some spoken language and Makaton signs, and he understands simple instructions. He likes a familiar routine and quickly becomes upset if things change suddenly. Tom enjoys adult attention, particularly from Amy, his key person in nursery.

1. Explain how different methods could be used to monitor Tom's development in nursery.

2. Explain how Tom's disability may affect his development and why his development may not follow the expected pattern.

3. Explain how different types of intervention could promote positive outcomes for Tom.

Keep your notes as evidence towards your assessment.

Your assessment criteria:

4.1 Analyse the importance of early identification of speech, language and communication delays and disorders and the potential risks of late recognition

4.2 Explain how multi-agency teams work together to support speech, language and communication

4.3 Explain how play and activities are used to support the development of speech, language and communication

Why is it important to identify speech, language and communication disorders?

Speech, language and communication difficulties are discussed Chapter 16, page 402. It is extremely important to recognise potential problems and identify difficulties with speech and language, as this can affect all other areas of development, both in the short term and over longer periods of time. If communication disorders are not identified at an early stage, it can lead to a wide range of problems, including:

▶ difficulties in learning and understanding information, which can seriously affect educational progress

▶ problems in being understood and difficulties in making friends

▶ low levels of confidence and self-esteem

▶ problems with expressing feelings, leading to frustration, anger or anti-social behaviour.

In the longer term, this can lead to children not reaching their full potential, experiencing difficulties in making and sustaining relationships and long-term problems with behaviour.

Supporting children's speech, language and communication

There are many different professionals who can provide support for children and young people with speech, language and communication difficulties and for their parents, as highlighted in Figure 5.7.

It is very important for all the professionals involved to work together and use a multi-agency approach in providing support for the child and family. Multi-agency working is also discussed in Chapter 10, page 268.

Play and activities can also be extremely important in supporting speech, language and communication. For example, songs and rhymes, books and stories, puppets, role play and group games can all help children and young people to practise saying different words, communicate with each other and develop their use of language.

Puppets can be particularly helpful for children who are reluctant to speak; some puppets are especially designed for helping children to make mouth movements or specific sounds. Some books use rhyme and repetition to reinforce certain words and sounds and others use interactive techniques such as 'lift the flap' or pressing the picture to make a sound and encourage children's communication.

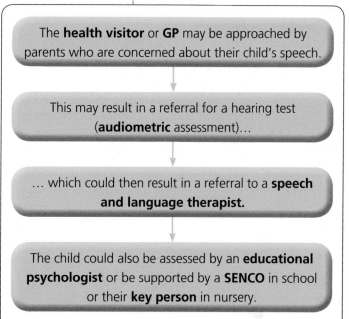

The **health visitor** or **GP** may be approached by parents who are concerned about their child's speech.

This may result in a referral for a hearing test (**audiometric** assessment)…

… which could then result in a referral to a **speech and language therapist.**

The child could also be assessed by an **educational psychologist** or be supported by a **SENCO** in school or their **key person** in nursery.

Figure 5.7 Professionals who can provide support for children and young people with SLC difficulties, and their parents

Knowledge Assessment Task   4.1   4.2   4.3

Polly is three years old. She is cared for by a child minder every morning and attends Treetops nursery every afternoon. Polly enjoys creative play, especially painting, singing and dancing, and she loves stories and picture books. Polly's child minder has recently expressed some concerns about Polly's speech development. She is worried that Polly does not speak very clearly and that it is sometimes difficult to understand what Polly says. This is particularly evident with words beginning with the letters 's', 'sh' and 'y'. For example, Polly says 'thand' instead of 'sand', 'thoos' instead of 'shoes' and 'lellow' for 'yellow'. At nursery, Polly's key person has noticed that Polly sometimes gets frustrated when other children do not seem to understand her.

1. Why is it important for Polly's speech, language and communication (SLC) difficulties to be identified?

2. Describe the potential risks for Polly if these difficulties are not recognised.

3. Explain how multi-agency teams might work together to support Polly's SLC difficulties.

4. Give some examples of play activities and explain how they could be used to support Polly's SLC development.

Keep your notes as evidence towards your assessment.

Over to you!

▶ Investigate some well-known children's nursery rhymes or songs that use the repetition of words or sounds with actions, for example, 'The wheels on the bus'.

▶ Make a list of some titles and learn the words and actions yourself!

How can transitions affect children and young people's development?

Change is a part of life for all children and young people. As they grow and develop, their bodies change, their friendships and relationships change and they will experience a variety of different situations involving transitions, including:

▶ *emotional transitions*, for example, bereavement, going into foster care, changing carers, new baby in the family

▶ *physical transitions*, for example, moving house, changing schools

▶ *physiological transitions*, for example, puberty, long-term medical conditions, going into hospital

▶ *intellectual transitions*, for example, moving between nursery–primary–secondary–college–work.

All children will experience transitions such as changing schools, but some transitions, such as going into foster care, will only affect some children or young people.

Children and young people respond to transitions in different ways, both positively and negatively. Transition can affect all aspects of development and behaviour but, in most cases, the effects are short-lived and temporary. It is very important that adults who work with children and young people deal sensitively with transition situations and provide support if necessary.

Some of the negative effects of transitions on the development of children and young people include:

▶ *regression* – going back to the development or behaviour of a younger child, for example, bed-wetting or 'baby talk'

▶ *changes in behaviour* – this can include becoming withdrawn or clingy, but also aggressive or attention-seeking behaviour

▶ *physical problems*, for example, food refusal, anorexia or bulimia, or sleep disturbances, including nightmares

▶ *speech problems*, for example, stuttering or **selective mutism**

▶ *mental problems*, for example, lack of concentration, depression or even suicidal tendencies or self-harm (including the misuse of drugs or risky sexual behaviour among young people).

Your assessment criteria:

5.1 Explain how different types of transitions can affect children and young people's development

5.2 Evaluate the effect on children and young people of having positive relationships during periods of transition

Key terms

Selective mutism: a severe childhood anxiety disorder in which the child is unable to speak in given situations, or to specific people

The importance of positive relationships during periods of transition

Change can be very unsettling and can cause children and young people to feel anxious and insecure. During times of uncertainty, children need consistency and familiarity and they need to know that someone will continue to provide security for them. A strong attachment relationship with a trusted adult is extremely important for children and young people during times of transition. In most situations, their parents or main carers will fulfil this role but, in circumstances where children are separated from their main carers, then an alternative attachment relationship becomes even more important.

For young children in early years' settings, this will frequently be their key person; for children in hospital it may be their designated nurse or play specialist and, for many young people in the care system, this could be a youth worker or learning mentor. It is the responsibility of this key person to provide support, reassurance and stability for children or young people who are experiencing transitions. This is particularly important for looked-after children (children in care), who may sometimes experience multiple transitions in very short periods of time.

Over to you!

▶ Think about the different transitions in your own life. Make a list of both the positive and negative effects of those transitions for you.

▶ What has helped you to deal with change in your own life?

Knowledge Assessment Task   5.1   5.2

Create a poster, leaflet or webpage for professionals, which provides information about:

▶ how different types of transitions can affect children and young people's development

▶ the effect on children and young people of having positive relationships during periods of transition.

You can illustrate your work with suitable images and keep all your notes as evidence towards your assessment.

Are you ready for assessment?

AC	What do you know now?	Assessment task	✓
1.1	The sequence and rate of each aspect of development from birth to 19 years	Page 137	
1.2	The difference between sequence of development and rate of development and why the difference is important	Page 137	
2.1 2.2	How children and young people's development is influenced by a range of personal factors and external factors	Page 145	
2.3	How theories of development and frameworks to support development influence current practice	Page 145	
3.1	How to monitor children and young people's development using different methods	Page 151	
3.2	The reasons why children and young people's development may not follow the expected pattern	Page 151	
3.3	How disability may affect development	Page 151	
3.4	How different types of interventions can promote positive outcomes for children and young people where development is not following the expected pattern	Page 151	
4.1	The importance of early identification of speech, language and communication delays and disorders and the potential risks of late recognition	Page 153	
4.2	How multi-agency teams work together to support speech, language and communication	Page 153	
4.3	How play and activities are used to support the development of speech, language and communication	Page 153	
5.1	How different types of transitions can affect children and young people's development	Page 155	
5.2	The effect on children and young people of having positive relationships during periods of transition	Page 155	

There is no practical assessment for this unit, but your tutor or assessor may question you about some of the following points.

What can you do now?   ✓

Can you apply your knowledge about the development of children and young people to your practice in the real work environment?

Do you have any examples to share with your assessor as evidence of this?

Can you apply your knowledge about early intervention and monitoring the development of children and young people to your practice in the real work environment?

Do you have any examples of observations or other evidence of this?

Can you apply your knowledge about the effects of transitions on the development of children and young people in the real work environment?

Could you tell your assessor about this?

6 | Promote child and young person development (CYP 3.2)

Assessment of this unit

This unit is about assessing and promoting the development of children and young people. It covers the importance of development plans and appropriate working practices to meet individual needs and explores different approaches to supporting positive behaviour. It also examines the role of practitioners in supporting children and young people who are experiencing different types of transitions.

The assessment of this unit includes both knowledge (things that you need to know about) and competence (things that you need to be able to do in the real work environment).

In order to complete this unit successfully, you will need to produce evidence of your knowledge and competence. The charts below and opposite explain what you need to know and do, alongside the relevant assessment criteria.

Your tutor or assessor will help you to prepare for your assessment, and the tasks suggested in this chapter will help you to create the evidence you need.

AC What you need to know

4.1	How your own working practice, institutions, agencies
4.2	and services can affect children and young people's development

CHAPTER 6

AC What you need to do

1.1   Explain the factors that need to be taken into account when assessing development

1.2   Assess a child's or young person's development in the following areas: physical;
1.3   communication; intellectual/cognitive; social, emotional and behavioural; moral and explain the selection of the assessment methods used

1.4   Develop a plan to meet the development needs of a child or young person in the work setting

2.1   Implement the development plan for a child or young person according to your own role and responsibilities, taking into account that development is holistic and interconnected

2.2   Evaluate and revise the development plan in the light of implementation

2.3   Explain the importance of a person-centred and inclusive approach and give examples of how this is implemented in your own work

2.4   Listen to children or young people and communicate in a way that encourages them to feel valued

2.5   Encourage children or young people to participate actively in decisions affecting their lives and the services they receive, according to their age and abilities

3.1   Explain the features of an environment or service that promotes the development of children and young people

3.2   Demonstrate how your own work environment or service is organised to promote the development of children or young people

5.1   Demonstrate how you work with children and young people to encourage positive behaviour

5.2   Evaluate different approaches to supporting positive behaviour

6.1   Explain how to support children and young people experiencing different types of transitions

6.2   Demonstrate provision of structured opportunities for children or young people to explore the effects of transitions on their lives

---

This unit links with some of the other mandatory units:

CYP 3.1   Understand child and young person development

CYP 3.7   Understand how to support positive outcomes for children and young people

EYMP 1   Context and principles for early years provision

EYMP 2   Promote learning and development in the early years

Some of your learning will be repeated in these units and will give you the chance to review your knowledge and understanding.

Your assessment criteria:

1.1 Explain the factors that need to be taken into account when assessing development

What factors need to be considered when assessing development?

Assessing development is a highly skilled task and an important part of the job for anyone who works with children or young people. The information from assessment can be used for monitoring progress, creating development plans and sharing with parents or carers.

It is very important that assessments are carried out carefully; the following factors need to be considered.

▶ Information should be recorded reliably and accurately.

▶ Confidentiality should be maintained regarding all information, ensuring the security of assessment records and appropriate sharing of information.

▶ Permission should be gained from parents or carers (or young people themselves).

▶ Children's own feelings and individual needs should be respected; for example, if a child has specific developmental needs or a disability.

▶ Assessments should be recorded in an **objective** way in order to avoid **subjective** judgements.

▶ Assessments should be recorded in a range of different situations, and over a period of time, in order to create a balanced picture of the child or young person.

Key terms

Objective: not influenced by emotion or personal bias

Subjective: based on personal opinion or experience

Assessing development

Assessments of children and young people may focus on many different areas of development or behaviour, including:

- *physical skills,* for example, how children control their bodies and co-ordinate their movements, or how a child uses hand–eye co-ordination and manipulative skills

- *intellectual (cognitive) skills,* for example, how a toddler uses problem-solving skills, how a child learns to read, write and count or how a young person achieves in academic tests

- *communication skills,* for example, how toddlers learn to use language to communicate their needs, how a child starts to learn the rules of grammar, or the communication skills a young person uses to negotiate with their parents

- *social, emotional and behavioural skills,* for example, how toddlers develop independence, how children learn to share and play together or how young people learn to express and manage their feelings

- *moral development,* for example, how a child learns about right and wrong or acceptable and unacceptable behaviour.

One of the most important ways that information is collected for assessing the development of children and young people is through the process of observation. There are many different ways to carry out and record observations; some methods are more effective than others. Figure 6.1 overleaf summarises some of the main recording methods and why they might be used.

Development can also be assessed by means of **standardised tests**, for example IQ tests or Standard Assessment Tests (SATs) in schools. These tests can be useful in measuring the abilities of children and young people against the expected level for their age, but it is important to remember that standardised tests can only provide a snapshot of the child's abilities on the day the test is performed.

Development plans

Assessment is a very useful tool and can provide a lot of information about children and young people. In a work setting, observations and assessments are frequently used to identify the development needs of children and young people. This information can then be used to plan individual support and activities to encourage learning and development. In most settings, this will be done with parents or carers and, in some cases, with children or young people themselves. Most plans will include the information in Figure 6.2 on page 162.

Key terms

Standardised test: a test designed so that the questions, conditions for administering, scoring procedures and interpretations are consistent

Over to you!

Consider the following statements and decide which are objective and which are subjective.

1. *He looks happy.*
2. *He uses a pincer grasp with his left hand to pick up the bead.*
3. *She is a very bright girl .*
4. *She walks up the steps, one foot at a time.*
5. *She loves painting with the blue paint.*

Why is it important to be objective when recording assessments on the development of children or young people?

Figure 6.1 The main recording methods and why they might be used

Recording method	Advantages	Disadvantages
Written record (also called narrative or free description)	Flexible and can be used for observing several areas of development together; observer can be unobtrusive	Can be difficult to record everything the child does or says; can be very subjective
Time sample (observing regularly over a period of time)	Helps to focus on specific skills; very useful for observing behaviour patterns	Some aspects of development or behaviour can be missed
Event sample (recording specific aspects of behaviour)	Useful for observing specific behaviour (e.g. biting) or social interaction	Not detailed enough to explain reasons for specific behaviour
Checklists or tick sheets	Useful for structured assessments and routine check-ups on development and for monitoring progress against expected milestones	Can be quite limiting as a recording method and children can feel as if they are being 'watched'
Photographs/Filming	Can be used to obtain a wide range of information about children's development or behaviour; an excellent way of sharing observations with parents or carers	Observer can be very selective about what to record; important to obtain all the necessary permissions; visual images of children or young people should never be disclosed outside of the setting
Audio recording	Digital recording devices can be a useful way to assess a child's language development at different stages	Observer can be very selective about what to record; children can be conscious of being recorded
Target child (recording one child's activity over time)	Useful for gaining an overall picture of an individual child's holistic development	Observer selects when to record and may choose a time when the child is not showing typical behaviour
Information from parents and carers	Parents see children engaged in different activities in their own home	Some parents may record and report inaccurately or subjectively

Over to you!

Referring to Figure 6.1, explain which methods would be most effective for assessing:

▶ *the behaviour of a toddler who is experiencing separation anxiety on leaving their main carer every morning*

▶ *the gross motor skills of a four-year-old*

▶ *the literacy and numeracy abilities of a seven-year-old.*

In your placement or work setting, think about the different methods that are used to assess the development of children and young people and what factors need to be taken into account when assessing development.

Select different methods to carry out observations and assessments of all aspects of children's development (physical, communication, cognitive, social, emotional, behavioural and moral) and discuss these with other staff in the setting.

Use the information from your observations and assessments to develop plans that meet children's development needs.

Keep your observations and plans to share and discuss with your assessor.

Your evidence for this task must be based on your practice in a real work environment and must be witnessed by or be in a format that is acceptable to your assessor.

Your assessment criteria:

1.1 Explain the factors that need to be taken into account when assessing development

1.2 Assess a child or young person's development in the following areas: physical, communication, intellectual/cognitive, social, emotional and behavioural, moral

1.3 Explain the selection of the assessment methods used

1.4 Develop a plan to meet the development needs of a child or young person in the work setting

Figure 6.2 An example of a development plan

Child's name: _____	Age: _____
Key person: _____	Date: _____

Observed interests/individual needs of the child:

For example, enjoys looking at books; playing with trains; being outdoors; playing with specific children; developing manipulative skills in using scissors; gaining confidence in climbing stairs; starting to put words together in simple sentences

Information from parents/carers/child:

For example, what the child currently likes to do at home

Aims/targets: For example, to develop fine motor skills; build confidence in new situations; encourage language; support social interaction; develop body co-ordination and balance

Suggested experiences/activities:	**Resources/equipment:**
For example, threading beads to develop fine motor skills; building a den outside to encourage co-operation; sharing books about trains to build on individual interests and promote learning	For example, beads of different sizes, shapes and colours; den-building materials outside (poles, fabric, blankets, etc.); 'Thomas the Tank Engine' books

Practitioner role:

For example, ensure safety; provide a variety of resources; use praise and encouragement; ask open-ended questions to encourage language and new vocabulary

Timescale/review date:

Be able to promote the development of children or young people

How can development plans be used?

Development plans can be extremely useful for promoting the learning and development of children and young people. Plans can be used to:

- focus on the individual interests and needs of children or young people

- make suggestions for experiences, activities and resources to promote learning and development and meet individual needs

- identify the role of the practitioner in supporting learning and development

- gather ideas from parents, carers, children or young people

- share with other professionals who may be involved in supporting learning and development.

Involving children and young people in planning

When working with children or young people, it is very important to involve them in the planning process. This way of working ensures that individual interests and needs are fully considered and that children's and young people's ideas are treated with respect. It also transfers some of the decision-making and control of the planning process to children and young people themselves, which is very important for building confidence and self-esteem. Actively involving the participation of children and young people is called a person-centred (or child-centred) approach and is an important element in the United Nations Convention on the Rights of the Child. (See Chapter 3, page 68.)

In order to include children and young people effectively, it is extremely important to communicate and listen in a way that makes them feel valued. This involves setting aside time, being genuinely interested in what they have to say and making sure that their ideas are represented in the planning process. This is also discussed in Chapter 11, page 286.

Evaluating development plans

Planning is a continuous process. A development plan should be reviewed regularly, to ensure it still meets its aims. Ongoing observation is a vitally important part of this process to determine how effective the plan is in meeting the child's needs. Plans will continually be revised and adapted, as the needs of children and young people change; the timescale for review will vary with the child's age and stage of development. Ideally, the evaluation of a development plan should take into account the views of everyone involved, including parents or carers and the child or young person themselves.

Your assessment criteria:

2.1 Implement the development plan for a child or young person according to own role and responsibilities, taking into account that development is holistic and interconnected

2.2 Evaluate and revise the development plan in the light of implementation

2.3 Explain the importance of a person-centred and inclusive approach and give examples of how this is implemented in own work

2.4 Listen to children or young people and communicate in a way that encourages them to feel valued

2.5 Encourage children or young people actively to participate in decisions affecting their lives and the services they receive according to their age and abilities

Listed below are some of the factors that should be considered when reviewing a development plan.

- ▶ Does the child seem to be benefiting from the plan and enjoying the suggested activities?
- ▶ Do the suggested activities seem to be promoting the child's development?
- ▶ What are the comments from the child, young person or parents and carers?
- ▶ What other activities, experiences or resources could be added?
- ▶ When should the plan next be reviewed?

Case study

Jenny works at the Alphabet nursery and is the key person for Raol, aged four years. She has noticed that Raol always chooses to play outside, by himself, and that his play consistently involves a fantasy game about being a superhero. Jenny is aware that Raol's play is very repetitive and that he is not accessing other nursery activities or playing with other children. She would like to encourage his social interaction and involve him more in mark-making, books and stories, construction and creative play. Jenny decides that she will discuss this with Raol's dad when he comes to pick up Raol at the end of the day.

1. How could Jenny use Raol's specific interests to plan different activities for Raol and support his holistic development?
2. How could Jenny involve Raol in the planning process?

Practical Assessment Task

2.1 2.2 2.3 2.4 2.5

In your placement or work setting, create and implement a development plan for a specific child or young person. Carry out observations of the child or young person and then evaluate and revise your plan, taking into account what you have observed.

Think about how you would involve the child or young person in reviewing their plan, using a person-centred approach.

Consider how you would listen and communicate with the child or young person and how you might encourage them to participate actively in making decisions.

Keep your observations and plans to share and discuss with your assessor.

Your evidence for this task must be based on your practice in a real work environment and must be witnessed by or be in a format that is acceptable to your assessor.

Your assessment criteria:

3.1 Explain the features of an environment or service that promotes the development of children and young people

3.2 Demonstrate how own work environment or service is organised to promote the development of children or young people

How does the environment promote the development of children and young people?

Many different features in the physical and emotional environment can influence the development of children and young people. Physically, development will be promoted by opportunities for physical activity, both indoors and outdoors, a variety of stimulating, inclusive activities and space to move around safely. Emotionally, development can be influenced by a positive staff approach, an organised routine and encouragement for children's efforts and achievements. This is also discussed in Chapter 12 (page 310) and Chapter 13 (page 332).

It is important for practitioners to organise the work environment and provide services that will promote development and improve outcomes for children, young people and their families. Some of the ways this can be done are summarised in Figure 6.3.

Figure 6.3 How the environment promotes the development of children and young people

Feature	What to consider	Organising the work environment or service
Physical environment		
Design and layout of the environment, both indoors and outdoors	Space to move around; access to all areas; safety and supervision; providing appropriate risk and challenge	Planning the environment; risk assessment; policies and procedures to meet regulatory requirements
Provision of activities and resources	Variety of interesting resources; activities that are inclusive, age/stage appropriate and safe; opportunities for children to make their own choices	Development plans to meet individual needs; storage and accessibility of resources; opportunities for child-initiated activities; regular safety checks
Emotional environment		
Appearance and atmosphere of the environment	Attractive, welcoming, inclusive surroundings; balancing periods of calm and stimulation; an organised routine	Planning daily routines; attractive displays of children's work; creating security and a sense of belonging
Staff approach	Professional and positive; caring and respectful; providing praise and encouragement and supporting participation	Key person system; involving children and young people in decision making
Working closely with parents and carers	Encouraging involvement; providing support and information; signposting to different services	Providing a parent room; regular, ongoing communication; multi-agency support

Practical Assessment Task   3.1 3.2

In your placement or work setting, think about the features of the environment that promote the development of children and young people. Use Figure 6.3 to help you.

Make notes about specific examples from your setting to highlight the organisation of the environment or service and how this helps to promote the development of children or young people.

Keep your notes as evidence towards your assessment.

Your evidence for this task must be based on your practice in a real work environment and must be witnessed by or be in a format that is acceptable to your assessor.

How can working practices affect the development of children and young people?

Adults who work with children and young people have an extremely important role in supporting and promoting development. This could be through their work in a specific setting, such as a nursery, school or out of school club, or in the provision of other services, such as speech and language therapy, developmental assessments or behaviour support. Ways in which working practices can affect the development of children and young people include:

▶ practitioners who have a sound knowledge of child development

▶ systems for observing children and young people in order to monitor development

▶ practitioners who can recognise and respond to deviations from the expected pattern of development

▶ providing experiences, activities and resources to promote development

▶ planning that meets individual needs and interests and promotes development

▶ policies and procedures that support the welfare and safety of children and young people

▶ sound referral systems for reporting concerns about the development of children and young people

▶ procedures for integrated and multi-agency working and sharing information

▶ working closely with parents and carers.

This also links with Chapter 3 (page 68) Chapter 10 (page 268) Chapter 11 (page 286).

Institutions, agencies and services can also affect the development of children and young people. This is discussed in more detail in Chapter 10, page 286.

Your assessment criteria:

4.1 Explain how own working practice can affect children and young people's development

4.2 Explain how institutions, agencies and services can affect children and young people's development

Figure 6.4 Quiz

	1 = extremely well
	2 = fairly well
	3 = not very well

How well do I ...

1. Giggle and laugh with the children to show I am relaxed and enjoying their company   1   2   3

2. Show children I am interested in their play – without necessarily joining in   1   2   3

3. Just sit down with children to enjoy a moment of peace and relaxation   1   2   3

4. Show real appreciation of their achievements, whatever form it may take   1   2   3

5. Follow the flow of what children want to learn about today   1   2   3

6. Show children that I am really listening to them   1   2   3

7. Make every day a happy and social event, for every child   1   2   3

Knowledge Assessment Task   4.1   4.2

Sam is eight years old and attends a local primary school. His class teacher, Miss Sykes, is concerned about Sam's behaviour, which she describes as 'erratic, hyperactive and inappropriate at times'. Miss Sykes discusses this with Sam's mother and discovers that his mother is also very concerned. Together they decide that it would be a good idea for Sam to be assessed and they arrange for him to be seen by the educational psychologist. Sam and his mother attend the assessment and the educational psychologist confirms that Sam does have some behavioural difficulties. It is agreed that further investigations will be conducted and that the school special educational needs co-ordinator (SENCO) will provide additional help for Sam in school. The school SENCO will work with the class teacher and Sam's mother to provide advice about strategies for managing Sam's behaviour at home.

1. Explain how the working practices of Sam's class teacher and the school SENCO could have an impact on Sam's development.

2. Explain why it is important for Sam's development that he has access to other services and agencies.

Keep your notes as evidence towards your assessment.

Over to you!

▶ Think about your own working practice with children or young people and try to answer the quiz in Figure 6.4 as honestly as possible. For each numbered statement, make a note of your score, using the key on the right.

▶ Compare your responses with those of others in the group. What improvements do you think you could make to your own working practices?

Be able to support children and young people's positive behaviour

What is positive behaviour?

Positive behaviour is often referred to as *acceptable* or *appropriate*, meaning that it conforms to expected values and beliefs. Many different factors influence our understanding of positive behaviour, including family background and culture, but, in general, positive behaviour is defined as being helpful and constructive. It can be demonstrated through actions, speech or non-verbal behaviour, for example, sharing, being polite, or smiling as a welcoming greeting.

Supporting positive behaviour

In order to support positive behaviour, it is important for adults to have a sound understanding of holistic development and realistic expectations of children and young people. For example, it would be unrealistic to expect a baby to understand the danger of touching a hot iron, just as it would be impractical to suggest that most nine-year-olds need adult help to dress themselves. This knowledge and understanding helps us not only to have realistic expectations, but also to implement appropriate strategies to support positive behaviour. Young children need to learn how to behave appropriately, just as they learn to walk and talk, and it is important to remember that they need adult help to do this. Some of the ways that adults can support positive behaviour include:

▶ being a good role model, through your own language and behaviour

▶ giving positive attention, using lots of praise and encouragement and **positive reinforcement**

▶ using positive language, tell children what you want them to do, rather than what you don't want them to do (for example, *'Remember to keep away from the hot fire,'* rather than *'Don't touch the hot fire!'*)

▶ being consistent, providing constant messages and reliable boundaries

▶ giving choices, supporting children and young people to make their own decisions

▶ providing stimulating activities, keeping children and young people engaged with a variety of interesting activities will reduce the likelihood of inappropriate behaviour through boredom

▶ having inclusive behaviour policies, which clearly outline staff roles and responsibilities and expectations for the children or young people.

Your assessment criteria:

5.1 Demonstrate how you work with children and young people to encourage positive behaviour

5.2 Evaluate different approaches to supporting positive behaviour

Key terms

Positive reinforcement: giving encouragement to a particular behaviour, with the result that it is more likely to be repeated

Over to you!

Think about your own behaviour with children or young people in your placement or work setting.

▶ *Are you always polite?*

▶ *Do you model appropriate language?*

▶ *How do you model appropriate behaviour for the children or young people in your setting?*

Share some actual examples from your placement or work setting with a colleague.

Positive reinforcement

Praise is extremely important in encouraging positive behaviour. When children or young people feel that they have been rewarded for their behaviour, it encourages them to behave in that way again. This is positive reinforcement and is linked to Skinner's theory of operant conditioning (see chapter 5, page 124). Rewarding positive behaviour supports children in learning about what is acceptable and appropriate, it helps them to feel valued and builds their self-esteem. The most important reward of all is positive attention from caring adults and most children will respond extremely well to smiles and encouraging words. There are many other ways to reward positive behaviour, including stickers, star charts and special badges.

When using positive reinforcement, it is important to remember that it is sometimes easier to pay attention to children who are behaving inappropriately, for example, scolding a child for pushing, snatching or being rude. It is more challenging to remember to make the effort to praise a child who is sitting quietly, showing consideration to others or responding in a thoughtful way. Rewards also need to be immediate, particularly with young children, who have very little concept of time. If children are rewarded straight away, they are more likely to link it with their behaviour. If rewards are saved until the end of the day, then it is likely that the behaviour will be forgotten.

For children with some special needs, visual prompts can help to reinforce the rules and boundaries for behaviour. For example, using pictures or special charts can help to promote positive behaviour and support children with acceptable behaviour patterns.

Over to you!

In your own placement or work setting, think about the different ways in which you support positive behaviour when dealing with children and young people.

► Do you use positive reinforcement?
► What kind of rewards have you seen being used to promote positive behaviour of children and young people?
► How effective do you think these are?

Share your ideas with others in the group.

Other approaches to support positive behaviour

Positive reinforcement is a very important approach for supporting behaviour. However, different strategies can also be effective, depending on the age and stage of development of the child or young person. Very young children will often respond to a simple diversion, whereas older children may react more positively to reasoning and reflecting on their own behaviour. Some alternative approaches for supporting positive behaviour are outlined in Figure 6.5.

Your assessment criteria:

5.1 Demonstrate how you work with children and young people to encourage positive behaviour

5.2 Evaluate different approaches to supporting positive behaviour

Figure 6.5 Some alternative approaches for supporting positive behaviour

Approach	Example
Diversion	Useful with infants and very young children, for example, distracting their attention away from a potentially dangerous, troublesome or conflict situation to defuse the problem.
Boundary setting	Important for children and young people to understand expectations for their behaviour, for example, *'We don't hurt each other'*, *'We take turns with the bikes outside'*, *'You need to be home by 8pm'*; these need to be consistent and fair.
Involvement	Involving children and young people in creating boundaries for their own behaviour and reflecting on the consequences; this provides them with an opportunity to make decisions and take some ownership of the rules about behaviour, resulting in these being more likely to be followed.
Verbal and non-verbal communication	Eye contact or facial expression can be very effective in expressing both approval and disapproval of behaviour; saying the child's name with the right degree of verbal intonation can act as a warning or disapproval of behaviour, particularly when combined with facial expression.

Young children need support to develop positive behaviour

Practical Assessment Task   5.1   5.2

In your placement or work setting, think about how you work with children and young people to encourage positive behaviour.

Make notes on specific examples from your practice that demonstrate how you:

▶ support positive behaviour with specific children or young people

▶ use different approaches to encourage positive behaviour with children or young people.

Keep your notes as evidence towards your assessment.

Your evidence for this task must be based on your practice in a real work environment and must be witnessed by or be in a format that is acceptable to your assessor.

What are the different transitions children and young people may experience?

Your assessment criteria:

6.1 Explain how to support children and young people experiencing different types of transitions

Children and young people will experience many different transitions during their lives.

As they grow and develop, their friendships and relationships change and they will experience a variety of different situations, both within and outside their family. Some transitions, such as starting school, will affect most children; however, other transitions, such as parental divorce or the death of a parent or close family member, will only affect some children and young people.

Transitions affecting most children include:

► starting pre-school, nursery or school

► moving rooms or classes

► moving from primary to secondary school

► changes in routine

► puberty.

Transitions affecting only some children include:

► changes in main carer or moving into foster care

► the arrival of a new baby in the family

► illness or hospitalisation

► parents separating or divorcing

► bereavement

► moving house

► changing country

► going to boarding school.

Supporting transitions

The effects of transitions on children and young people are discussed in Chapter 5, page 124. When children and young people are experiencing changes in their lives they need consistent support; adults need to make sure that, as far as possible, children have some degree of stability to help them cope. Some of the ways that children and young people can be supported with transitions are summarised in Figure 6.6.

Over to you!

Think about some of the major transitions in your own life. Create a timeline to show when the transitions happened. Can you remember how the different transitions affected you? What helped you to cope?

Figure 6.6 Some ways that children and young people can be supported with transitions

Type of support	Example
Providing information	Explaining what is going to happen and what that might mean for the child: with young children, it is important to use simple language and not provide too much information at once.
Listening	Allowing time for information to be taken in and for children to respond: some children will need more time than others to process information and it is important not to rush this.
Being honest	Being truthful with children and young people is very important, especially when answering their questions, even if this is difficult. When children and young people are experiencing transitions, they need to be able to trust the adults in their lives. This helps them to feel more secure with the changes that are happening.
Acknowledging feelings	It is normal for children and young people to express a variety of feelings when they are dealing with transitions. Often these are negative feelings such as frustration or anger. Adults will sometimes dismiss children's feelings and say things like, 'Don't cry.' It is important to acknowledge feelings with children and young people and to give them the opportunity to express themselves.

Your assessment criteria:

6.1 Explain how to support children and young people experiencing different types of transitions

6.2 Demonstrate provision of structured opportunities for children or young people to explore the effects of transitions on their lives

Over to you!

Investigate a range of books that would help to support children or young people experiencing:

▶ *parental divorce or separation*

▶ *going in to hospital*

▶ *having a new baby in the family.*

For each example, list the title, author, date of publication and recommended age range.

The following websites might help you to get started.

www.booktrustchildrensbooks. org.uk/

www.bookstart.org.uk/

Exploring the effects of transitions

Children and young people need time and structured opportunities to explore the effects of transitions on their lives.

Importance of play

Expressive, creative and imaginative play can all provide opportunities for children to explore different ideas and express their feelings, for example, playing at doctors and nurses in preparation for going into hospital, or sharing a book about babies when a new baby is expected in the family. Puppets, painting, small-world play, sand play and stories can all help children to understand and come to terms with changes in their lives.

Resource packs and information

These are produced by many organisations and can be a useful source of support for some children, young people and their families. For example:

▶ the Who Cares? Trust (www.thewhocarestrust.org.uk/) supporting children and young people in care

▶ National Children's Bureau (www.ncb.org.uk/) supporting the rights of children and young people

▶ Winston's Wish (www.winstonswish.org.uk/) supporting children and young people coping with bereavement.

Case study

Hassan is four years old and lives with his mum, dad, grandma and two older brothers. He attends a local pre-school group every morning and he enjoys playing with a small group of friends. Hassan's mother is expecting a new baby in two months' time and she is anxious that Hassan is well prepared and supported through this exciting event in their family.

1. Explain why it is important for Hassan to be prepared for the arrival of the new baby.

2. Give examples of some of the ways in which Hassan's mother could help to prepare him for the new baby's arrival.

3. Explain how the staff at the pre-school group could support Hassan after the new baby is born.

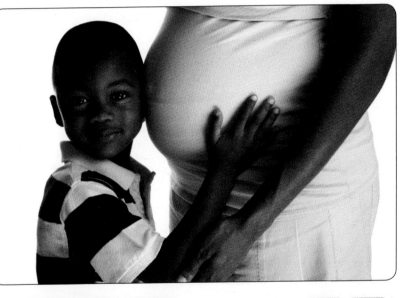

Practical Assessment Task

In your placement or work setting, think about how you support children and young people who are experiencing different types of transitions.

In preparing for your assessment, make notes about specific examples of how you have provided activities and structured opportunities for children or young people to cope with and explore the effects of transitions on their lives.

Keep your notes as evidence towards your assessment.

Your evidence for this task must be based on your practice in a real work environment and must be witnessed by or be in a format that is acceptable to your assessor.

Are you ready for assessment?

AC	What do you know now?	Assessment task	✓
4.1 4.2	How your own working practice, institutions, agencies and services can affect children and young people's development	Page 169	

Your tutor or assessor may need to observe your competence in your placement or work setting.

AC	What can you do now?	Assessment task	✓
1.1	Explain the factors that need to be taken into account when assessing development Could you discuss actual examples of this with your assessor?	Page 163	
1.2 1.3	Assess a child or young person's development in the following areas: physical; communication; intellectual/cognitive; social, emotional and behavioural; moral Explain the selection of the assessment methods used. Do you have examples to share with your assessor?	Page 163	
1.4	Develop a plan to meet the development needs of a child or young person in the work setting Do you have examples to share with your assessor?	Page 163	
2.1	Implement the development plan for a child or young person, according to your own role and responsibilities, taking into account that development is holistic and interconnected Do you have examples to share with your assessor?	Page 165	
2.2	Evaluate and revise the development plan in the light of implementation Do you have examples to share with your assessor?	Page 165	

AC	What can you do now?	Assessment task	✓
2.3	Explain the importance of a person-centred and inclusive approach and give examples of how this is implemented in your own work Could you discuss this with your assessor?	Page 165	
2.4	Listen to children or young people and communicate in a way that encourages them to feel valued	Page 165	
2.5	Encourage children or young people to participate actively in decisions affecting their lives and the services they receive according to their age and abilities Do you have any specific examples to share with your assessor?	Page 165	
3.1	Explain the features of an environment or service that promotes the development of children and young people Could you discuss this with your assessor?	Page 167	
3.2	Demonstrate how your work environment or service is organised to promote the development of children or young people	Page 167	
5.1	Demonstrate how you work with children and young people to encourage positive behaviour	Page 173	
5.2	Evaluate different approaches to supporting positive behaviour Do you have any specific examples to share with your assessor?	Page 173	
6.1	Explain how to support children and young people experiencing different types of transition Could you discuss this with your assessor?	Page 177	
6.2	Demonstrate provision of structured opportunities for children or young people to explore the effects of transitions on their lives Do you have any specific examples to share with your assessor?	Page 177	

7 | Understand how to safeguard the wellbeing of children and young people (CYP 3.3)

Assessment of this unit

This unit is about safeguarding the wellbeing of children and young people. It covers legislation, safeguarding policies and the roles and responsibilities of different organisations involved in keeping children and young people safe. It also examines how to recognise and respond to evidence or concerns that a child or young person has been abused, harmed or bullied, including the importance of e-safety. In addition, this unit explores how to support children's and young people's self-confidence, self-esteem and resilience in helping them to protect themselves.

The assessment of this unit is all knowledge based (things that you need to know about), but it is also very important to be able to apply your knowledge practically in the real work environment.

In order to complete this unit successfully, you will need to produce evidence of your knowledge. The charts on pages 181–2 explain what you need to know, alongside the relevant assessment criteria.

Your tutor or assessor will help you to prepare for your assessment and the tasks suggested in this chapter will help you to create the evidence you need.

AC	What you need to know
1.1	Current legislation, guidelines, policies and procedures within your own UK Home Nation affecting the safeguarding of children and young people
1.2	The importance of child protection within the wider concept of safeguarding children and young people
1.3	How national and local guidelines, policies and procedures for safeguarding affect day-to-day work with children and young people
1.4	When and why inquiries and serious case reviews are required and how the sharing of the findings informs practice
1.5	How the processes used by your own work setting or service comply with legislation that covers data protection, information handling and sharing
2.1 **2.2**	The importance of safeguarding children and young people and the importance of a child or young person-centred approach
2.3	What is meant by partnership working in the context of safeguarding
2.4	The roles and responsibilities of the different organisations that may be involved when a child or young person has been abused or harmed
3.1 **3.2**	Why it is important to ensure children and young people are protected from harm within the work setting and the policies and procedures that are in place to protect children and young people and adults who work with them
3.3	Ways in which concerns about poor practice can be reported whilst ensuring that whistle-blowers and those whose practice or behaviour is being questioned are protected
3.4	How practitioners can take steps to protect themselves within their everyday practice in the work setting and on off-site visits
4.1	The possible signs, symptoms, indicators and behaviours that may cause concern in the context of safeguarding
4.2	The actions to take if a child or young person alleges harm or abuse in line with policies and procedures of own setting
4.3	The rights that children, young people and their carers have in situations where harm or abuse is suspected or alleged
5.1	Different types of bullying and the potential effects on children and young people
5.2	The policies and procedures that should be followed in response to concerns or evidence of bullying and explain the reasons why they are in place
5.3	How to support a child or young person and/or their family when bullying is suspected or alleged

continued...

AC   What you need to know

6.1	How to support children and young people's self-confidence and self-esteem
6.2	The importance of supporting resilience in children and young people
6.3	Why it is important to work with the child or young person to ensure they have strategies to protect themselves and make decisions about safety
6.4	Ways of empowering children and young people to make positive and informed choices that support their wellbeing and safety
7.1	The risks and possible consequences for children and young people of being online and of using a mobile phone
7.2	Ways of reducing risk to children and young people from social networking, internet use, buying online, using a mobile phone

There is no practical assessment for this unit, but your tutor or assessor may question you about some of the following points.

What you need to do

Apply your knowledge about safeguarding policies and procedures in the real work environment

Be clear about your own responsibilities in the case of any evidence or concerns about safeguarding issues in the work environment

Apply your knowledge about supporting children and young people's self-confidence, self-esteem and resilience in the real work environment

This is an extremely important unit of study and it links with many of the other mandatory units:

SHC 31	Promote communication in health, social care or children's and young people's settings
SHC 34	Principles for implementing duty of care in health, social care or children's and young people's settings
CYP 3.4	Support children and young people's health and safety
CYP 3.5	Develop positive relationships with children, young people and others involved in their care
CYP 3.6	Working together for the benefit of children and young people
CYP 3.7	Understand how to support positive outcomes for children and young people
EYMP 3	Promote children's welfare and wellbeing in the early years

Some of your learning will be repeated in these units and will give you the chance to review your knowledge and understanding.

HM Government

Working Together to Safeguard Children

A guide to inter-agency working to safeguard and promote the welfare of children

What is the main guidance for safeguarding children and young people?

Some of the main legislation related to safeguarding children began with the Children Act (1989). This was updated with the Children Act (2004), which included the principle of **integrated children's services** and incorporated the five main principles of **Every Child Matters** (2003).

The Act also introduced **Local Safeguarding Children Boards**, which are statutory organisations in England and operate within each local area to ensure that services co-operate to promote the welfare of children and young people.

In 2010, another key document was updated and published by the government. Called 'Working Together to Safeguard Children', it outlines the key responsibilities for professionals in protecting children from harm and keeping them safe.

A very important organisation involved in safeguarding the welfare of children and young people is the **Independent Safeguarding Authority (ISA).** This organisation operates the **Vetting and Barring Scheme** and is responsible for helping to prevent unsuitable people from working with children or young people. One of the ways it does this is to carry out **Criminal Records Bureau (CRB)** checks on anyone who works with or applies to work with children or young people.

Legislation and policy development varies among the four UK nations and it is important to be familiar with the guidance for the country in which you live.

Your assessment criteria:

1.1 Outline current legislation, guidelines, policies and procedures within your own UK Home Nation affecting the safeguarding of children and young people

1.2 Explain child protection within the wider concept of safeguarding children and young people

Key terms

Criminal Records Bureau (CRB): a Home Office agency, providing access to criminal record information (see also Disclosure Scotland and Access Northern Ireland)

Every Child Matters: a UK government initiative launched in 2003 to improve outcomes for children and young people

Integrated children's services: different services working together to support children, young people and their families

Independent Safeguarding Authority (ISA): a public body that is responsible for checking the suitability of those who wish to work with children or young people

Over to you!

Investigate more about legislation and policies about safeguarding children and young people in the country where you live.

England: www.isa-gov.org.uk/
N. Ireland: www.deni.gov.uk/index/21-pupils-parents-pg/21-child-protection-2.htm
Scotland: www.scotland.gov.uk/Topics/People/Young-People/children-families/17834
Wales: www.awcpp.org.uk/areasofwork/safeguardingchildren/awcpprg/index.html

The wider concept of safeguarding

Safeguarding the welfare of children and young people is extremely important. It involves more than just protecting children from abuse – it also includes promoting their interests, keeping them safe and protecting their rights. The 'Staying Safe' action plan, published by the government in 2008, highlighted a number of different areas for concern, including:

▶ road safety and safety on the streets

▶ bullying

▶ safety in using the internet and other technology

▶ young runaways and missing children

▶ substance misuse by young people

▶ guidance for safeguarding disabled children.

Young children are extremely vulnerable. It is very important for anyone who works with children or young people to be aware of safeguarding procedures and to know how to respond to any concerns about children's welfare and safety. All children and young people have a right to grow up in safety; adults have a duty to protect them from being harmed or abused in any way.

Every child matters

Key terms

Local Safeguarding Children Boards: statutory organisations that oversee service provision for promoting the welfare of children and young people

Vetting and Barring Scheme: a scheme set up to help prevent unsuitable people from working with children and vulnerable adults

Policies and procedures

National legislation and guidance influence the development of local policies and procedures that affect everyday work with children and young people. It is very important for workplace settings to have clear policies and procedures that cover all aspects of safeguarding. Policies must cover the protection of all children and young people under the age of 18 and the content of the policy must be reviewed annually. Some key issues are summarised in Figure 7.1.

Figure 7.1 A summary of the key issues of safeguarding policies

Policy requirement	Example content
Staff responsibilities	A key member of staff being the 'named person' as the main contact for all safeguarding issues; regular training and updating on all aspects of safeguarding; the importance of all staff knowing their own role and responsibilities; all staff to undertake CRB checks
Contact with children	Clear procedures for managing personal care with children (e.g. changing nappies or helping them with toileting); clear procedures about appropriate physical contact with children and young people (e.g. cuddling children or restraining young people); clear policies about taking photographs or filming children, including the use of mobile phones in the work setting
Security and safety	Security measures for protecting children, (e.g. CCTV, webcams, biometric access devices such as fingerprint recognition); clear arrangements for confirming the identity of parents or carers who are collecting children and checking the identity of any visitors to the setting; clear procedures for risk assessment (e.g. regular checking of equipment for damage and to make sure it is safe)
Information	Clear policies about sharing information and confidentiality procedures; arrangements to liaise with the Local Safeguarding Children Board; contact details for a parent or carer for all children under the age of 18
Empowering children and young people	Activities to empower and educate children and young people (e.g. about confidence with their own bodies or being assertive in making decisions); the importance of observation and listening to children and young people, building self-confidence and self-esteem

Your assessment criteria:

1.1 Outline current legislation, guidelines, policies and procedures within your own UK Home Nation affecting the safeguarding of children and young people

1.2 Explain child protection within the wider concept of safeguarding children and young people

1.3 Analyse how national and local guidelines, policies and procedures for safeguarding affect day-to-day work with children and young people

1.4 Explain when and why inquiries and serious case reviews are required and how the sharing of the findings informs practice

Key terms

Biometrics: using physical characteristics for the purpose of personal identification

What are serious case reviews?

The Local Safeguarding Children's Board (LSCB) will conduct a serious case review if a child dies and abuse or neglect are known or suspected. The LSCB must also consider conducting a serious case review where:

▶ a child sustains a potentially life-threatening injury through abuse or neglect

▶ a child has been subject to particularly serious sexual abuse

▶ the case gives rise to concerns about inter-agency working to protect children from harm.

The purpose of a serious case review is:

▶ to establish whether there are any lessons to be learnt from the case about inter-agency working

▶ to identify clearly what these lessons are, how they will be acted upon and what is expected to change as a result

▶ to improve inter-agency working to safeguard and promote the welfare of children.

The review brings together all the organisations involved in the case, including the local authority children's service, the police, health, education and social services as required. Each organisation involved conducts an independent inquiry into their management of the case and recommendations are made for future improvements. Figure 7.2 shows the children who were the subject of a serious case review between 1 April 2009 and 31 March 2010, the majority of whom were under one year of age.

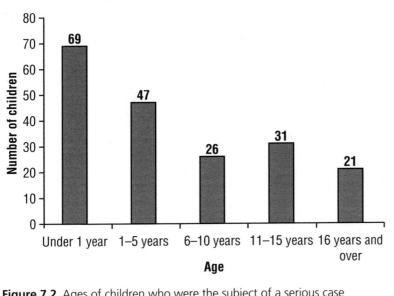

Figure 7.2 Ages of children who were the subject of a serious case review evaluated by Ofsted between 1 April 2009 and 31 March 2010

Lessons to be learnt

The death of Peter Connelly (Baby P) in 2007 led to the publication of a review by Lord Laming, in 2009, which seriously criticised child protection services and other agencies involved in the case.

A serious case review into the death of Alex Sutherland (aged 13 months), also in 2009, found that the case was poorly managed throughout and led to disciplinary investigations involving four members of staff.

Some of the consistent findings from serious case reviews over recent years have highlighted a number of lessons to be learnt, including:

▶ failure to implement good practice even though established frameworks were available

▶ failure to share sources of information that could have contributed to a better understanding of children and their families

▶ insufficient consideration of the child's individual views and needs; the voice of the child is not always heard.

Your assessment criteria:

1.1 Outline current legislation, guidelines, policies and procedures within your own UK Home Nation affecting the safeguarding of children and young people

1.2 Explain child protection within the wider concept of safeguarding children and young people

1.3 Analyse how national and local guidelines, policies and procedures for safeguarding affect day-to-day work with children and young people

1.4 Explain when and why inquiries and serious case reviews are required and how the sharing of the findings informs practice

1.5 Explain how the processes used by your own work setting or service comply with legislation that covers data protection, information handling and sharing

Case study

Read this extract from a serious case review.

It concerned three children aged five, 11 and 14. Their mother had a long history of being abused as a child herself and had been in care. She married young and had children by three different partners. The mother began to take illicit drugs and then developed an alcohol problem. She moved into various houses, often because the former house was in such poor condition that she requested a move. The young woman suffered violence from each of her partners. As her children began school, concerns arose about their behaviour and attendance and often the children arrived at school hungry and dirty. Records were inconsistent because the children moved through several different schools. The serious case review was in fact triggered by sexual abuse of one of the children by a neighbour. However, the review concluded that there had been missed opportunities for the children to have been removed and placed in care, and protected from further preventable abuse and neglect.

1. Outline the factors that could have contributed to the problems and difficulties in this family.

2. Describe the concerns that could have been highlighted in relation to the children in this family.

3. Identify some of the criticisms that may have been made about the professional involvement in this case.

Information sharing and data protection

Settings that provide services for children and young people need to have clear processes for sharing information; this is particularly important in relation to safeguarding issues. The procedure should include clear policies about confidentiality and data protection relating to both paper-based and electronic records, for example:

▶ how, why and where information should be recorded and stored

▶ who can have access to information and how this is monitored

▶ obtaining permission to share information or take photographs of children and young people

▶ strict policies on confidentiality and the importance of not discussing confidential information outside the work setting.

The Data Protection Act (1998) regulates the recording and storage of personal information, to make sure that settings work within the law. It is extremely important that any personal or confidential information relating to children, young people or their families is accurate, stored securely in the work setting and only used when needed.

Over to you!

Think about your placement or work setting.

▶ *Where is the information about children or young people kept?*

▶ *How is this information securely stored and who has access to it?*

▶ *Who is responsible for keeping the information up to date?*

Compare your experiences with those of others in your group.

Knowledge Assessment Task | 1.1 | 1.2 | 1.3 | 1.4 | 1.5

Investigate the safeguarding policy in your placement or work setting. Imagine that you have been asked to review that policy in order to update it.

Write a document that could be used to revise the safeguarding policy and includes:

▶ the current, relevant legislation and guidelines affecting the safeguarding of children and young people

▶ an explanation of child protection in the wider context of safeguarding children and young people

▶ how the guidelines affect your day-to-day work with children and young people

▶ when and why serious case reviews are required and how the findings can inform practice

▶ how processes comply with legislation relating to data protection and information sharing.

Keep your notes as evidence towards your assessment.

Why is partnership working important in safeguarding children and young people?

Safeguarding the welfare of children and young people is a complex process, which relies on effective partnership working between different agencies. There may be several different services involved with the family, including health, education, social services and voluntary agencies, each with their own area of responsibility. It is extremely important that all these professionals work together and share information in order to co-ordinate support for the child or young person and their family. It is equally important that professionals work closely with the child or young person and their family, to make sure they are fully involved in any decision-making and that consideration is given to the needs and wishes of the individuals concerned. This way of working ensures that the whole process centres on the child or young person and provides an opportunity for their voice to be heard.

Roles and responsibilities

Professionals within different agencies and organisations all have specific responsibilities regarding safeguarding children and young people. The concept of **integrated working** involves everyone who works with children and young people, and is a central part of the Every Child Matters agenda. Using integrated working, practitioners can:

- identify needs early
- deliver a co-ordinated package of support that is centred on the child or young person
- help to secure better outcomes for children, young people and their families.

Integrated working is achieved through collaboration at all levels and across all services. The roles and responsibilities of the different organisations involved in safeguarding children and young people are summarised in Figure 7.3.

Your assessment criteria:

2.1 Explain the importance of safeguarding children and young people

2.2 Explain the importance of a child or young-person centred approach

2.3 Explain what is meant by partnership working in the context of safeguarding

2.4 Describe the roles and responsibilities of the different organisations that may be involved when a child or young person has been abused or harmed

Key terms

Integrated working: everyone supporting children, young people and families works together effectively to put the child at the centre, meet their needs and improve their lives

Figure 7.3 Organisations involved in safeguarding children and young people

Organisation	Professional roles and responsibilities
Health services	*Health visitors* have a responsibility for the health and development of children under the age of five. They usually have contact with families both in the clinic or health centre and on home visits. Health visitors may often be the first people to identify concerns about a child's safety, health or welfare.
	General practitioners (GPs) have a responsibility for the general health of registered patients in their local community. They usually have contact with children and families in the surgery or health centre, and may identify safeguarding concerns as a result of a routine visit or general health check-up.
	Hospital staff may be involved in safeguarding issues if a child or young person attends the accident and emergency department as the result of a non-accidental injury.
	Child psychology services may be involved in supporting children or young people who have been abused.
Social services	*Social workers* have a responsibility to provide services for vulnerable children and their families. This might be because parents are struggling to care for their children or when families are trying to cope with challenging situations such as imprisonment or alcohol and other drug use. Social workers will always be involved in situations of abuse or harm to do with children or young people.
	Residential care workers have a responsibility for children who are living in residential care homes and not with their own families. (These are often called 'looked-after' children.) Children and young people in care are particularly vulnerable; residential care workers have a specific duty to safeguard their health and welfare.
	Family support workers have a responsibility to provide support for vulnerable children and their families. They will usually have contact with families, both at the local children's centre and on home visits, and are often called upon to monitor families when there are concerns about safety, health or welfare.
Education services	*Teachers* have a responsibility for the education and welfare of children and young people. Their work involves close observation of pupils in the classroom and this can frequently trigger concerns about health or welfare.
	Children's service workers may work in schools, pre-schools, nurseries or out-of-school clubs. They have a responsibility for the safety and welfare of children and young people and may often be the first people to identify safeguarding concerns.
Legal and criminal services	*Police* have a responsibility for the safety and protection of the general public. They will be involved in any criminal proceedings that may result from safeguarding situations.
	Probation officers have a responsibility to support the rehabilitation of some offenders in the community. This will involve monitoring people convicted of offences against children, to ensure that they do not continue to pose a threat.
Voluntary services	A wide range of voluntary organisations and groups may be involved in safeguarding the welfare of children and young people. These include the NSPCC, Childline, Kidscape, Scout/Cub and Guide/Brownie leaders, sports coaches.

Integrated working

The Children's Workforce Development Council states that: 'Integrated working involves everyone who works with children and young people, part or all of the time; whether employed, self-employed or in a voluntary capacity. Integrated working is at the centre of making a real difference to the lives of children, young people and their families. It is a central part of the *Every Child Matters* agenda and the One Children's Workforce Framework.'

Your assessment criteria:

2.1 Explain the importance of safeguarding children and young people

2.2 Explain the importance of a child or young-person centred approach

2.3 Explain what is meant by partnership working in the context of safeguarding

2.4 Describe the roles and responsibilities of the different organisations that may be involved when a child or young person has been abused or harmed

Knowledge Assessment Task   2.1   2.2   2.3   2.4

Ryan is eight years old. His father is currently in prison for drug-related offences and his mother, who has recently given birth to a baby girl, is suffering with depression. Ryan is now living with his mother and her current boyfriend and his attendance at the local primary school is erratic. When Ryan does come to school, he is usually dirty, always hungry and his behaviour is aggressive and unco-operative. He frequently hits and kicks other children and adults and has become more and more isolated. Before his father's imprisonment, Ryan had always been an outgoing, boisterous boy, who enjoyed football and social play with his friends. There have been some concerns expressed about Ryan's safety and welfare and this is currently being investigated.

1. Explain why it is important to safeguard Ryan's welfare and safety.

2. Describe the roles and responsibilities of different organisations that may be involved with Ryan and his family.

3. Explain what is meant by 'partnership working' in the context of safeguarding.

4. Explain why it is important to work closely with Ryan and his family to ensure a child-centred approach and enable Ryan's voice to be heard.

Keep your notes as evidence towards your assessment.

Over to you!

▶ Investigate the work of some of the voluntary groups involved with safeguarding children and young people.

▶ Make a list of some of their key areas of work in promoting children's welfare and keeping them safe.

Kidscape: www.**kidscape**.org.uk/

Childline: www.**childline**.org.uk

NSPCC: www.**nspcc**.org.uk

Understand the importance of ensuring children's and young people's safety and protection in the work setting

Why is it important to ensure children and young people are protected from harm?

One of the most important characteristics of anyone who works with children and young people is that they can be trusted. Parents need to be absolutely certain that their children will be safe and protected from harm when in any kind of professional care. Understanding the duty of care is an important part of being a practitioner working with children and young people and is a fundamental requirement of any job related to that area. See also Chapter 4, page 102.

Concerns about poor practice

It is extremely important that everyone who works with children and young people fully understands and complies with safeguarding procedures. Most people would take this for granted as a vital part of the job, but there have been situations where practitioners fail to follow procedures or, in some cases, actually inflict harm or abuse on children or young people.

A nursery worker was jailed in 2009 for sexually abusing young children in her care. The review of that case stated that the nursery provided 'an ideal environment' for the abuse to take place. It is extremely important that settings have rigorous policies and procedures on all aspects of safeguarding and that staff are fully aware of their roles and responsibilities.

Everyone who works with children and young people has a professional responsibility to report any concerns about colleagues who do not follow safeguarding procedures. This practice is usually referred to as 'whistle-blowing' and it is important to know how to go about it.

▶ Identify *exactly* the poor practice you have witnessed.

▶ Tell your manager, supervisor or named safeguarding member of staff.

▶ If possible, put your concerns in writing, with details including names, dates and places

Anyone who whistle-blows has a legal right to protection; managers have a duty to support members of staff who report any incidents of unprofessional conduct or poor practice that puts children's welfare at risk. It should also be acknowledged that anyone who is subject to an unproven allegation about abuse has the right to full protection for the duration of any investigation.

Your assessment criteria:

3.1 Explain why it is important to ensure children and young people are protected from harm within the work setting

3.2 Explain policies and procedures that are in place to protect children and young people and adults who work with them

3.3 Evaluate ways in which concerns about poor practice can be reported whilst ensuring that whistle-blowers and those whose practice or behaviour is being questioned are protected

3.4 Explain how practitioners can take steps to protect themselves within their everyday practice in the work setting and on off-site visits

Case study

Simon works in an out-of-school club every day from 3pm to 6.30pm. He is responsible for a small group of 'key children' aged from six to nine years and he knows them all very well. At the end of one day, as Simon is busy putting some playthings away, he notices an unfamiliar man has come to collect William, aged seven. The man says that he is William's uncle and he has been asked by William's mother to pick him up. Simon does not recognise this man, but he observes Gemma, who also works at the out-of-school club, saying that this will be fine and helping William to collect his things, ready to leave.

1. Explain what Simon should do in this situation.
2. Describe why it is important for Simon to report what he has observed.

Over to you!

Look again at Figure 7.3 on page 191, which outlines the key points about safeguarding policies and procedures in work settings. What are the policies in your placement or work setting regarding:

▶ staff use of mobile phones
▶ taking photographs of children and young people
▶ physical contact with children and young people?

Share your experiences with others in your group.

Practitioners protecting themselves

Adopting a professional, common-sense approach is the best way for practitioners to protect themselves against any accusations or suspicions of abuse. Staff should always make sure that they fully understand safeguarding policies and how they should be applied, both inside the setting and for off-site visits.

Over to you!

Think about the safeguarding policies in your placement or work setting and describe how you would respond to the following situations.

▶ A colleague asks you to take a child to the toilet, which is outside of the room and out of view.
▶ A manager asks you to take children, one at a time, into a separate room, to work on letters and sounds.
▶ A parent asks you to take their child to the out-of-school club at the end of the school day.

Compare your responses with those of others in your group.

Knowledge Assessment Task | 3.1 | 3.2 | 3.3 | 3.4

Prepare an information pack that could be used for new students in children's and young people's services. The pack should include information about:

▶ why it is important to ensure that children and young people are protected from harm within the work setting
▶ how practitioners can take steps to protect themselves from safeguarding-related accusations in their everyday practice
▶ how to report concerns about poor practice and why this is important
▶ the policies and procedures in place to ensure that children, young people and the adults who work with them are protected.

Keep your notes as evidence towards your assessment.

Your assessment criteria:

4.1 Describe the possible signs, symptoms, indicators and behaviours that may cause concern in the context of safeguarding

4.2 Describe the actions to take if a child or young person alleges harm or abuse in line with policies and procedures of your own setting

4.3 Explain the rights that children, young people and their carers have in situations where harm or abuse is suspected or alleged

What are the signs and symptoms that may cause concern?

Abuse, harm or bullying of children and young people can take many different forms.

Generally, the four main types of abuse are categorised as:

▶ physical

▶ emotional

▶ sexual

▶ neglect.

Bullying can include physical, emotional or sexual abuse and this is considered in more detail on page 200.

There are many possible signs, symptoms, indicators and behaviours that may cause concern about abuse or harm of a child or young person, as outlined in Figure 7.4.

Figure 7.4 Signs, symptoms, indicators and behaviours that may cause concern about abuse or harm

Cause for concern	Could indicate	Characteristics
Unexplained injuries, bruising or burns; reluctance or refusal to undress (e.g. for PE, games or a medical exam); wearing layers of clothing or heavy clothes to cover injuries, aggressive behaviour; fear of physical contact	Physical abuse	Hitting, shaking, throwing, burning or scalding, beating with objects or otherwise causing physical harm or injury It can result in pain, bruising, broken bones and sometimes disability or even death.
Lack of confidence, particularly in new situations; becoming very withdrawn; delayed development; repetitive, nervous behaviour (e.g. fidgeting or rocking back and forth)	Emotional abuse	Shouting, swearing and negative criticism; withholding love and affection; bullying, including cyber-bullying; causing children to feel worthless and useless It can result in low self-esteem and extreme fearfulness.
Disturbed behaviour including self-harm, personality changes, regression, inappropriate sexual behaviour; medical problems such as repeated urinary infections; insecurity and lack of trust	Sexual abuse	Forcing or enticing into sexual activities; viewing pornographic material, including on the internet; encouraging inappropriate physical touching; sexual harassment It can result in depression, guild, anxiety, post-traumatic stress disorder and sexual promiscuity or an eating disorder.
Constant hunger; tiredness (always falling asleep); poor personal hygiene; inadequate or inappropriate clothing; poor interpersonal and social skills	Neglect	Not providing food, clothing, warmth, shelter, basic hygiene, care or protection It can result in **failure to thrive** and developmental delay.

Key terms

Failure to thrive: not growing or gaining weight at the expected rate

Responding to evidence or safeguarding concerns

It is extremely important for anyone who works with children or young people to understand fully the action to take in response to evidence or concerns about abuse or harm.

One of the most important things to remember is that, if you ever have concerns about the welfare of a child or young person, you should always make those concerns known to the appropriate person, following the procedures of the setting. Many children living in abusive or harmful situations are in a constant state of anxiety and fear and it can therefore be very difficult for them to talk to anyone about it.

The act of a child or young person telling you or suggesting that they have been abused, harmed or bullied is called **disclosure**. The details can be distressing to hear, but knowing how to respond to disclosure is an important part of professional practice. Your key actions should include some of the following.

▶ Listen carefully, without showing shock or disbelief.

▶ Do not ask leading questions, such as: *'Where did he hurt you?'*

▶ Accept what the child or young person says and do not rush them.

▶ Reassure them and emphasise that they have done the right thing by telling someone.

▶ Never promise that you will keep what they have said a secret.

▶ Follow the procedure for your work setting (which will usually involve telling your supervisor in the first instance, and you may be required to write a report).

Your assessment criteria:

4.2 Describe the actions to take if a child or young person alleges harm or abuse in line with policies and procedures of your own setting

4.3 Explain the rights that children, young people and their carers have in situations where harm or abuse is suspected or alleged

Key terms

Disclosure: revealing sensitive information

The rights of children, young people and their carers

The voice of the child or young person should always be at the heart of any decision making involving safeguarding issues, even in cases of traumatic abuse, when the circumstances can be very distressing. Practitioners have an important responsibility, not only to listen sensitively, but also actively to create opportunities for children and young people to express themselves and feel secure.

Children and young people have the right to:

▶ be given accurate information and help to understand it

▶ express themselves and be heard

▶ participate in decision making

▶ refuse repeated medical examinations and questioning (e.g. following allegations of physical or sexual abuse)

▶ be consulted and kept fully informed of proceedings and decisions about their future.

Knowledge Assessment Task   4.1   4.2   4.3

Karl works at an out-of-school club. He has been building dens outside with a group of children and they have decided to come inside for a drink and a snack. Aaron, aged nine years, is hanging back from the rest of the group and Karl waits for him to catch up. Aaron tells Karl that his dad 'gave him a right belting' last night and Aaron is feeling anxious about going home tonight.

1. Describe the actions that Karl should take in response to Aaron's disclosure.

2. Explain the rights that Aaron and his family have in this situation.

3. Describe the possible signs, symptoms, indicators or behaviours that Karl should be aware of, in the context of safeguarding, with the children in his care.

Keep your notes as evidence towards your assessment.

Over to you!

▶ *Make sure that you fully understand the safeguarding policy at your placement or work setting.*

▶ *For further information, investigate the document 'Working Together to Safeguard Children' at: www.education. gov.uk/publications// eOrderingDownload/00305-2010DOM-EN.PDF*

What is bullying?

Bullying is the use of aggression with the intention of hurting another person. Bullying includes intimidation, harassment and discrimination and results in pain and distress to the victim. It can be carried out by an individual or a group and frequently involves aggressive, dominant children or young people taking advantage of more vulnerable ones. The charity **Kidscape** estimates that one in 12 children are so badly bullied that it affects their education, relationships and even their prospects for jobs in later life.

Types of bullying

Bullying can take many different forms, all of which can have devastating effects on the lives of children and young people. There is an increasing concern about the extent of cyberbullying, particularly among young people, and this is discussed on page 208.

Different types of bullying and the potential effects on children and young people are outlined in Figure 7.5.

Your assessment criteria:

5.1 Explain different types of bullying and the potential effects on children and young people

5.2 Outline the policies and procedures that should be followed in response to concerns or evidence of bullying and explain the reasons why they are in place

Figure 7.5 Types of bullying and potential effects on children and young people

Type of bullying	Example	Potential effects on children and young people
Physical	Pushing, kicking, hitting, pinching and other forms of violence or threats	• low self-esteem • depression • becoming withdrawn and isolated • lack of concentration • poor academic achievement • attempted suicide
Verbal	Name-calling, insults, sarcasm, spreading rumours, persistent teasing	
Emotional	Humiliation, excluding, tormenting, ridicule, spreading lies	
Cyberbullying	Using information and communication technology (ICT), including mobile phones, the internet and social networking sites, deliberately to upset someone else	
Targeted bullying	Homophobia, racism, gender or disability discrimination	

Responding to concerns about bullying

Everybody has the right to be treated with respect and no one deserves to be a victim of bullying. Children or young people who bully need to learn different ways of behaving; settings have a responsibility to respond promptly and effectively to any incidents involving bullying. All schools are required by law to have anti-bullying policies; most will take a 'zero tolerance' approach towards bullying in any form. The government document, 'Safe to Learn: Embedding anti-bullying work in schools' recommends that anti-bullying policies are developed as part of the school's wider behaviour policy and should involve children and young people as well as staff, parents and carers. The Welsh Assembly has developed anti-bullying guidance called 'Respecting Others', which aims to provide information on tackling bullying in schools. The recommendations for responding to concerns or evidence of bullying include these guidelines.

- ▶ Report bullying incidents to an appropriate member of staff.

- ▶ In serious cases, inform parents and ask them to come to a meeting to discuss the problem.

- ▶ If necessary and appropriate, consult the police.

- ▶ The bullying behaviour or threats of bullying must be investigated and the bullying stopped quickly.

- ▶ An attempt will be made to help the bully (bullies) change their behaviour.

- ▶ The bully (bullies) may be asked to apologise, genuinely and sincerely.

- ▶ If possible, the children or young people will be reconciled.

- ▶ After the incident/incidents have been investigated and dealt with, each case will be monitored to ensure that repeated bullying does not take place.

Key terms

Kidscape: a charitable organisation dedicated to keeping children safe from bullying and abuse

Your assessment criteria:

5.1 Explain different types of bullying and the potential effects on children and young people

5.2 Outline the policies and procedures that should be followed in response to concerns or evidence of bullying and explain the reasons why they are in place

5.3 Explain how to support a child or young person and/or their family when bullying is suspected or alleged

Supporting the child or young person and their family

Dealing with bullying incidents can be very distressing for everyone concerned, particularly the individual who is being bullied. It is important to treat each situation seriously and remember that both the victim and the bully, in addition to their family, will need support.

The victim

Any victim of bullying is likely to feel frightened and upset and may find it very difficult to tell anyone. The victim needs to know that the bullying will be fully investigated and they will be supported throughout the process. They also need to be reassured that the bullying will not be allowed to continue.

The bully

Anyone involved in bullying behaviour towards someone else also needs support. They need to understand that their behaviour is not acceptable and needs to change. Research from the NSPCC suggests that many bullies have experienced family problems themselves and have difficulty in managing positive relationships. They need consistency and support in order to develop more positive behaviour patterns.

The family

The families of both victims and bullies also need support. It can be very stressful for parents to realise that their child has been involved in bullying, either as a victim or a bully, and they will need information, advice and guidance. Parents need to be fully informed and involved in the investigation and should be given a copy of the anti-bullying policy followed in the setting. Organisations such as Kidscape and the NSPCC are excellent sources of support for families dealing with bullying.

Case study

Mischa works as a teaching assistant at Woodlands primary school and she frequently supervises the children at break times, when they are playing outside. Vicky is an eight-year-old child who attends Woodlands school. She is tall for her age and very overweight. Mischa has noticed that a small group of girls have started teasing Vicky about her size and calling her names such as 'Fatty'. These children exclude Vicky from their games and Mischa has observed that Vicky is often left on her own at play times. One lunch-time, Mischa finds Vicky in the toilets, sobbing and extremely distressed about her treatment from the other girls.

1. Describe the action Mischa should take in response to this situation.

2. Explain how Mischa could support Vicky.

3. Outline sources of support that could help Woodlands primary school in dealing with this bullying incident.

Preventing bullying

It is recognised that one of the best ways to address bullying is to help prevent it in the first place. Children and young people can be involved in this process by:

▶ creating the rules about behaviour

▶ signing a behaviour contract

▶ writing stories or poems or drawing pictures about bullying

▶ reading stories about bullying or having them read to a class or assembly

▶ making up role-plays

▶ having discussions about bullying and why it matters.

Knowledge Assessment Task   5.1   5.2   5.3

Imagine that you have been asked to review the anti-bullying policy at your placement or work setting. Create an outline, which could be used to review the policy that includes:

▶ different types of bullying and the potential effects on children and young people

▶ the procedures that should be followed in response to concerns or evidence of bullying and the reasons why these need to be in place

▶ how to support the child, young person and their family when bullying is suspected or alleged.

Keep your notes as evidence towards your assessment.

Your assessment criteria:

6.1 Explain how to support children's and young people's self-confidence and self-esteem

6.2 Analyse the importance of supporting resilience in children and young people

6.3 Explain why it is important to work with the child or young person to ensure they have strategies to protect themselves and make decisions about safety

6.4 Explain ways of empowering children and young people to make positive and informed choices that support their wellbeing and safety

Why is it important to support children's and young people's wellbeing?

A sense of wellbeing comes from feeling good about yourself and having a positive outlook on life. It embraces a range of positive feelings, including enjoyment, vitality and self-esteem. Children and young people who have a positive sense of wellbeing are confident and less likely to be vulnerable to abuse, harm or bullying. It is therefore extremely important to encourage children and young people's wellbeing.

Supporting self-confidence, self-esteem and resilience

Self-esteem

This relates to how positively or negatively an individual feels about themself.

Self-confidence

This relates to how an individual projects that feeling through their personality and behaviour.

Resilience

This is defined as the ability to deal with the ups and downs of life and the capacity to recover from setbacks. It is based on secure early attachments and positive relationships with family and friends. Research has shown that children and young people with high levels of self-esteem and self-confidence are more resilient and better able to deal with life as they get older.

Over to you!

▶ *Think about how you encourage self-confidence, self-esteem and resilience in children or young people in your placement or work setting.*

▶ *Give two examples from your own practice that demonstrate how you encourage self-confidence, self-esteem and resilience in children or young people in your placement or work setting.*

▶ *Share your examples with a colleague.*

The role of practitioners

Practitioners can support the development of self-confidence, self-esteem and resilience in many different ways in children and young people. Some suggestions are listed in Figure 7.6.

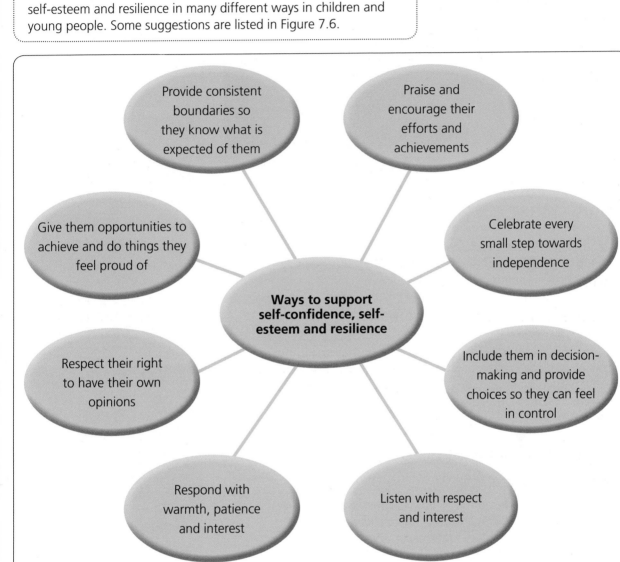

Figure 7.6 How practitioners can support self-confidence, self-esteem and resilience

Your assessment criteria:

6.1 Explain how to support children's and young people's self-confidence and self-esteem

6.2 Analyse the importance of supporting resilience in children and young people

6.3 Explain why it is important to work with the child or young person to ensure they have strategies to protect themselves and make decisions about safety

6.4 Explain ways of empowering children and young people to make positive and informed choices that support their wellbeing and safety

Supporting children and young people to protect themselves

Children and young people have the right to feel safe. It is important for them to develop strategies to protect themselves and make decisions about their own safety. Young children need to learn about danger and risk and older children need to learn about being assertive and resisting peer pressure. In order to do this, children and young people need:

- ▶ *accurate, reliable information* about their own bodies and about appropriate and inappropriate behaviour, and they need to know what help and support services are available

- ▶ *encouragement* to share their worries or concerns about their safety and welfare

- ▶ *trust and respect* that their concerns will be treated seriously

- ▶ *support* in positive decision making.

Kidscape have produced the 'Keepsafe Code', which provides a useful guide for young children. Older children may need more detailed information, for example, about sexual health, relationships or drug use.

Empowering children and young people to make informed choices

Children and young people need to learn how to assess and manage risk in order to make positive decisions and keep themselves safe. This process starts at a very young age. For example, when children first learn to climb up stairs, adults will provide support and safeguards in order to manage the risk and minimise the danger. As children learn about the risks involved, they will gradually become more independent and assess the danger for themselves. Equally, if young people are supported in their decision making, they will be empowered to make informed choices, for example, in relation to sexual health or drug use.

Over to you!

- ▶ *Make a list of some of the decisions you make every day, for example, what to eat, what to wear or what you are going to do with your friends.*

- ▶ *Think about how you make these decisions and the factors that influence your choices.*

- ▶ *Compare your responses with those of others in the group.*

Case study

Read this extract from a blog, posted on a support website for young people.

I am 15, I like doing things with my friends and we always do stuff together. A new girl has just started at our school and has joined our group. She likes doing different things and always persuades my friends to go with her. Some of the things she suggests, I don't want to do, like going to the pub, but if I don't go, then I get left out from the rest of the group. I still want to do things with my friends, but I don't want to get into trouble.

What should I do?

Amy

(Unhappy and confused)

1. Discuss some of the reasons why Amy is feeling unhappy and confused.
2. What advice would you give Amy to help her deal with this situation?

Knowledge Assessment Task   6.1   6.2   6.3   6.4

Design an advertising campaign that focuses on empowering children and young people and supporting their self-confidence and self-esteem. Your campaign could include a TV commercial, designs for a billboard, poster or information leaflet, and should include information about:

▶ how children and young people can be empowered to make informed choices that support their safety and wellbeing

▶ the importance of supporting children and young people's self-confidence, self-esteem and resilience

▶ the importance of helping children and young people to develop strategies to protect themselves.

Keep your notes and details of your campaign as evidence towards your assessment.

Your assessment criteria:

7.1 Explain the risks and possible consequences for children and young people of being online and of using a mobile phone

7.2 Describe ways of reducing risk to children and young people from: social networking, internet use, buying online, using a mobile phone

Over to you!

▶ *Think about your own use of technology, including the internet and social networking sites.*

▶ *What measures do you take to protect yourself online?*

What are the risks of using technology for children and young people?

Children and young people are particularly at risk from some forms of technology, which can present a threat to their safety and welfare.

The internet is a powerful tool but it can also expose children and young people to unsuitable sites and potentially harmful material. Social networking sites can encourage young people to post personal and private information online, making them vulnerable to exploitation.

Many children and young people have access to mobile phones and the benefits of being able to communicate with them can be a great reassurance to parents. However, mobile phones can also be an instrument for cyber-bullying, and this has caused a great deal of distress for many young people and their parents.

Video games and online gaming can also present risks for children and young people, particularly in relation to the classification of violent content. Children and young people need to be aware of the possible dangers from using all types of technology and adults have a responsibility to ensure that children are protected.

Reducing the risk

In 2008, the Byron Review 'Safer Children in a Digital World' made a number of recommendations about reducing the risk from technology to children and young people. It concluded that, while no one can completely eliminate the risks, there are a number of measures that can improve e-safety, including:

- improving knowledge, skills and understanding about e-safety regarding children, young people, their parents and other adults (such as teachers)

- supporting children and young people to be aware of the dangers and have the confidence and skills to use the internet more safely

- restricting access and increasing parental supervision and content controls to block out unsuitable material.

Case study

Dale is seven years old and has an older brother aged 11. He enjoys playing video games, especially car racing and football games, which he sometimes plays with his brother. Dale and his brother have a computer in their bedroom and, although their parents try to limit the amount of time spent on it, invariably the boys end up spending a couple of hours every night in front of the screen. Dale has only experimented with the internet, but his brother is a more practised user and often encourages Dale to view some of the material he finds on more 'risky' sites, stating that their parents: *'Don't know enough to check on what we're doing.'*

1. Explain the risks to which Dale and his brother could be exposed.

2. Describe how Dale's parents could reduce the risks for both Dale and his brother.

Knowledge Assessment Task   7.1   7.2

Create a factsheet that could be used as part of an information website for parents about the importance of e-safety for children and young people. Your factsheet should include:

- the risks and possible consequences for children and young people of being online and using mobile phone technology

- ways of reducing risk to children and young people from using technology, including social networking, internet use, buying online and using mobile phone technology.

Keep your factsheet as evidence towards your assessment.

Are you ready for assessment?

AC	What do you know now?	Assessment task	✓
1.1	Current legislation, guidelines, policies and procedures within own UK Home Nation affecting the safeguarding of children and young people	Page 189	
1.2	The importance of child protection within the wider concept of safeguarding children and young people	Page 189	
1.3	How national and local guidelines, policies and procedures for safeguarding affect day-to-day work with children and young people	Page 189	
1.4	When and why inquiries and serious case reviews are required and how the sharing of the findings informs practice	Page 189	
1.5	How the processes used by own work setting or service comply with legislation that covers data protection, information handling and sharing	Page 189	
2.1 2.2	The importance of safeguarding children and young people and the importance of a child or young person-centred approach	Page 193	
2.3	What is meant by partnership working in the context of safeguarding	Page 193	
2.4	The roles and responsibilities of the different organisations that may be involved when a child or young person has been abused or harmed	Page 193	
3.1 3.2	Why it is important to ensure children and young people are protected from harm within the work setting and the policies and procedures that are in place to protect children and young people and adults who work with them	Page 195	
3.3	Ways in which concerns about poor practice can be reported whilst ensuring that whistle-blowers and those whose practice or behaviour is being questioned are protected	Page 195	
3.4	How practitioners can take steps to protect themselves within their everyday practice in the work setting and on off-site visits	Page 195	
4.1	The possible signs, symptoms, indicators and behaviours that may cause concern in the context of safeguarding	Page 199	
4.2	The actions to take if a child or young person alleges harm or abuse in line with policies and procedures of your own setting	Page 199	

AC	What do you know now?	Assessment task	✓
4.3	The rights that children, young people and their carers have in situations where harm or abuse is suspected or alleged	Page 199	
5.1	Different types of bullying and the potential effects on children and young people	Page 203	
5.2	The policies and procedures that should be followed in response to concerns or evidence of bullying and explain the reasons why they are in place	Page 203	
5.3	How to support a child or young person and/or their family when bullying is suspected or alleged	Page 203	
6.1	How to support children and young people's self-confidence and self-esteem	Page 207	
6.2	The importance of supporting resilience in children and young people	Page 207	
6.3	Why it is important to work with the child or young person to ensure they have strategies to protect themselves and make decisions about safety	Page 207	
6.4	Ways of empowering children and young people to make positive and informed choices that support their wellbeing and safety	Page 207	
7.1	The risks and possible consequences for children and young people of being online and of using a mobile phone	Page 209	
7.2	Ways of reducing risk to children and young people from social networking, internet use, buying online, using a mobile phone	Page 209	

There is no practical assessment for this unit, but your tutor or assessor may question you about some of the following points.

What can you do now?	✓
Apply your knowledge about safeguarding policies and procedures in the real work environment	
Do you have any examples from your own practice to share with your assessor?	
Be clear about your own responsibilities in the case of any evidence or concerns about safeguarding issues in the work environment	
Could you discuss this with your assessor?	
Apply your knowledge about supporting children and young people's self-confidence, self-esteem and resilience in the real work environment	
Do you have any examples from your own practice to share with your assessor?	

3 | Support children and young people's health and safety (CYP 3.4)

Assessment of this unit

This unit focuses on the main aspects of health and safety that you need to know in order to be able to protect the children and young people in your care from harm. It explains the relevant legislation, policies and procedures and how to fulfil legal requirements in your working practice. It also explains the steps of the risk assessment and management process and explores how this must be balanced with the need for children and young people to learn how to experience challenges safely. It equips you to respond appropriately in the event of illness, accident, injury, incident and emergency.

To complete this unit successfully you will need to produce evidence of your knowledge, as shown in the 'What you need to know' chart opposite. You also need to produce evidence of your practical ability, as shown in the 'What you need to do' chart. The 'What you need to do' criteria must be assessed in a real work environment by a vocationally competent assessor. Your tutor or assessor will help you to prepare for your assessment and the tasks suggested in this unit will help you to create the evidence you need.

CHAPTER 8

AC   What you need to know

1.1	The factors to take into account when planning healthy and safe indoor and outdoor environments and services
1.2	How health and safety are monitored and maintained and how people in the work setting are made aware of risks and hazards and encouraged to work safely
1.3	Sources of current guidance for planning healthy and safe environments and services
1.4	How current health and safety legislation, policies and procedures are implemented in your own work setting or service
3.1	Why it is important to take a balanced approach to risk management
3.2	The dilemma between the rights and choices of children and young people and health and safety requirements
3.3	Examples from your own practice of supporting children or young people to assess and manage risk
4.1	The policies and procedures of the setting or service in response to accidents, incidents, emergencies and illness
4.2	The correct procedures for recording and reporting accidents, incidents, injuries, signs of illness and other emergencies

AC   What you need to

2.1	Demonstrate how to identify potential hazards to the health, safety and security of children or young people, families and other visitors and colleagues
2.2	Demonstrate ability to deal with hazards in the work setting or in off-site visits
2.3	Undertake a health and safety risk assessment in your own work setting or service, illustrating how its implementation will reduce risk
2.4	Explain how healthy and safety risk assessments are monitored and reviewed

This unit links with other mandatory units as shown below.	
SHC 34	Principles for implementing duty of care in health, social care or children's and young people's settings
CYP 3.3	Understand how to safeguard the wellbeing of children and young people
CYP 3.7	Understand how to support positive outcomes for children and young people
EYMP 3	Promote children's welfare and wellbeing in the early years
Some of your learning will be repeated in these units and will give you the chance to review your knowledge and understanding.	

Your assessment criteria:

1.1 Describe the factors to take into account when planning healthy and safe indoor and outdoor environments and services

What are the key factors to consider when planning healthy and safe environments and services?

In your work with children and young people you will need to prepare safe areas where they can play. You will also need to organise a range of different activities in which they will be able to take part safely. There are a number of health and safety requirements to include in your planning for both indoors and outside.

The principles for providing safe play areas and activities

Common sense is one of the most important qualities you need when providing play areas and activities that are healthy and safe for children and young people. Use your personal experience and accumulated knowledge about potential hazards to inform you. Figure 8.1 outlines the key health and safety principles you must consider.

Differing needs

Each child and young person is a unique individual, meaning that each will have differing needs, abilities and level of understanding. This is influenced by the age and stage of development each child has reached. If you care for children of a mixed age range you may need to section off certain areas or have activities placed at different physical levels. This would prevent, for example, a child who is crawling from getting access to a climbing frame or unsupervised water-play area. You also need to bear in mind the different wishes of parents who may have strong opinions about their child participating in certain types of play, particularly adventurous play, which they may view as being too risky.

Figure 8.1 Health and safety principles

Special needs

Some children and young people have special needs related to a physical condition, a disability, sensory impairment or a learning difficulty. Keeping these children safe while providing them with equal opportunities to play, explore and be active is an additional challenge that requires careful thought. You may need to adapt play equipment or find suitable enabling or protective aids. Consider also how to make sure the children understand safety instructions and can follow them sufficiently well.

Specific risks

There may be particular risks to bear in mind. For example, if you're working with a colleague who is pregnant, or individuals with a sensory impairment, you will need to make allowances. There may also be specific risks associated

with particular activities, so make sure you use the relevant safety equipment and give appropriate safety instructions in preparation. For example, if you are starting a baking session, don't begin without making sure that aprons and oven gloves are available, that children know who may use matches and how to use them safely, that they only open the oven when an adult is present, and understand the importance of personal hygiene while cooking.

Duty of care

Your **duty of care** means you are legally obliged to look out for the welfare and safety of the children in your care, and of others such as your colleagues. This must be at the forefront of every decision you make.

Function and purpose

Only use equipment in the way it was intended for use because, as well as the potential dangers involved, insurance will not cover accidents that occur as a result of misuse. Being creative, for example, using a plank of wood to make a slide, might seem like a good idea but will not be much fun if the children then get splinters. Make sure that all equipment is fit for purpose and in good working order and that you know how to operate it safely.

Desired outcomes

Keep in mind your aims and objectives for the activities you plan and the play environments you prepare. Think about what you are trying to achieve through these, especially in relationship to the age and stage of the child or young person and the required outcomes within which you are obliged to work, such as the Early Years Foundation Stage for children under the age of five.

Lines of responsibility and accountability

Part of health and safety is to know exactly what responsibility you hold, to whom you must report and who is in overall charge. Be aware of colleagues with particular responsibility, such as the named person responsible for safeguarding and child protection, should you need to report suspected abuse. It is also important to know to whom to go if this person is away. If you work alone you need to know to whom to report with specific concerns.

Your assessment criteria:

1.1 Describe the factors to take into account when planning healthy and safe indoor and outdoor environments and services

Key terms

Duty of care: the legal obligation to act toward others with careful attention and reasonable caution to protect their wellbeing and prevent harm occurring

Knowledge Assessment Task 1.1

There are a number of health and safety requirements to include when you plan indoor and outdoor areas and services for children and young people.

Describe the key factors you will need to take into consideration to prepare a healthy and safe indoor and outdoor environment for the following three scenarios.

1. A group of Brownies, aged nine to 10 years, are joining other local Brownie packs, to take part in a sponsored swim at a local leisure centre. They will walk together to the event, but individual parents will collect their child at the end. The girls are excited to hear that a photographer from the local paper will be there to take a whole-group photo.

2. A nursery outing has been planned to visit the library, which is local and within walking distance. The children will have some stories read to them and the library is providing a drink and snack.

3. A Year 2 primary school class is being taken by coach for a day trip to the zoo. Extra parent helpers have been requested. They will have the chance to visit the petting zoo just before lunch and should get to see the popular 'penguin parade' before they have to leave.

Keep your written work as evidence towards your assessment.

Over to you!

▶ Make notes of some of the differing needs, special needs and particular risks among the children and young people you work with, as well as their families and your colleagues. Remember not to use real names, in order to maintain confidentiality.

▶ Are there any particular measures you need to take to accommodate the needs of others?

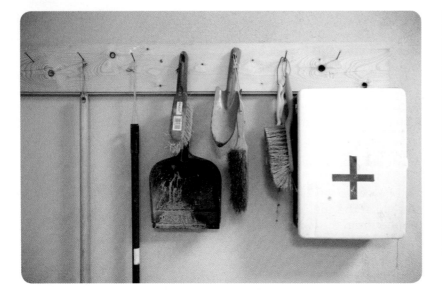

Key terms

Infection control: procedures
and systems designed to
prevent or limit organisms that
cause disease from passing
between people and objects

How do you monitor and maintain health and safety in the work setting and encourage safe working practices?

All care settings must have systems in place so that each aspect of
health and safety concerning the workplace and working practice
are checked regularly. These should be itemised as part of a health
and safety policy and include details about how often the checks
should take place, who should make the checks and how the
information must be recorded and reported.

Case study

Ben is a paid Sunday school worker who oversees the adult volunteers
and children who attend. There are three classes: a crèche, a primary
group and a secondary group. Most parents attend church services,
but some older children come independently to Sunday school. They
do craft activities and dress up and act out plays. Following an appeal
to the congregation they have received play equipment, toys and
dressing-up clothes, all of which need sorting. The church's children's
committee have asked Ben to develop some basic health and safety
procedures to do with cleanliness and health and safety.

1. What health and safety procedures do you think Ben should
   include?

2. What should Ben do to ensure that the donated toys and
   dressing-up clothes are safe for the children to use?

3. What can be done to make sure play equipment, toys and
   dressing-up clothes remain safe?

Monitoring systems

The different areas that require monitoring are set out in Figure 8.2.

Figure 8.2 Health and safety monitoring systems

Area	People responsible
• *Cleanliness*: regular cleaning of facilities, equipment, toys; rolling programme of deep cleaning	• Owner/landlord
• *Emergencies*: fire/first aid/evacuation/missing child equipment; drills; training	• Facility manager
• *Equipment*: product safety marks (see page 227); items in good working order	• Specialist professional, such as electricians
• *Furniture*: fit for purpose; no slip, trip and fall hazards; safe furniture storage systems (such as chairs and tables stacked correctly to a specified height); in good condition	• Practitioners and care workers
• *Gas and electrical equipment*: checked regularly by qualified technician	• Caretaker/cleaning staff
• *Hazardous equipment*: knives/matches/chemicals safely stored, handled, disposed of	• Catering staff
• *Heat*: adequate, comfortable temperature; maintained by qualified technician	
• *Hygiene and sanitary arrangements*: sufficient toilets, hand basins, etc. to the number of people	
• Infection control *measures*: hygiene products, protective clothing (aprons/hair covering)	
• *Light*: adequate; maintained by qualified technician, sockets and socket covers	
• *Outdoor areas*: cleared of rubbish, dog excrement, hazardous obstacles or areas, poisonous plants	
• *Pets and other animals*: safe, clean, no access to water/sand-play areas; hand-washing after touching	
• *Routines*: monitoring children during playtime, meal times, when sleeping; pick-up/drop-off times	
• *Rubbish disposal*: receptacles, storage, handling and disposal	
• *Security*: locks; system for checking visitors in and out, staff badges; boundaries and gates	
• *Safety*: information and warning notices; drills; proper use of specialist equipment for children	
• *Space*: ratio of individuals to space/facilities adequate	
• *Ventilation*: adequate; air conditioning maintained by qualified technician	
• *Water*: Legionella procedures in place; temperature; safe drinking water, water-play areas, water hazards (ponds, rivers)	
• *Windows/doors*: safety glass, safety catches for windows; access monitored	

Keeping people safe

Every member of staff has a right to have their health and safety protected and holds an equal responsibility to protect the health and safety of others. This includes the children and young people in your care, their families, your colleagues, visiting practitioners and other visitors.

For example, a tradesperson such as an electrician might need to do repair or maintenance work during the working day of a playgroup. During the electrician's visit the children need to be kept safe from dangers such as tools and exposure to electricity, and the electrician must be kept safe from accidents and incidents, such as falling over a dropped toy or slipping in spilt juice. In addition, the electrician may not be known to you and is a visitor, so should not be left to wander around or interact inappropriately with children.

Figure 8.3 shows ways of keeping people safe within your workplace.

Your assessment criteria:

1.2 Explain how health and safety is monitored and maintained and how people in your work setting are made aware of risks and hazards and encouraged to work safely

1.3 Identify sources of current guidance for planning healthy and safe environments and services

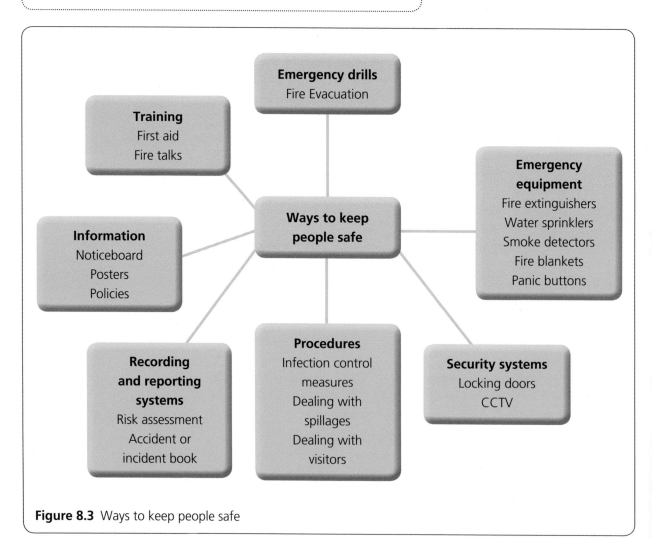

Figure 8.3 Ways to keep people safe

Case study

The children and parents of Viewlands primary school have been fundraising for a year to have a traverse climbing wall installed in the playground. At last they have collected enough money and the company is coming to the school to install the wall. Nenita has been asked to meet the climbing wall team, show them the playground and make sure they have what they need. She must also make any arrangements necessary to keep the children and the workers safe while the team continues to work over playtime.

1. What steps must Nenita take to make sure that the children are safe during playtime while the climbing wall is being installed?

2. What must she do to keep the climbing wall team safe?

3. What other information would you want to find out before the team leave and the children can play on the new equipment?

Over to you!

▶ *How many notices posted up at your placement or work setting publicise information aimed at keeping you safe?*

▶ *Make a point of reading these and checking that you are working according to safe guidelines.*

Where can you find guidance about planning healthy and safe environments?

Health and safety considerations will be an important element of nearly every situation you encounter when you work with children and young people. It is impossible to have an answer for each potential situation, but there are resources available to guide and support you.

Sources of guidance

There are a number of different sources of information available to you. Your place of work and your local library are good starting points, and a great deal of information can be found on the internet.

People

▶ *Colleagues* – some of your colleagues may have specialist knowledge or a wealth of experience from which you can benefit.

▶ *Visiting practitioners* – people who practice in other professions but come to your workplace as part of the service provision may be able to give you different insights.

Documents

▶ *Legislation documents* explain the ways in which health and safety law relates to your place of work and your work role.

▶ *Policies* describe under-running principles for safe working. There will be a specific health and safety policy, as well as other related policies, such as safeguarding and moving and handling.

▶ *Procedures* set out detailed instructions about what must happen in particular circumstances, such a fire alarm sounding, or if the building is to be evacuated, or in the event of a child or young person going missing.

▶ *Other professions* such as the police, social services or healthcare can be contacted by letter to request specific relevant information.

Public information

▶ *Health and Safety Executive (HSE)* is a national independent watchdog for work-related health, safety and illness. Its role is to enforce legislation, provide information and advice and run an advocacy service that supports individuals who have been injured at work to go through a complaints procedure.

▶ *British Safety Council (BSC)* is a UK charity offering information and guidance on health, safety and environmental issues.

▶ *Health Protection Agency (HPA)* is an independent UK organisation set up to protect the public from infectious disease and environmental hazards. It offers advice and information and

Key terms

Legislation: laws and legal regulations

produced the Children's Environment and Health Action Plan for the UK (2009).

▶ *Child Accident Prevention Trust* is a charity working to reduce the number of children and young people killed, disabled and seriously injured as a result of accidents.

▶ *CEOP (Child Exploitation and Online Protection Centre)* is a section of UK policing dedicated to preventing sexual abuse of children online. It provides information and training about safe internet use, as well as tracking known sex offenders.

In addition you can look at government, family and education websites for the country within the UK in which you work, as well as your local authority website, which will have information that is particular to your local area. There are also specialist magazines published for those who work with children and young people that carry articles and interviews and often run an in-depth focus on a particular topic. Back copies may be available in your local community library or college library.

Over to you!

Start a box-file in which you gather useful health and safety resource information, about aspects of child and young people care, that are relevant to you. This could include leaflets and website information about your area of work.

Case study

At a recent committee meeting for the Little Tots playgroup it is reported that the local council have agreed to the playgroup using a section of rough ground just outside the village hall for the children to enjoy outdoor play. The parents who are present at the meeting are delighted and some offer to help to improve the space. Doug talks about the need for clearing the rubbish and putting up fencing, and Sandeep wants to make a sandpit and water-play area, while Isabel is keen to plant some shrubs and herbs and to include the children in this activity.

1. Does each of these improvements raise any specific health and safety issues?
2. What measures can Isabel take to make sure the children remain safe and well when they help with the gardening?
3. What sources of information might be available for this group of parents to seek advice about health and safety requirements?

Knowledge Assessment Task   1.2   1.3

There must be systems in place to monitor and maintain the health and safety of both care settings and work practices, and there are a number of sources available that give guidance about healthy and safe environments and services.

To complete this assessment task, make a table of information to:

▶ explain how health and safety is monitored and maintained where you work
▶ explain how staff members and visiting practitioners are made aware of risks and hazards and encouraged to work safely
▶ identify sources of current guidance for planning healthy and safe environments and services.

Keep your written work as evidence towards your assessment.

How are health and safety legislation, policies and procedures implemented at work?

Health and safety is an area that is surrounded by laws. This reflects how important it is. Local authorities, private companies and other employers must interpret these laws and offer guidance to their employees to ensure that they work within the law. This is the purpose of policies and procedures in the workplace. Be aware that some laws differ in the four countries of the UK: England, Wales, Scotland and Northern Ireland.

Health and safety laws and legal regulations

You do not need to know the detail about all the health and safety laws that concern your workplace, but you are obliged to understand those elements that concern your work role. Figure 8.4 sets out the main laws.

Over to you!

▶ Are you aware of the ways in which the laws in Figure 8.4 relate to your role in your placement or work setting?

▶ Look through the table and work out how each law impacts on each area of your working practice.

Case study

Mal is working on a Saturday evening at the Youth Centre, where Joe and Mohammed, both aged 12, have been playing pool. When they run out of change they try to dismantle the coin mechanism on the underside of the table to release the balls without paying. They use Joe's penknife but it slips, slicing the top of his middle finger. There is a lot of blood and both Joe and Mohammed panic. You are the first staff member to arrive on the scene.

1. How does health and safety law relate to real-life situations, such as this one, that occur in a work setting?

2. In what ways would policy and procedure inform and guide your response to this particular situation?

3. What changes might you suggest to the youth club policy as a result of this incident?

Figure 8.4 Laws and regulations

Law	About the law
The Health and Safety at Work Act 1974 (Great Britain)	• The foundation for all health and safety law – gathering previous law together and giving coherent guidance • Everyone at work has duties and responsibilities
The Health and Safety at Work Order 1978 (NI)	• The welfare of workers is protected • Created the Health and Safety Executive (HSE) to provide guidance, manage health and safety issues and apply the law
The Management of Health and Safety at Work Regulations 1999	• Introduced the concept of risk assessment
Childcare Act 2006	• Focused on improving the early years of children. Introduced the 'five outcomes' of 'Every Child Matters', one of which is health and another safety. Introduced the Early Years Foundation Stage (EYFS) that covers every aspect of health and safety and safeguarding children
The Manual Handling Operations 1992	• Avoid lifting and carrying children where possible • Risk assess before you lift or carry a child • Use the correct technique to lift and carry children
The Education (School Premises) Regulations 1999 (England and Wales)	• Sets out minimum health and safety standards for schools, covering issues such as temperature, toilet facilities for pupils, ventilation and lighting
Control of Substances Hazardous to Health 2002 (COSHH) (includes cleaning solutions and medicines)	• Protect children from accessing dangerous chemicals and exposure to them • Make sure chemicals are correctly labelled and stored away from children's reach • Protect young people in work or on work experience
Reporting of Injuries, Diseases and Dangerous Occurrences Regulations 1995 (RIDDOR)	• All schools must have in place a system for reporting to the Health and Safety Executive (HSE) • Has particular relevance for young people in work or on work experience
Motor Vehicles (wearing of seatbelts) Regulations 2006	• Details the rules about babies, children and young people being transported, using correct carseats and belts and in appropriate area of vehicle
Health and Safety First Aid Regulations 1981	• There must be adequate equipment, facilities and trained personnel to act in the event of illness or injury, within and outside the premises
Fire Precautions Act 1971 and Fire Regulations (1997; 1999)	• Covers all aspects of safety related to preventing fires, responding in the event of a fire and emergency evacuation

The responsibility of the employee

As an employee you are legally obliged to follow the guidance of your employer in safety matters. You also need to adopt the following practices.

- ▶ Take reasonable care of your own health and safety.
- ▶ Wear protective clothing as necessary.
- ▶ Follow hygiene guidelines.
- ▶ Take care not to put others at risk.
- ▶ Attend recommended health and safety training.
- ▶ Report accidents, incidents, injuries and illness.
- ▶ Do not interfere with protective and safety equipment.
- ▶ Inform your employer of anything that might affect your ability to work (such as becoming pregnant or being injured).

Safety equipment

There are a number of products available to help keep children and young people safe. Some items, such as smoke alarms and cycle helmets, are protective and these are relevant whatever your age, but others are specifically aimed at different age groups of children. For example, safety gates and cupboard and window locks make the home safer for toddlers, while playground surfaces that are impact-absorbing help protect older children when they're playing outside.

Other items do not have a protective function, but are designed in ways that ensure the product itself is safe and reaches required standards. All items should display a product-safety logo, such as the **safety Kitemark**.

All items must display the **CE Mark** to show that they meet European health and safety standards. In addition, some products must give warnings, such as: 'Not suitable for children under the age of three,' or 'Contains small parts and may be a choking hazard.'

Some manufacturers still choose to show the British safety Kitemark, although this has been superseded by the CE Mark.

Your assessment criteria:

1.4 Explain how current health and safety legislation, policies and procedures are implemented in your own work place, setting or service

Figure 8.5 The British Kitemark symbol

Key terms

CE Mark: a symbol that is the manufacturer's declaration that a product complies with essential requirements of European health, safety and environmental protection legislation

Safety Kitemark: a symbol stamped on products to indicate each reaches an acceptable standard of safety and quality for the UK, which has now been superceded by the CE Mark

Figure 8.6 The CE Mark – this one shows a safety warning symbol

Knowledge Assessment Task   1.4

Health and safety law requires employers to put policies and procedures in place to ensure that work environments are safe, healthy and secure, and employees are required to make sure that their working practice reflects these policies and procedures.

For this task, select an aspect of your working practice to explain how current health and safety legislation is implemented. For example, this could be about handling food and serving meals for the children and young people in your care, or providing first aid, or making sure toys and equipment for activities are safe. Think about how health and safety legislation, policies and procedures are implemented in your placement or work setting. Make a public information poster for new members of staff to explain:

▶ the health and safety aspects of this area of your working practice
▶ how health and safety legislation relates to this area
▶ how policies and procedures guide practice in this area.

Your assessment criteria:

2.1 Demonstrate how to identify potential hazards to the health, safety and security of children or young people, families and other visitors and colleagues

2.2 Demonstrate ability to deal with hazards in the work setting or in off-site visits

How do you identify and deal with potential health, safety and security hazards at work and during off-site visits?

Recognising a hazard is the first important step towards managing it. In every work setting there will be potential hazards that pose a risk to children and young people, as well as to the adults you work with. Equipment and buildings could also be at risk of damage, which could then pose a health and safety risk. Outside the work setting, the environment is less predictable and less easy to control and there will be additional hazards to face.

Hazards in the work place

Hazards can be present in many different forms in a children's and young person's setting. You should be aware of the main areas shown in Figure 8.7.

Figure 8.7 Hazards in the workplace

Key terms

Hazard: any object or situation that has the potential to cause injury or ill health

Risk: the chance, high or low, that somebody could be harmed by a hazard, together with an indication of how serious the harm could be

Physical objects

This refers to furniture and equipment that could cause trips, slips or falls if they become an obstacle left in a person's way, such as a filing cabinet drawer left open, a discarded toy or a trailing wire. Physical objects also pose a risk if they are damaged, causing uneven surfaces or splinters to flake off. Check as well for curtain or blind cords that a young child could wrap around their neck, causing strangulation.

Fire

Fire is always a risk, be it from discarded matches, electrical faults, cooking equipment or flammable liquids.

Food safety

Pathogens (germs) can be present and multiply in foodstuffs in food preparation areas and on individuals who prepare food. When contaminated food is eaten, the pathogens enter the body and cause illness, which can even lead to death.

Security

Security ensures that only authorised people can enter an area. This can be breached through unlocked windows and doors and poor security checks involving lost pass codes and keys that get into the wrong hands, for example.

Personal safety

Individual safety is threatened through accident, injury or ill health. People are also vulnerable to those who seek to inflict hurt and harm.

Key terms

Pathogens: micro-organisms (such as bacteria) that cause illness and disease in the body

Over to you!

If you are asked to prepare food for the children or young people in your care, what precautions would you take to avoid the hazard of food contamination?

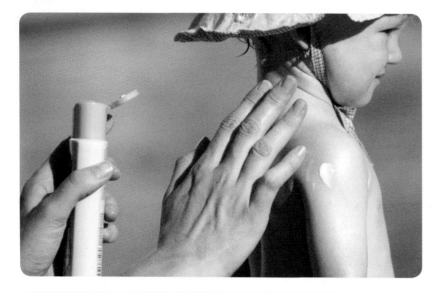

The hazards of off-site visits

Some visits outside the work environment hold similar risks to those in the workplace but there are likely to be additional risks, as shown in Figure 8.8.

Transport

Getting from the work setting to the place you are visiting will involve transport of some description, even if it is walking. Traffic will be a major hazard to negotiate, whether on foot or travelling in cars or on public transport.

Weather

Being out of doors means you are exposed to the elements, for example hot, cold or wet, as well as potentially extreme conditions such as high winds or electrical storms.

Animals and insects

Insect stings and dog bites are a common hazard wherever you go but, especially if you are visiting a more remote location, there may be more unusual animal life to be aware of, such as snakes.

Environment

Different environments carry different hazards such as water at the seaside or riverside and falling rocks in a mountainous area. Less wild environments, such as the park, can still involve hazards such as paddling pools or steps. Similarly, indoor environments can present hazards such as escalators or lifts.

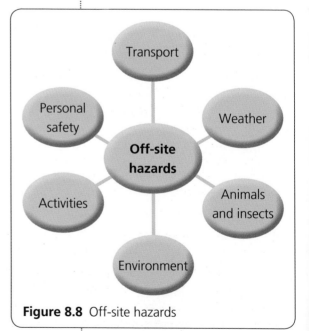

Figure 8.8 Off-site hazards

Activities

The activities you and the children and young people you care for take part in during an outdoor visit may be of an adventurous nature and therefore present more hazards, such as rock climbing or canoeing, but even going for a walk and having a picnic can present some hazards.

Personal safety

When you are out and about you will be exposed to many more risks to your personal safety than in a contained environment and it is also less possible to have control over these risks.

Over to you!

► *Think about the hazards you face in everyday life.*

► *What hazards do you face when you travel on public transport, or when you spend a hot day on the beach?*

Case study

Volunteers from a local church have arranged an all-day visit for their kids' club to a wildlife park that has indoor and outdoor play facilities, as well as opportunities to feed and pet the animals. There will be a total of 18 children aged between three and 16 years, with five adult helpers. Moira feels that the park is a bit young for the older children, but Francine points out that the teenagers will enjoy helping with the little ones and can also go off on their own. Shani comments that his son will bring a football for his friends to have a kick about. They decide to ask parents to contribute food for a group picnic, but are a bit concerned about the Nesbit twins who they know have some sort of allergy to certain foods. Emanual says it will be much easier if parents drop their children off at the park and pick them up later, rather than taking the club minibus for them to travel together.

1. What potential hazards have been mentioned during the planning discussion?
2. How do you suggest each hazard should be managed to minimise the risk of harm occurring?
3. What are the positive and negative aspects of taking the club minibus versus relying on parents to drop off their children?

Practical Assessment Task

2.1 2.2

It is important for practitioners working with children and young people to be able to identify potential hazards to the health, safety and security of those they look after and work with and be able to deal with these, both in the work setting and during visits away from the workplace. For this task you must demonstrate your ability both to recognise and to deal with health and safety hazards.

► Select an activity that takes place in your work setting or a visit to an area outside your workplace.

► Make an information poster to illustrate the potential hazards. (Remember to include hazards to do with both the environment and the activity.)

► For each hazard, include explanatory notes that describe why it is a hazard and what must be done to remove or reduce it to an acceptable level.

Your evidence for this task must be based on your practice in a real work environment and must be witnessed by or be presented in a format that is acceptable to your assessor.

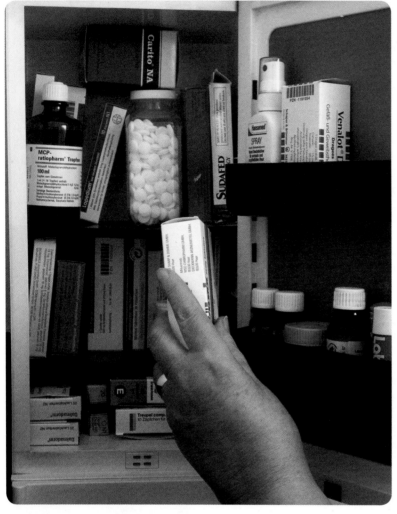

What hazards could the contents of this cupboard pose?

Your assessment criteria:

2.3 Undertake a health and safety risk assessment in your work setting or service illustrating how its implementation will reduce risk

How can a health and safety risk assessment help to reduce risk?

A health and safety risk assessment is a careful examination of any hazards or situations that could cause harm to people or damage to buildings or equipment. In carrying out a risk assessment you have the opportunity to recognise potential risks before harm occurs and to take measures to avoid or minimise the impact.

How to carry out a risk assessment

You carry out informal risk assessments many times a day, often without really thinking, such as every time you cross the road or drive a car. A formal risk assessment process uses a structure to identify and assess the risk and find ways to avoid or reduce it to an acceptable level. The process is summarised in Figure 8.9.

Key terms

Risk assessment: the process of identifying risk and considering measures to take to reduce risk to a safe limit

IDENTIFY HAZARDS
Walk around; check with others; check with a source of information such as a Health and Safety Executive (HSE); think about long-term and short-term hazards

IDENTIFY WHO IS AT RISK AND HOW
Identify every person who might be harmed and how each might be affected; for example, the younger children, or colleagues who are pregnant

REVIEW
Check regularly; change as needed

RECORD FINDINGS AND IMPLEMENT ACTION
Write down the results; share with others; implement action

EVALUATE RISK AND TAKE MEASURES TO REDUCE IT
Ask, 'Can I get rid of the hazard altogether? If not, how can I control the risks so that harm is unlikely?' (for example, wear protective clothing, or have extra helpers)

Figure 8.9 The risk assessment process

Practical Assessment Task — 2.3

Carrying out a risk assessment gives you the opportunity to identify potential health and safety risks before harm occurs and to take measures to avoid or minimise their impact. For this task you must undertake a health and safety risk assessment in your work setting or service.

▶ Select an activity or area within or outside of your placement or work setting.
▶ Carry out a detailed health and safety risk assessment.
▶ Record the process of your risk assessment, using Figure 8.9 as a guide.
▶ Show in detail exactly how implementation of your risk assessment will reduce risk, giving examples of the ways in which health and safety will be improved for the children or young people, the staff and other visitors.

Your evidence for this task must be based on your practice in a real work environment and must be witnessed by or be presented in a format that is acceptable to your assessor.

Over to you!

▶ *Raise your awareness to those times during the day when you carry out an informal risk assessment, such as when boiling the water in a kettle for a cup of tea.*

▶ *Use the risk assessment process shown in Figure 8.9 to practise making a formal record of your risk assessment.*

Your assessment criteria:

2.4 Explain how health and safety risk assessments are monitored and reviewed

How are health and safety risk assessments monitored and reviewed?

Risk assessment is an ongoing process that needs continuous review until the risk is over. The law does not expect you to eliminate all risk, but you are required to protect people as far as is *'reasonably practicable'* and this means monitoring risks and keeping them under review.

Monitoring and reviewing risk assessments

When you work with children and young people the workplace does not usually stay the same from day to day. Different people are around at different times and each individual will have different needs on different occasions. Also, over the weeks, new equipment and new activities will probably be introduced. This means there can be no 'once and for all' risk assessment. Regular monitoring and reviewing keeps up with changes, allowing risk assessments to be adjusted and adapted as necessary.

When considering how risk assessments might need to be changed, think about:

▶ the children and young people taking part

▶ the staff members who are involved

▶ other people who are around, such as family members, visitors or strangers

Over to you!

▶ *Think about activities that take place at your placement or work setting that need to take into account the weather conditions, for example, sunny, wet or cold conditions. These impact on break-time and lunch-time play for primary school children.*

▶ *How does a risk assessment help you identify and respond to the risks associated with different weather conditions?*

- ▶ the weather conditions
- ▶ time of day
- ▶ the previous activity and how it may impact on this one
- ▶ any new potential hazards that have arisen.

Ask the opinion and advice of others, who may spot things you overlook, or have a different viewpoint. Check what has worked well on other occasions and always learn from previous mistakes.

Case study

At Caterpillar drop-in crèche the staff want to encourage the children to help to clear up the hall at the end of the morning session, but it can be a chaotic affair! It depends on the mix of children there that day. Yesterday, while the staff were busy washing up beakers and plates, the children had great fun trying to stack the chairs as high as they could reach. Luckily Emma, a new staff member, noticed and intervened before the pile toppled. Once a week the sand and water-play areas are emptied, which the children think is great fun, but the staff are always concerned because spilt sand and water are slippery underfoot. The children also love spraying antiseptic spray and wiping the tables, but tend to fight over it and spray too much around. When Emma raises her concerns about clear-up time being potentially dangerous, the manager of the crèche explains that the activity has been risk-assessed and tells Emma not to worry.

1. If you were Emma, would this put your mind at rest?
2. How might you introduce the idea of monitoring and reviewing the risk assessment?
3. What aspects of the clean-up time would be safer if they were continually monitored and reviewed?

Practical Assessment Task   2.4

Regular monitoring and reviewing of health and safety risk assessments ensure that they are current by keeping up with changes to equipment, new activities, different groups of children and young people and variations in the staff team.

Investigate how health and safety risk assessments are monitored and reviewed in your placement or work setting. Write a reflective account that explains the process for reviewing risks assessments and how this is carried out.

Your evidence for this task must be based on your practice in a real work environment and must be presented in a format that is acceptable to your assessor.

What does a balanced approach to risk management mean?

Living is risky. To avoid risk completely could mean missing out on a full life. A balanced approach involves weighing the benefits against the chances of harm occurring so you take risks as safely as possible. This means you don't allow excessive risks to be taken but you don't avoid every risk for fear of harm occurring.

The individual child and risk

Children and young people are not usually as well placed as adults to assess risk accurately. They may not have the physical capability, the knowledge or the life experience to inform their judgement. Their desire to do something may also outweigh a sensible decision. Adults hold the responsibility to make decisions about the safety and wellbeing of children.

Finding a balance

There may be a tendency for some adults to label certain activities as high risk without looking more deeply at what these involve. For example, a high ropes course or rock climbing have many risks reduced or removed by routine safety measures, such as wearing helmets and protective clothing, being roped to an instructor and undertaking a training course.

In our desire to keep children and young people safe we might deprive them of opportunities for personal challenge and the chance to explore and experiment, all of which extend their learning and development, self-confidence and enjoyment. Being over-protective risks denying a child his or her full potential and can lead to creeping anxiety about real or imagined dangers, which results in risk avoidance. This can reduce a child or young person's confidence and sense of self-esteem.

Rights and choices

When making a judgement about whether to allow a more risky activity you are obliged to consider the United Nations Convention on the Rights of the Child. This states that decisions should be made in the best interests of the child. It also acknowledges that children have the right to express their opinions and to have these heard and acted upon when appropriate and that their lives should not be subject to excessive interference.

Recognise that children learn and build confidence and self-esteem through trying out new experiences, facing challenges and learning about their own limitations.

Your assessment criteria:

3.1 Explain why it is important to take a balanced approach to risk management

3.2 Explain the dilemma between the rights and choices of children and young people and health and safety requirements

Over to you!

Think of activities you have undertaken recently with children or young people in your care that have challenged them and advanced their learning and understanding.

▶ *Did these activities require them to take some risks?*

▶ *Do you think the risks were reasonable?*

Knowledge Assessment Task　3.1　3.2

A balanced approach to risk taking involves weighing the benefits of an action against the chances of harm occurring and taking measures to reduce this to an acceptable level. It also requires you to find a balance when the rights of a child or young person conflict with health and safety requirements.

1. Read the first scenario set out in a table (as below).

2. Complete the second scenario with your ideas, copying the format of the first.

3. Explain how, for each scenario, it is important to take a balanced approach to risk management.

4. Explain how the rights and choices of the children and young people in each scenario conflict with health and safety requirements.

HAZARD	RISK	BENEFIT	MEASURES	DECISION
Example: The nursery children want to play outside, but it is the hottest day on record.	• Sunburn • Dehydration • Sunstroke	• The children enjoy the weather • Physical benefits of reasonable exposure to fresh air and sun • Space to play more physical activities	**Conditions:** • Sunscreen applied • Sun-hats worn • Drinking water available and encouraged • Find or make shade • Avoid hottest part of day • Limit time in sun • Have water-play activities	☑ yes ☐ no
Three staff call in sick one morning but the Year 4 class was promised a cookery session today and will be really disappointed to have it cancelled. The teacher wonders if she can manage without her staff assistance.			**Conditions:**	☐ yes ☐ no

Your assessment criteria:

3.3 Give an example from your own practice of supporting children or young people to assess and manage risk

How have you supported a child or young person to assess and manage risk?

All children and young people are different, but many do exercise a natural caution when trying out a new experience or challenge. This can be seen as a self-protective instinct. Risky behaviour often comes about when a child has been over protected and not exposed to any risk, so has not learnt how to assess risk.

Ways of supporting risk assessment

Learning about risk assessment and risk management is a gradual process in which there should be an increasing number of mini-steps along the route to independence. If a child is allowed to 'get it wrong' sometimes, as long as it is within a controlled environment where they cannot come to too much harm, they will learn from their mistakes. There are a number of ways that you can help to support a child or young person to assess and manage risks safely.

► *Be present* to physically support a young child physically as they try out new skills, for example, standing behind a very young child to give confidence as they negotiate stairs and to be there if they fall.

► *Be a positive role model,* for example, by holding a safety rail/ wearing a bike helmet/ using safety belts and explaining why these precautions are necessary.

▶ *Be encouraging* by praising effort and highlighting competence and achievement.

▶ *Create opportunities to practise* decision making, such as, when crossing a road, suggesting a child tells you when they think it is safe to do so.

▶ *Talk over the process* of assessing risk as you are carrying out tasks, for example, 'I'll use an oven glove so I don't burn myself on the cooker.'

▶ *Allow enough time* for the process of risk assessment to take place properly – if you rush a child they may not think it through properly.

▶ *Support parents* to let go as they allow their children to make more independent choices.

▶ *Increase opportunities* for independent decision making for children and young people as they get older.

Over to you!

Think back to when you were a child or young person and the first time you were allowed to take a step towards independence. Perhaps it was the first time you boiled a kettle to make a cup of tea, or went to the shops unaccompanied, or stayed in the house without an adult being present.

▶ *Do you remember how it felt?*
▶ *What supported you and gave you confidence to manage the risks involved?*

Knowledge Assessment Task   3.3

▶ Write a report about a specific example from your own practice, where you have supported children or young people to assess and manage risk, for example, encouraging a child on the climbing frame or taking a group of children out walking in the local neighbourhood.

▶ Think about how you did this and be prepared to discuss this with your assessor.

Keep your report as evidence towards your assessment.

Your assessment criteria:

4.1 Explain the policies and procedures of the setting or service in response to accidents, incidents, emergencies and illness

How do policies and procedures guide responses to accidents, incidents, emergencies and illness?

Accidents and emergencies are unexpected and the first impact is often shock. It is difficult to think clearly when you are shaken up and that is where policies and procedures provide a useful framework to guide your response. Also, the consequences of accidents can be very serious and by following policy and procedure you will be acting according to best practice guidelines and remain within the law. In addition, policies and procedures can be used as evidence that you are fulfilling health and safety law and statutory requirements, such as those set out in the Early Years Foundation Stage.

Policies to guide responses to urgent situations

Most work settings for children and young people will have guidelines for responding to a number of urgent situations such as those listed on the next page.

Accidents

Accidents may involve, for example, vehicles, falls, falling objects, fire or heat and sharp objects. They may result in injuries such as broken bones, cuts, burns, shock and trauma.

Emergencies

Emergencies may include fire, drowning or missing children or young people.

Illness

Illness may include incidents of sudden onset, or may be due to an exacerbation or deterioration in a person's condition.

Incident

An incident might involve intrusion by a stranger, an aggressive outburst, the need to evacuate the building due to a gas leak and so on.

Required responses

It is important that each person knows what to do in response to an urgent situation. You need to act calmly, but with authority to manage the situation appropriately. Figure 8.10 shows examples of required responses.

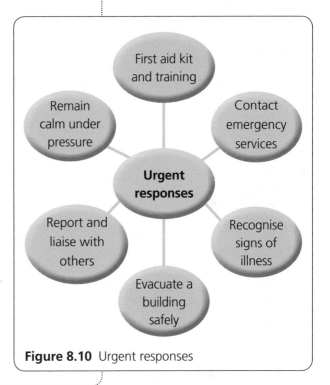

Figure 8.10 Urgent responses

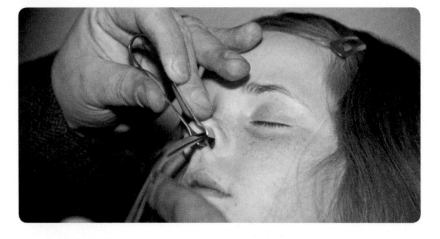

Your assessment criteria:

4.1 Explain the policies and procedures of the setting or service in response to accidents, incidents, emergencies and illness

First aid policy

Every children's and young people's setting will have a first aid policy that must include the following.

Information about the designated first aider

The designated first aider has responsibility to:

- ▶ respond to situations requiring first aid
- ▶ contact emergency services
- ▶ regularly check the first aid kit (although it is the responsibility of whoever uses an item to inform the first aider as soon as possible)
- ▶ if requested, check the first aid training status of other employees
- ▶ in some settings, organise or lead first aid training.

Information about the first aid kit

First aid kits are usually kept simple and include items to clean and cover minor cuts and scrapes. They also contain products to deal with more severe bleeding (including sterile gloves to protect the first aider), products to support a damaged limb and to wash out and protect an eye injury. All members of staff should:

- ▶ know where it is kept
- ▶ be familiar with its contents
- ▶ know how to use items appropriately.

Information about first aid training

All those who care for children and young people are recommended to take an approved course. The course should be reviewed and updated at least every three years.

Over to you!

Find out about the policies to do with illness, first aid and emergency responses in your placement or work setting.

- ▶ *Do you know who the designated first aider is in your work setting?*
- ▶ *Do you know where the first aid kit is and what it contains?*

Information about the situations to be prepared for

Information should prepare care workers for:

- ▶ recognising and responding appropriately to **anaphylactic shock**, bites and stings, bleeding, burns and scalds, choking, electric shock, extreme effects of heat and cold, eye injuries, **febrile convulsions**, **foreign bodies** in eyes, ears and nose, head, neck and back injuries, poisoning, suspected fractures

- ▶ recognising and dealing with the effects of shock

- ▶ the care of an unconscious person

- ▶ resuscitation procedures appropriate to the age of children you care for, as well as adults.

Fire policy

Every children's and young people's setting will have a fire policy that must include information about:

- ▶ fire drills – how often these are carried out, along with a record that is kept in the fire drill book

- ▶ fire training for staff

- ▶ fire exits and the need to keep these clear and accessible

- ▶ emergency evacuation and the procedure in every room of the building, including the evacuation of infants and children and young people with mobility difficulties or other special needs

- ▶ child or young person register, to check for the presence of each individual

- ▶ fire extinguishers and other fire-fighting equipment that must be readily available and regularly serviced.

Sickness policy

The sickness policy is concerned for the safety and wellbeing of any individual who is unwell and those who come into contact with them who are therefore also vulnerable to infection. The policy will include information about:

- ▶ children who are unwell, who should not attend and return only when fully better

- ▶ children who have been kept at home with infections, who must be verified by a GP as being fit to return

- ▶ management of children's prescribed medicine

- ▶ parents and carers, who need to make arrangements for emergency care to be available should their child become unwell during the day, and leave adequate contact numbers.

Anaphylactic shock: an extreme allergic reaction, usually to certain foods, drugs or insect stings, which results in rapid chemical changes in the body that, if not treated quickly, can be fatal

Febrile convulsion: a convulsion, with a high temperature (fever), that occurs in some children

Foreign body: an object lodged in a body orifice, passage or organ; in the case of children it is commonly inserted into a body opening, inhaled or swallowed

Your assessment criteria:

4.1 Explain the policies and procedures of the setting or service in response to accidents, incidents, emergencies and illness

Procedures to guide urgent responses

Procedures set down in a step-by-step manner the ways to respond appropriately and according to best practice when faced with a range of urgent situations. Emergencies happen relatively rarely, yet it is usual to carry out regular drills to practise. Your response to an emergency situation may make the difference between saving or losing a life.

In the event of accidents

When an accident occurs it is vital that you assess the situation before rushing in. Calm and quick-thinking actions may save the life of a child or young person in your care or prevent an injury becoming worse.

▶ If it is clear that an ambulance is required, phone 999 (or 112, which is also used across Europe) or get someone else to do so without delay.

▶ Check whether the person is breathing and has a pulse. If not, resuscitation must be commenced immediately.

▶ Check whether the person is conscious. If not, make sure their airway remains open, which can be achieved by placing the person in the recovery position.

▶ If the person is conscious, be reassuring and try to keep them calm.

▶ Check for signs of bleeding, head injury, broken bones, shock and do what you can (using the first aid kit) to manage injuries.

▶ See also 'Calling emergency services' (page 248 and 249).

Key terms

Recovery position: a number of methods of positioning an unconscious person in order to keep their airway open

In the event of illness

Children and young people can become seriously ill very suddenly. Depending on their age and ability they may not be able to let you know if they are feeling unwell, so you must always be alert to changes from their normal behaviour, as well as excessive sleepiness, or grumpy responses, which might indicate a child is in pain, or feeling sick or dizzy.

Signs of acute illness can include:

▶ difficulty breathing

▶ blue around lips

▶ high fever

▶ cold extremities

▶ pale and clammy skin

▶ floppy or unresponsive/unconscious.

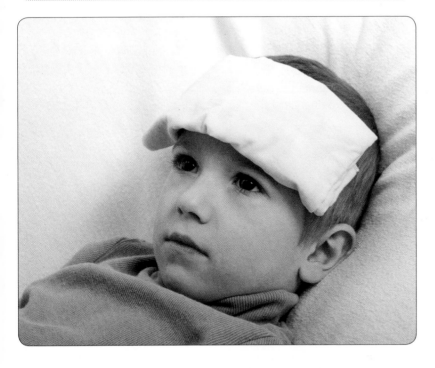

Over to you!

Have a look through the accident and incident book where you work.

▶ *What sorts of accidents and incidents occur most frequently?*

▶ *Do you know the procedures for completing the accident and incident book and informing those individuals who need to know what has happened?*

Focus on meningitis and meningococcal septicaemia

Meningitis is a serious illness causing inflammation to the covering of the brain. It may lead to septicaemia (blood poisoning) that can result in loss of limbs, deafness, blindness and even death. Children under the age of five and young people aged from 15 to 24 are in the age groups most at risk. The onset of meningitis is very quick, which is why it is important for childcare workers to recognise the classic signs and symptoms and seek immediate emergency help.

Symptoms can differ slightly between babies and young children and young people, and are not all present in every case. The range of symptoms is described in Figure 8.11.

Figure 8.11 The range of symptoms for meningitis and meningococcal septicaemia

Child 0–5	Shared symptoms	Young person 15–24
• Refusing food • Fretful and dislikes being handled • Blank, staring expression • High-pitched cry	• Fever with rigors (episodes of severe, uncontrollable shaking) • Cold hands and feet and pale blotchy skin • Vomiting • Stiff neck – cannot put chin to chest • Very drowsy – difficult to wake • Rash that does not fade under pressure (tested with a glass pressed against the skin)	• Headache • Confusion • Irritability • Joint and muscle pain • Photophobia – dislike of bright lights

Your assessment criteria:

4.1 Explain the policies and procedures of the setting or service in response to accidents, incidents, emergencies and illness

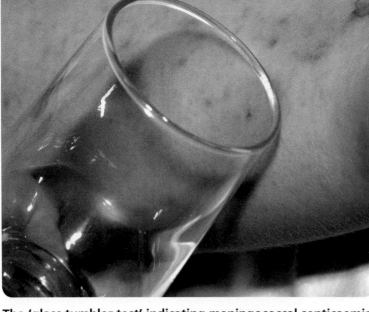

The 'glass tumbler test' indicating meningococcal septicaemia when the rash does not fade under pressure

Emergency needs of children with chronic medical conditions

If you look after children with chronic medical conditions you need to know how to provide appropriate ongoing care. You also need to be aware of the potential for an acute episode or flare-up.

Figure 8.12 Emergency needs of chronic medical conditions

Condition	Emergency need
Epilepsy	Epileptic fit (seizure)
Asthma	Acute asthma attack (when use of child's prescribed inhaler has not worked)
Allergy	Allergic reaction and anaphylactic shock
Diabetes	Hypo-glycaemia (low blood sugar) or hyper-glycaemia (high blood sugar)
Sickle cell anaemia	Sickle cell crisis

Key terms

Asthma: a respiratory condition characterised by recurring attacks of wheezing, shortness of breath, difficulty breathing out and an irritated cough

Diabetes: a condition in which the pancreas does not produce sufficient insulin, needed to process glucose

Epilepsy: abnormal electrical activity in the brain, causing recurrent spontaneous seizures (fits) that are not associated with triggers (such as fevers or head injury)

Sickle cell anaemia: a genetic blood disease mostly affecting children of black African, Caribbean and Asian descent, causing acute pain, drowsiness and fever during sudden episodes known as a **sickle cell crisis**

Your assessment criteria:

4.1 Explain the policies and procedures of the setting or service in response to accidents, incidents, emergencies and illness

Procedures in the event of emergencies

All work settings have to be prepared for an emergency and inform staff of appropriate procedures.

Calling emergency services

The person who calls 999 (or 112) for the emergency services should have all the relevant details in front of them so that they can give a clear picture of what has happened and the care that is required. You will need the child's name and age and details of any underlying condition and medication.

If you are the only person present remember that it is sometimes necessary to phone 999 first, so that expert help is on its way while you are giving first aid.

It may be necessary to meet the emergency vehicle to show them where to come and if you are out and about you will need to know the name and preferably the postcode of your destination.

Evacuation of a building

There are a number of reasons why a building may need to be evacuated, for example:

▶ fire

▶ intruder(s)

▶ bomb scare

▶ gas leak.

In most cases the evacuation will be caused by a false alarm, but it should be recognised that these, as well as routine drills, offer a useful opportunity to test the procedure and uncover any areas that need to be improved. Encourage children and young people to take drills seriously, to remain calm and keep quiet so that they can listen to instructions.

Make sure you explain to young children what is going on and reassure them that there is nothing to worry about.

Whoever is in charge of an evacuation needs to keep a register of all people in the building to check that everyone is present at the assembly point. No one should return to the building unless authorised by the person in charge and/or the emergency services personnel. Equally, no one should leave the assembly point until dismissed.

In case of fire

If you are the first person on the scene at a fire, the first action to take is to raise the alarm either by phoning 999 yourself or instructing someone else to do so. Other actions to take are as follows.

▶ Close doors and windows to prevent through-draughts that could fan flames.

▶ Only tackle the fire if it is small and manageable and you have the correct equipment.

▶ Do not leave children or young people alone at any time.

▶ If it is appropriate, or you are instructed to do so, evacuate the building, reassure the children and keep them calm.

▶ Be aware that after an emergency situation, both the adults and children or young people will need to have a debriefing.

Over to you!

Do you know where the assembly points are at your placement or work setting?

Key terms

Assembly point: an agreed place where everyone in an area must go when they are evacuated away from potential danger in an emergency

Debriefing: an opportunity to talk over what happened and ask questions, in order to understand events and let go of any associated anxiety

Over to you!

▶ *Have you ever taken part in a fire or other evacuation drill at your placement or work setting?*

▶ *What happened and how did you feel about it?*

▶ *Share your experiences with others in the group.*

Your assessment criteria:

4.1 Explain the policies and procedures of the setting or service in response to accidents, incidents, emergencies and illness

Lost or missing children

Children and young people do get lost or go missing, although it is relatively rare. A child might wander away or become separated in a crowd during an outing, or a young person may walk out when emotionally upset. Prevention is always best and it is hoped that the security measures in place where you work mean that children and young people remain safe at all times.

In the event of a child or young person becoming lost or going missing, the procedure for your place of work must be initiated immediately in an attempt to find the child or young person before they get into further danger or come to harm. The procedure should include the following.

▶ Inform the person in charge.

▶ Begin an immediate and systematic search. Staff should be instructed on which areas to search and have a method of keeping in touch, such as walkie-talkies or mobile phones.

▶ At the same time, all the other children or young people must also be supervised and remain safe.

▶ If the child or young person is not located immediately the person in charge must make decisions about informing parents or carers and the police.

▶ If the police are involved they will require information such as age, sex, height, distinguishing features and clothes worn.

▶ Following the event risk assessments, policies and procedures will need to be reviewed.

Intruders

This is a rare event, but it has happened in the past with tragic consequences, when an intruder has entered a childcare setting intending harm to both children and adult workers. Most procedures guard against this, including the following.

- ▶ Only one entrance and exit.

- ▶ Entry for visitors only via a security system, such as a keypad or locked door.

- ▶ Use of a bell or buzzer on the threshold to alert staff to the presence of a visitor.

- ▶ Identity badges to be worn by visitors.

- ▶ All staff must politely challenge any stranger who is not wearing a badge.

- ▶ Children only released at pick-up time to a named and authorised person (parents/child-minder/other relative).

Knowledge Assessment Task   4.1

Following policy and procedure when illness, accidents, incidents and emergencies occur provides a framework to ensure that your actions are appropriate and correct, where you act according to best practice guidelines and within the law.

To complete this assessment, explain what you would do in each of the following circumstances, with reference to the policies and procedures in place at your work setting or placement.

1. A person you have never seen before appears at your workplace and is hanging around, talking with anyone who cares to listen.

2. You smell burning and can see smoke coming from the coffee- and tea-making area.

3. Your colleague has slipped and fallen. Although she is conscious, she appears very distressed, her leg is at a strange angle and she can't move.

4. One of the children or young people you care for seems very sleepy and doesn't want to join in with activities, which is out of character. Minutes later they are sick and you realise they are also very hot.

Keep your written work as evidence towards your assessment.

How do you record and report accidents, injuries, illness and emergencies?

Your assessment criteria:

4.2 Identify the correct procedures for recording and reporting accidents, incidents, injuries, signs of illness and other emergencies

All accidents, illnesses and emergencies must be recorded and reported, but the type and amount of reporting depends on the seriousness of the incident.

Accident and incident records

Most of the time you will be required to fill out an accident and incident book as soon as possible after an event, while your memory is still fresh. This is to record what happened, who was involved, the nature of injuries or symptoms of illness, the action taken and the outcome. It is important to complete this even if you assess an injury or illness to be minor. This is because there might be more serious consequences in the future and the notes provide a record of what happened and evidence of your actions.

It is important to write accurately. If you were not present or did not see exactly what happened you need to state this. You should ask for witness accounts and include their names. You must always sign and date the report.

Reviewing records and procedures

The person in charge should regularly review the accident and incident book to check whether action needs to be taken to minimise the risk of a repeat occurrence. This might mean introducing new training, equipment, or a different procedure.

Reporting an accident or incident

Following a serious accident or incident there is a hierarchy of people to be informed by the senior manager. This might include the management structure, any governing body or committees and the responsible government department such as Ofsted (England), Estyn (Wales), Education & Training inspectorate (Northern Ireland) and the Care Commission (Scotland). In the most serious cases the Health and Safety Executive (HSE) must be notified and the matter may need to be formally investigated.

Informing the parents or carers

In all cases the parents or carers should be informed about what has occurred as soon as possible, either by phone or a note that accompanies the child or young person home that day. In some circumstances they will need to take the child or young person home or on to a doctor or the hospital.

When you speak to a parent or carer remember to be calm and give them the necessary information clearly. If their child is not badly hurt reassure them of this at the beginning of the conversation. If the situation is more serious, reassure them that everything that should be done is being done and make sure they know where to go and what to do to reach their child.

On occasion the child's or young person's parents or carers will not be available. In this instance there should be an emergency contact name and number to call, stored on your records.

Over to you!

It is only when you are involved in assisting at an accident or emergency that you realise how important it is to have good records. Information such as up-to-date contact numbers for parents and accurate information about a child or young person, such as vaccination records and allergies can be crucial.

▶ *Do you know where this information is stored or how regularly it is updated at your placement or work setting?*

Case study

Charlotte is a lunchtime supervisor at a primary school. A group of first-year girls who were in the queue suddenly realise they haven't washed their hands and all race to the nearby bathroom at once. In the rush, four-year-old Teresa is pushed into the wall and bangs her head. Charlotte just saw the girls run and as she followed them she heard Teresa cry out, but she did not see what actually happened. Luckily Teresa does not seem much hurt – just a small mark on her forehead – and she is soon laughing over her lunch with her new friends.

1. If you were Charlotte, would you get help and, if so, what kind of help?

2. Would you call Teresa's parents?

3. What procedure would you follow?

Knowledge Assessment Task

4.2

All accidents, injuries, signs of illness and emergencies must be recorded and reported according to correct procedures. Accurate records help to make sure the correct responses are made and can be useful at a later date for reference purposes.

To complete this assessment task, imagine that you have been asked by your manager to help present a health and safety workshop. You will be in charge of the session on correct procedures for recording and reporting accidents, injuries, signs of illness, incidents and emergencies. In preparation you need to follow these steps.

▶ Make notes on the correct procedures for recording and reporting accidents, injuries, signs of illness, incidents and emergencies in your work setting.

▶ Make up three short scenarios, relevant to your placement or work setting, that you can use to test the participant's knowledge about correct recording and reporting. Make sure you have thought out the correct responses so that they can check their answers.

Keep all your notes as evidence towards your assessment.

Are you ready for assessment?

AC	What do you now know?	Assessment task	✓
1.1	Describe the factors to take into account when planning healthy and safe indoor and outdoor environments and services	Page 217	
1.2	Explain how health and safety are monitored and maintained and how people in the work setting are made aware of risks and hazards and encouraged to work safely	Page 223	
1.3	Identify sources of current guidance for planning healthy and safe environments and services	Page 223	
1.4	Explain how current health and safety legislation, policies and procedures are implemented in your own work setting or service	Page 227	
3.1	Explain why it is important to take a balanced approach to risk management	Page 237	
3.2	Explain the dilemma between the rights and choices of children and young people and health and safety requirements	Page 237	
3.3	Give example from your own practice of supporting children or young people to assess and manage risk	Page 239	
4.1	Explain the policies and procedures of the setting or service in response to accidents, incidents, emergencies and illness	Page 251	
4.2	Identify the correct procedures for recording and reporting accidents, incidents, injuries, signs of illness and other emergencies	Page 253	

Your tutor or assessor may want to observe you actually doing this in your placement or work setting.

AC	What can you now do?	Assessment task	✓
2.1	Demonstrate how to identify potential hazards to the health, safety and security of children or young people, families and other visitors and colleagues	Page 231	
2.2	Demonstrate ability to deal with hazards in the work setting or in off-site visits	Page 231	
2.3	Undertake a health and safety risk assessment in your own work setting or service illustrating how its implementation will reduce risk	Page 233	
2.4	Explain how healthy and safety risk assessments are monitored and reviewed	Page 235	

9 | Develop positive relationships with children, young people and others involved in their care (CYP 3.5)

Assessment of this unit

This unit is about developing positive relationships with children, young people and others involved in their care, for example, parents and carers, colleagues and external partners. It covers the importance of effective communication, valuing and respecting individuality and evaluating your own effectiveness in building relationships.

The assessment of this unit is all competence based (things you need to be able to do in the real work environment).

In order to complete this unit successfully, you will need to produce evidence of your competence. The charts opposite explains what you need to know and do, alongside the relevant assessment criteria.

Your tutor or assessor will help you to prepare for your assessment and the tasks suggested in this chapter will help you to create the evidence you need.

CHAPTER 9

What you need to know

The importance of positive relationships with children and young people and how these are built and maintained

The importance of positive relationships with people involved in the care of children and young people

AC What you need to do

1.1	Explain why positive relationships with children and young people are important and how these are built and maintained
1.2	Demonstrate how to listen to and build relationships with children and young people
1.3	Evaluate own effectiveness in building relationships with children or young people
2.1	Explain why positive relationships with people involved in the care of children and young people are important
2.2	Demonstrate how to build positive relationships with people involved in the care of children and young people

This unit links with some of the other mandatory units:

SHC 31	Promote communication in health, social care or children's and young people's settings
SHC 33	Promote equality and inclusion in health, social care or children's and young people's settings
CYP 3.7	Understand how to support positive outcomes for children and young people

Some of your learning will be repeated in these units and will give you the chance to review your knowledge and understanding.

Be able to develop positive relationships with children and young people

Why are positive relationships important?

Children and young people need to feel confident and secure in their relationships with adults. A positive relationship is important because it:

▶ helps children and young people to feel valued and builds their self-esteem

▶ encourages the development of independence

▶ promotes a positive outlook

▶ builds trust and respect

▶ enables practitioners to identify and respond to children's individual needs.

Building and maintaining positive relationships

There are many different factors involved in building and maintaining positive relationships with children and young people, as summarised in Figure 9.1.

In most early years settings, providing care for children from birth to age five years, children will be allocated a **key person**. The role of a key person is to develop a close relationship with the child and to take on a greater responsibility for the child's welfare in the setting. It is a requirement of the Early Years Foundation Stage (EYFS) that all children in registered settings have a key person.

'Positive relationships' is also one of the four main themes of the EYFS (see Chapter 13, page 332). This theme states that children need positive relationships with their parents or carers and other significant people in their lives. Positive relationships help children to feel safe, secure and loved.

This is also underpinned by **attachment theory**, which is discussed in Chapter 5, page 124.

Key terms

Attachment theory: a theory concerning the formation of an emotional bond between children and their significant carers

Key person: a person who relates closely with the child and takes responsibility for their welfare in the setting

Figure 9.1 Factors involved in building and maintaining positive relationships with children and young people

Factor	Example
Appropriate communication: using verbal, non-verbal and active listening skills (see Chapter 1, page 2)	Comforting a crying baby; laughing and singing with a toddler, providing reassurance for an anxious pre-school child; listening sensitively to an older child; providing information for a young person
Consistency and fairness: always responding in a reliable, dependable way and resolving conflicts and disagreements	Developing secure attachments with babies; implementing a consistent key-person approach with young children; developing reliable rules and boundaries; avoiding favouritism; negotiating and compromising with older children and young people
Showing respect and courtesy: keeping promises and maintaining confidentiality (where appropriate)	Applying a sensitive approach to personal care routines with babies; offering choices and involving children in decision making; honouring commitments; being honest, truthful and sincere; respecting children's own views, decisions and participation
Valuing and respecting individuality: acknowledging and appreciating individual differences	Being responsive to children's individual likes, dislikes, interests and needs; understanding different attitudes and beliefs; welcoming and celebrating diversity
Monitoring impact of own behaviour on others: recognising and responding appropriately to the balance of power underpinning relationships	Not taking advantage or dominating situations to do with children and young people; adapting own behaviour to individual children's preferences and needs

Evaluating your own effectiveness in building relationships

It can sometimes be difficult to assess the effectiveness of your own practice in developing relationships with children and young people.

In your placement or work setting, think about your work with children or young people and try to answer the statements in Figure 9.2 as honestly as you can, selecting the appropriate number from the key.

Your assessment criteria:

1.1 Explain why positive relationships with children and young people are important and how these are built and maintained

1.2 Demonstrate how to listen to and build relationships with children and young people

1.3 Evaluate own effectiveness in building relationships with children or young people

1 = always
2 = sometimes
3 = never

Figure 9.2 Evaluating your own effectiveness

I welcome children warmly into the setting, every single day	1	2	3
I pay attention and listen actively when children communicate with me	1	2	3
I use facial expressions and body language to show that I am interested in children and what they are doing	1	2	3
I am consistent and fair in my dealings with all children	1	2	3
I show respect for children's own ideas and allow them to make decisions	1	2	3
I keep the promises I make to children and follow through on my commitments	1	2	3

Case study

Heidi is three years old and it is her first day at nursery. She arrives with her mother and seems very anxious. Heidi is not crying, but she does look very upset and clings to her mother's coat as they enter the main room of the nursery.

Julie is Heidi's key person in the nursery and she approaches Heidi and her mother as they enter the room.

1. Describe how Julie can start to build a positive relationship with Heidi in the nursery.

2. Explain why it is important for Julie to build and maintain a positive relationship with Heidi.

Over to you!

Reflect on your responses to the questions in Figure 9.2 above.

▶ Where did you score 'always'? Can you highlight a specific example from your practice?

▶ Where did you score 'sometimes'? Can you highlight a specific example from your practice?

Make a list of improvements you could make to your own practice in building relationships with children and young people.

Practical Assessment Task 1.1 1.2 1.3

1. Using examples from your own practice, write a reflective
   report that explains why positive relationships with children
   and young people are important and how these are built
   and maintained. Keep your report as evidence towards
   your assessment.

2. Think about the effectiveness of your own practice in listening
   to and building relationships with children and young people.
   Be prepared to demonstrate and discuss your skills with
   your assessor.

Your evidence for this task must be based on your practice in a real
work environment and must be witnessed by or be in a format
that is acceptable to your assessor. Keep your notes as evidence
towards your assessment.

Be able to build positive relationships with people involved in the care of children and young people

Your assessment criteria:

2.1 Explain why positive relationships with people involved in the care of children and young people are important

2.2 Demonstrate how to build positive relationships with people involved in the care of children and young people

Who are the people involved in the care of children and young people?

Many different people may be involved in the care of children and young people, both directly and indirectly. These iclude:

▶ parents and carers, including grandparents, child minders, foster carers or nannies

▶ colleagues, managers and supervisors in the setting

▶ visitors to the setting, including advisors, inspectors or other official visitors

▶ other professionals such as health visitors, therapists and social workers.

Building positive relationships with people involved in the care of children and young people

It is very important to form positive relationships with all the people involved in the care of children and young people, to ensure a holistic approach and meet individual needs. This involves not only effective communication but also respect for the diverse experience and expertise of parents, carers and others.

Parents and carers are extremely important in the lives of all children and young people.

The influence of parents is probably the most significant factor in shaping children's wellbeing, achievements and life chances. For most children, parents provide security, support and guidance through being good role models and encouraging success.

Being a parent is very challenging and individual people carry out the role in different ways. However, the majority of parents and carers want the best for their children and work hard to provide opportunities for them to do well. It is extremely important for practitioners to build positive relationships with parents and carers, to work in partnership and enable children and young people to reach their full potential.

The main benefits of building positive relationships with other people involved in the care of children are that:

▶ information, skills and ideas can be shared more easily

▶ children's individual needs can be identified and met

▶ a holistic approach can be applied in working towards improving outcomes for children and their families.

Over to you!

Think about your relationship with your parents or other significant adults in your life. Make a list of:

▶ *the positive influences these adults have had on your life so far*

▶ *the qualities and characteristics you would like to pass on to your own children*

Share your experiences with those of others in the group and compare the similarities and differences.

Case study

John is nine years old and has lived with foster carers for the past three months. His birth mother has been receiving treatment for depression and she spends long periods of time in hospital. John has occasional visits with his birth mother but he has not seen his birth father for many years. John attends a local primary school and has additional support in class to assist with his behaviour and learning difficulties. He has been assessed by the educational psychologist and has an individual education plan that outlines his specific support needs. John has a very positive relationship with Tony, his additional support worker, in school and they work together to plan a schedule each week in order to meet John's individual needs.

1. Identify all the different people involved in John's care.

2. Explain why it is important for Tony to build positive relationships with all the people involved in John's care.

3. Describe some of the ways in which Tony could build positive relationships with the people involved in John's care.

Your assessment criteria:

2.1 Explain why positive relationships with people involved in the care of children and young people are important

2.2 Demonstrate how to build positive relationships with people involved in the care of children and young people

Developing positive relationships

There are many different ways of developing positive relationships with parents and others involved in the care of children and young people. It is important to remember that, for any relationship to be effective, there needs to be mutual respect. It is particularly important to be aware of the needs of parents and carers who may have special needs, for example, those parents whose first language is not English. Some of the main factors involved in building positive relationships are outlined in Figure 9.3.

Figure 9.3 Building positive relationships with people involved in the care of children and young people

Factor	Building positive relationships
Effective communication	Be open, friendly and approachable
	Make time to talk and listen to questions and concerns
	Be aware of parents or carers whose first language is not English and make alternative arrangements for communication (e.g. using an interpreter)
	Provide privacy for discussing personal issues
Accurate information	Keep parents and other carers informed about daily routines, activities and children's achievements
	Display current or important information clearly on notice boards and send out newsletters with information about the setting and forthcoming events
	Provide reports and updates on children's progress for other professionals involved in their care, for example, speech and language therapists
	Respond promptly to requests for information from other professionals (with due regard to confidentiality)
	Use text-messaging or email, for parents or carers who prefer this, and maintain an up-to-date website for the setting
	Organise coffee mornings or special sessions to provide updates on children's progress
Active involvement	Welcome parents, carers and visitors into the setting
	Provide a private room for parents, carers and visitors
	Encourage parents and carers to help out on a regular basis and take part in special events and fundraising
	Attend multi-agency meetings to discuss relevant issues
	Use parents' and carers' experiences, for example, inviting a grandparent to share stories with the children

Practical Assessment Task

2.1 2.2

In your placement or work setting, think about how you build positive relationships with parents and other people involved in the care of children and young people.

Make notes on specific examples, from your own practice, that you could share with your assessor. For example, how do you make the effort to communicate with other carers such as grandparents, child minders or nannies? Why is this important?

How would you communicate with other professionals involved in children's care, for example, a speech and language therapist? Why is it important for you to build positive relationships with other professionals?

Be prepared to demonstrate and discuss your skills with your assessor. Your evidence for this task must be based on your practice in a real work environment and must be witnessed by or be in a format that is acceptable to your assessor. Keep your notes as evidence towards your assessment.

Are you ready for assessment?

There is no knowledge assessment for this unit, but your tutor or assessor may question you about some of the following points.

What do you know now?	✓
The importance of positive relationships with children and young people and how these are built and maintained Could you discuss this with your assessor?	
The importance of positive relationships with people involved in the care of children and young people Could you explain this to your assessor? Do you have any specific examples to share with your assessor?	

Your tutor or assessor may need to observe your competence in your placement or work setting.

AC	What can you do now?	Assessment task	✓
1.1	Explain why positive relationships with children and young people are important and how these are built and maintained. Do you have any examples from your own practice to discuss with your assessor?	Page 261	
1.2	Demonstrate how to listen to and build relationships with children and young people	Page 261	
1.3	Evaluate own effectiveness in building relationships with children or young people Do you have any specific examples to discuss with your assessor?	Page 261	
2.1	Explain why positive relationships with people involved in the care of children and young people are important	Page 265	
2.2	Demonstrate how to build positive relationships with people involved in the care of children and young people	Page 265	

10 | Working together for the benefit of children and young people (CYP 3.6)

Assessment of this unit

This unit is about multi-agency and integrated working with children and young people. It covers the importance of professional communication, processes for recording, storing and sharing information and confidentiality.

The assessment of this unit includes both knowledge (things that you need to know about) and competence (things you need to be able to do in the real work environment).

In order to complete this unit successfully, you will need to produce evidence of your knowledge and competence. The charts opposite explain what you need to know and do, alongside the relevant assessment criteria.

Your tutor or assessor will help you to prepare for your assessment, and the tasks suggested in this chapter will help you to create the evidence you need.

CHAPTER 10

AC   What you need to know

1.1	The importance of multi-agency working and integrated working
1.2	How integrated working practices and multi-agency working in partnership deliver better outcomes for children and young people
1.3	The functions of external agencies with whom your work setting or service interacts
1.4	Common barriers to integrated working and multi-agency working and how these can be overcome
1.5	How and why referrals are made between agencies
1.6	The assessment frameworks that are used in own UK Home Nation

AC   What you need to do

2.1 **2.2**	Select and demonstrate the use of appropriate communication methods for different circumstances
2.3	Prepare reports that are accurate, legible, concise and meet legal requirements
3.1	Demonstrate own contribution to the development or implementation of processes and procedures for recording, storing and sharing information
3.2	Demonstrate how to maintain secure recording and storage systems for both paper-based and electronic information
3.3	Analyse the potential tension between maintaining confidentiality with the need to disclose information: • where abuse of a child or young person is suspected • when it is suspected that a crime has been/may be committed

This unit also links to some of the other mandatory units:	
SHC 31	Promote communication in health, social care or children's and young people's settings
CYP 3.2	Promote child and young person development
CYP 3.3	Understand how to safeguard the wellbeing of children and young people
EYMP 3	Promote children's welfare and wellbeing in the early years
Some of your learning will be repeated in these units and will give you the chance to review your knowledge and understanding.	

Understand integrated and multi-agency working

Your assessment criteria:

1.1 Explain the importance of multi-agency working and integrated working

1.2 Analyse how integrated working practices and multi-agency working in partnership deliver better outcomes for children and young people

What is meant by integrated and multi-agency working?

'Multi-agency' and 'integrated working' are terms used to describe the way in which services work together, in different ways, to meet the needs of children, young people and their families.

Multi-agency working involves different agencies, services or teams of professionals working together to provide services that meet the needs of children, young people and their families; for example, when practitioners from health, education and social services work together to provide support for a family and their child, who has Down's syndrome.

Integrated working involves different services joining together, usually in the same building, to offer more effective care for children, young people and families. For example, in a children's centre, parents may be able to seek advice from a health visitor, attend a play session with their toddler and access a training programme in order to improve their own education or employment prospects.

Over to you!

▶ *Make a list of all the different professionals you can think of who are involved in providing services for children, young people and their families.*

▶ *How many of these professionals have you experienced working with in your placement or work setting?*

▶ *Compare your list with those of others in your group.*

The importance of working together

The provision of services for children and young people can involve many different agencies, each with their own roles and responsibilities. Different professionals may work with children in a range of situations and will therefore gain different information.

In order to create a **holistic** view of the child or young person, it is extremely important that this information is shared, both between the practitioners themselves and with the child's parents or main carers. This holistic approach is an important part of the Every Child Matters framework in England, which clearly states that professionals should work together in order to improve outcomes for children and their families.

Key terms

Holistic: emphasising the importance of the whole child

Case study

Six-year-old Nasreen attends a local primary school every day. English is not Nasreen's first language and she receives support from a bilingual support worker, alongside the class teacher. After school, Nasreen attends an out-of-school club on three days a week and is looked after by Josh, the playworker. On the other two days of each week, Nasreen is picked up from school by her mum.

All these professionals experience Nasreen in different ways and gather different information about her and her family. The classroom teacher will see Nasreen engaged in learning and involved in the daily routine in school. The bilingual support worker may observe different aspects of Nasreen's learning and behaviour, for example, schoolwork that she finds difficult or situations in which she feels anxious. Josh will see Nasreen in a different environment and will observe her at play and interacting with other children, both indoors and outdoors.

1. Give two examples of information that the class teacher might have about Nasreen.

2. Describe how the bilingual support worker might provide support for Nasreen during the day.

3. Describe how Josh, the playworker, might support Nasreen at the out-of-school club.

4. Explain why it is important for these professionals to work together in order to improve outcomes for Nasreen and her family.

Functions of external agencies

Different professionals may offer a range of support services to meet the needs of children and their families. For example, a six-year-old boy with **autistic spectrum disorder (ASD)** may need support for his development, language and education, in addition to information, advice and guidance being offered his family. This might involve services from the family doctor (GP), a speech and language therapist, a special educational needs co-ordinator (SENCO) and an educational psychologist.

The functions of some external agencies that may be involved in providing support for children, young people and their families are summarised in Figure 10.1.

Barriers to effective partnership working

For integrated and multi-agency working to operate effectively, it is important for all the professionals involved to respect each other. This requires an understanding of different areas of expertise and experience, which is not always an easy process. There can sometimes be problems with partnership working, particularly when roles are not clearly defined, information is not shared or communication between partners is poor. Different professionals provide a wide range of services for children, young people and their families. If the approach is not co-ordinated, then it can result in duplication of services and confusion for everyone involved.

Some of the barriers to effective partnership working include:

▶ poor communication between partners

▶ lack of information-sharing between partners

▶ lack of co-ordination between different service providers

▶ inaccurate or inconsistent record-keeping

▶ ineffective policies and procedures

▶ lack of understanding about the roles or involvement of different partners

▶ lack of evaluation and no review process of service provision.

Your assessment criteria:

1.3 Describe the functions of external agencies with whom your work setting or service interacts

1.4 Explain common barriers to integrated working and multi-agency working and how these can be overcome

Key terms

Autistic spectrum disorder (ASD): a neuro-developmental disorder of varying degrees, characterised by inflexibility of thought and imagination, impaired social interaction and difficulties with communication

Over to you!

▶ *Investigate Sure Start Children's Centres at www.direct.gov.uk/*

▶ *Find out about the centres in your local area and the integrated services they offer for children and families.*

Case study

Angelina is three years old and her child minder brings her to the Alphabet nursery every morning. Jo is Angelina's key person at the nursery and she carries out regular observations to monitor Angelina's development and individual needs. Jo has noticed that Angelina is often reluctant to join in with group activities and can sometimes be very aggressive with other children. Jo has mentioned this to Angelina's child minder who said that Angelina's mum has just had a new baby and had to spend some time in hospital.

continued...

Jo discussed the situation with her manager, who suggested that a referral might be made to Angelina's health visitor. She also suggested that Angelina's mum might benefit from contacting a family support worker, who may be able to help the family.

Jo suggests this to the child minder, who sees Angelina's mum every day.

Together, they work out a plan to contact the health visitor for advice and arrange for the family support worker to visit. Jo records this information and plans to talk to Angelina's mum in two weeks' time.

1. Explain how effective partnership working in this situation could improve outcomes for Angelina and her family.

2. Identify the potential barriers to effective partnership working successfully in this situation.

Figure 10.1 The functions of some external agencies involved in supporting children, young people and their families

External agency	Professionals involved	Support provided
Health services	General practitioners (GP) Health visitors Midwives Speech and language therapists Hospital and health care staff	Support with health issues, medication or treatment; advice about development; support with language and communication
Education services	Specialist teachers Teaching assistants SENCOs Educational welfare officers Parent support advisor (PSA)	Support for a child or young person's educational progress; monitoring school attendance; support for children and young people with special educational needs, including behavioural difficulties; supporting families
Social services	Social worker Family support worker	Support with children's welfare or concerns about safety; help and support for families to access support and local services
Psychology services (child and adolescent mental health services, (CAMHS)	Educational psychologist Play therapist and other therapeutic services	Support with mental health issues; behaviour support; help and support for children and young people with learning difficulties
Youth services	Youth workers Playworkers Careers advisors	Support and mentoring for young people; play schemes; education and careers advice
Voluntary agencies	NSPCC; Kidscape Gingerbread	Support, advice and training for professionals, children, young people and families

The referral process

In order for professionals to provide effective support for children, young people and their families, they need to be fully aware of the help that is needed. This means that the various professionals involved need to communicate with each other, and with the family, through the process of **referral**. A referral can be made by a professional practitioner, a parent or main carer, or in some cases by the child or young person themselves. Referrals can be made verbally, in person or by telephone, or in writing, by letter or email. An example of the referral process is shown in Figure 10.2 opposite.

For example, a parent may have concerns about their child's development and take the child to see the health visitor at the children's centre. The health visitor may carry out some developmental checks and, if there are still concerns, would discuss these with the parents. A referral may then be made for the child to be seen at a specialist child development unit or the children's hospital. This may result in further referrals being made, for example, for a speech and language assessment, a hearing test or a physical examination. It is vitally important that professionals from all the different agencies involved in the referral process, and from the families, communicate effectively and share information with each other.

The Common Assessment Framework (CAF)

The Common Assessment Framework (CAF) was introduced in England in 2005. It is a standardised framework for assessing the needs of a child or young person. It is intended for use by practitioners in all agencies so that they can communicate and work more effectively together. The main aim of the CAF is to help practitioners make a holistic assessment of children's additional needs and to identify any support required. Where families are receiving support from different agencies, a **lead professional** will usually be appointed. The role of the lead professional is to:

▶ provide a single point of contact for families and help them to make choices

▶ ensure that families receive appropriate intervention when needed

▶ reduce overlap and avoid inconsistency from other practitioners.

The CAF summary should highlight the strengths and needs of the child and family and identify what is required to meet the needs of the child and family. The main sections include:

▶ development of the child – including health and progress in learning

▶ parents and carers – how well parents are able to support their child's development

▶ family and environmental – the impact of wider family and environmental elements, such as housing.

1.1 Explain the importance of multi-agency working and integrated working

1.2 Analyse how integrated working practices and multi-agency working in partnership deliver better outcomes for children and young people

1.3 Describe the functions of external agencies with whom your work setting or service interacts

1.4 Explain common barriers to integrated working and multi-agency working and how these can be overcome

1.5 Explain how and why referrals are made between agencies

1.6 Explain the assessment frameworks that are used in own UK home nation

Key terms

Lead professional: professional carer who takes on the role of co-ordinating all the other practitioners involved in the care of a child

Referral: the process of communicating with professional colleagues in order to co-operate in the care of a child or young person

Case study

Andy is nine years old. His father is currently in prison for drug-related offences and his mother, who has recently given birth to a baby girl, is being treated for depression. Andy is currently living with his mother and maternal grandmother, and he attends a local primary school.

Prior to his father's imprisonment, Andy had always been an outgoing, boisterous boy, who enjoyed football and social play with his friends; however, in school recently, he has become increasingly angry and unco-operative. He refuses to participate in any group activities and is aggressive towards other children, frequently punching, hitting and kicking. Andy often arrives late for school, he is frequently dirty and smelly and sometimes he does not attend at all.

1. Identify three main strengths of this family.
2. List and briefly describe the key professionals who may be involved in supporting and providing services for Andy and his family.
3. Describe the potential benefits of completing a Common Assessment Framework form in order to improve outcomes for Andy and his family.

Figure 10.2 An example of the referral process

	1.1	1.2
Knowledge Assessment Task 1.3	1.4	1.5	1.6

Create an information webpage that could be accessed by different professionals working in children's services. The information should include:

▶ the importance of multi-agency and integrated working
▶ how multi-agency and integrated working practices can improve outcomes for children, young people and their families
▶ the functions of different agencies involved in children's and young people's services
▶ common barriers to multi-agency and integrated working and how these can be overcome
▶ how and why referrals are made between agencies
▶ the importance of the Common Assessment Framework.

You can illustrate your webpage with appropriate images and should keep all your work as evidence towards your assessment.

Why is communication important in partnership working?

The importance of effective communication has been discussed in Chapter 1, page 2. In partnership working, it is extremely important that information is shared and communicated effectively between professionals, in order to meet the needs of children, young people and their families.

The integration and co-ordination of services relies on everyone working together. This requires all communication to be made clearly, shared appropriately and recorded accurately. It may involve all forms of written and verbal communication, as well as telephone messages, emails or other electronic communication systems. Some of the most tragic situations, often involving the death of children or young people, have highlighted failings in partnership working and a lack of effective communication among professionals.

Your assessment criteria:

2.1 Select appropriate communication methods for different circumstances

2.2 Demonstrate use of appropriate communication methods selected for different circumstances

Appropriate communication methods

Professionals who work with children, young people and their families use a wide range of communication methods as part of everyday practice. Communicating with children, young people, parents and carers, visitors and other professionals is a vitally important part of the job and it is essential to be able to choose appropriate communication methods for different circumstances. In using different communication methods, professionals may need to take account of:

▶ children, young people or adults whose first language is not English

▶ dealing with very private, personal or sensitive information

▶ the importance of confidentiality

▶ different levels of literacy and understanding of the written word

▶ the importance of respecting different attitudes, values and beliefs

▶ children, young people and adults who have varying levels of comfort and confidence with different communication methods (for example, speaking on the telephone or using email).

Over to you!

Think about the factors you would need to consider in the following communication situations.

▶ *Reporting routine events from a child's day in the nursery when the child's parents do not speak English as their first language*

▶ *Discussing your concerns about a child's speech and language development with the child's mother*

▶ *Informing parents and carers about a forthcoming open day at the nursery*

▶ *Contacting social services to report your concerns about a child's welfare*

▶ *Gathering the views of the staff team about proposed changes to the organisation of the outdoor play area*

▶ *Interacting with a group of children, aged four to five years, during circle time*

Share your ideas with others in the group.

Your assessment criteria:

2.1 Select appropriate communication methods for different circumstances

2.2 Demonstrate use of appropriate communication methods selected for different circumstances

2.3 Prepare reports that are accurate, legible, concise and meet legal requirements

Appropriate communication methods *continued*

Some of the factors to consider in selecting appropriate communication methods are summarised in Figure 10.3.

Figure 10.3 Communication methods

Communication method	Advantages	Disadvantages	Example in professional practice
Verbal • face-to-face • telephone	More personal; better suited to private or sensitive information	Can be misinterpreted; could lead to conflict; may need an interpreter for individuals whose first language is not English	Interacting with children, parents or colleagues; discussion in meetings or interviews; providing information to other professionals
Written • letters and notes • reports	Clear, accurate and official; less open to misinterpretation	More impersonal; could be difficult for individuals with literacy problems or whose first language is not English	Permission slips; newsletters; notice boards; accident reports; records of meetings; observations and assessments
Electronic/digital • emails • websites • text messages • videos	Professional; quick; clear, accurate and official; creates a permanent record that can be referred back to	Can be misinterpreted; care must be taken with confidentiality; permission must be obtained for digital/video recording of children or young people	Contacting parents or carers; updates or information about the setting; video recordings of children's learning and development
Sign language • baby signing • Makaton • British/Irish sign language	Inclusive communication method for children or adults with hearing impairments or learning difficulties; helps babies and toddlers to express their needs	Requires specialised training; different systems are used in different countries of the UK	Interacting with children, young people or adults; songs and rhymes and circle time with children

Preparing reports

Many different kinds of report are used in children's and young people's services. Reports present a summary of factual information and usually outline recommendations for action or future work. Report-writing is a skill that requires planning, clarity and accuracy, as the content and structure need to be fully understood by others. Some reports may also need to comply with legal requirements and could be used as evidence in situations involving concerns about the safety or welfare of children and young people.

Some of the different kinds of report used in children's and young people's services are outlined in Figure 10.4.

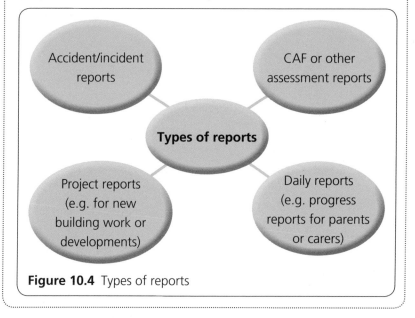

Figure 10.4 Types of reports

Practical Assessment Task   2.1   2.2   2.3

1. In your placement or work setting, think about the methods of communication that you select to use with parents and carers, colleagues or other professionals in different circumstances. What factors influence your choice of communication method?

   Make notes about specific examples, from your own practice, to discuss with your assessor. Be prepared to demonstrate different communication methods.

2. Collect examples of reports you have written that demonstrate your ability to prepare reports that are accurate, legible, concise and meet legal requirements. Be prepared to discuss these with your assessor.

Your evidence for this task must be based on your practice in a real work environment and must be witnessed by or be in a format that is acceptable to your assessor. Keep your notes as evidence towards your assessment.

Over to you!

Outline the information you might need to include in the following kinds of reports.

1. *An accident report, to record a child sustaining a knee injury as a result of a fall from the climbing frame outside.*

2. *A project report, submitting plans to develop a sensory garden at your nursery.*

Describe the factors you would need to consider in completing these reports.

Your assessment criteria:

3.1 Demonstrate own contribution to the development or implementation of processes and procedures for recording, storing and sharing information

3.2 Demonstrate how to maintain secure recording and storage systems for information:
- paper-based
- electronic

3.3 Analyse the potential tension between maintaining confidentiality with the need to disclose information:
- where abuse of a child or young person is suspected
- when it is suspected that a crime has been/ may be committed

What are the processes and procedures for recording, storing and sharing information?

Settings that provide services for children and young people need to have clear policies and procedures for recording, storing and sharing information. This should include processes for both electronic and paper-based records. Some of the main points to be considered about recording, storing and sharing information include:

▶ how, why and where information should be recorded

▶ how information should be securely stored within the requirements of the **Data Protection Act (1998)**

▶ who can have access to information and how this is monitored

▶ obtaining permission to share information or take photographs of children and young people

▶ the importance of privacy when discussing private information with families

▶ strict policies on confidentiality and the importance of not discussing confidential information outside the work setting

▶ dealing with conflicts in confidentiality.

Key terms

Data Protection Act (1998): an Act of Parliament that sets out a number of legal obligations that are imposed on anyone who handles personal information about individuals, to protect that information

Storage of information

It is extremely important that any personal or confidential information relating to children, young people or their families is stored securely in the work setting. This relates to both paper-based and electronic records. The Data Protection Act (1998) regulates the recording and storage of personal information to make sure that settings work within the law. Some of the main points relating to storing information include:

▶ only record information that is strictly relevant for the care and welfare of the child or young person

▶ always use secure, password-protected systems for electronic records

▶ always log-off from the computer after accessing electronic records

▶ always keep back-ups of electronic records

▶ maintain secure, locked storage for paper-based records

▶ never leave any memory sticks or paper-based records lying around in the setting

▶ always follow the setting's policy for storing photographs of children.

Conflicts with confidentiality

It is important for all settings to have a clear policy about confidentiality in respect to information about children, young people and their families. Private information is often disclosed in work settings. Families need to be sure that practitioners can be trusted to respect confidentiality. Professionals who work with children and young people should never gossip about families and should always be mindful of the regulations about confidentiality and information sharing.

However, there will be some situations when the procedures are not always straightforward for practitioners and there can be some conflict between maintaining confidentiality and the need to disclose information. For example, if there is ever any concern about the welfare of a child or young person, particularly relating to an abusive situation or a safeguarding issue, then it is extremely important to report this information to an appropriate person. This is discussed in detail in Chapter 7, page 180.

> **Over to you!**
>
> *In your placement or work setting, investigate and write down the policies for:*
>
> ▶ *accessing computer-based, electronic records*
>
> ▶ *the storage of paper-based records concerning children, young people and their families.*
>
> *Compare your experiences with those of others in the group.*

Conflicts with confidentiality *continued*

Equally, if it is known or suspected that a child or young person is involved in criminal behaviour, this information should be communicated according to the procedures of the setting.

Case study

Dale is a qualified playworker and he is running a holiday playscheme for children aged from five to 12 years. He has been building a den outside with a group of children and they have decided to take a bit of a break. Dale overhears Louis, aged 10 years, talking with some of the other boys about being out with his older brother the previous night. Louis tells the boys that he helped his brother and some friends to break into a car and then they drove it to the other side of the city and set it on fire. Louis talks about this behaviour as something to be proud of, because he and his brother: '*...didn't get caught by the police.*'

1. Describe what Dale should do in this situation.

2. Explain why it is important for Dale to understand the difference between maintaining confidentiality and the need to disclose information in such a situation.

Your assessment criteria:

3.1 Demonstrate own contribution to the development or implementation of processes and procedures for recording, storing and sharing information

3.2 Demonstrate how to maintain secure recording and storage systems for information:
- paper-based
- electronic

3.3 Analyse the potential tension between maintaining confidentiality with the need to disclose information:
- where abuse of a child or young person is suspected
- when it is suspected that a crime has been/ may be committed

Over to you!

Think about how you would deal with the following situations involving conflicts with confidentiality.

1. *A parent of a child at your setting asks you for the telephone number of another parent so that she can invite her child to a birthday party.*

2. *You answer the telephone in your setting and the caller states that he is an educational psychologist. He asks for the personal details of one of the children in your setting.*

3. *A five-year-old child in your setting tells you that she was locked in the house alone last night while her dad went to the pub.*

Compare your responses with those of others in your group.

Practical Assessment Task   3.1   3.2   3.3

1. In your placement or work setting, think about your own contribution to the processes and procedures for recording, storing and sharing information.

   Be prepared to demonstrate to your assessor how you maintain secure recording and storage systems for both paper-based and electronic information.

2. Write a brief report, outlining the potential conflict with confidentiality in situations involving:

   a) abuse

   b) actual or suspected criminal behaviour.

Keep your report as evidence towards your assessment.

Your evidence for this task must be based on your practice in a real work environment and must be witnessed by or be in a format that is acceptable to your assessor.

Are you ready for assessment?

AC	What do you know now?	Assessment task	✓
1.1	The importance of multi-agency working and integrated working	Page 275	
1.2	How integrated working practices and multi-agency working in partnership deliver better outcomes for children and young people Could you discuss this with your assessor?	Page 275	
1.3	The functions of external agencies with whom your work setting or service interacts Do you have any examples to share with your assessor?	Page 275	
1.4	Common barriers to integrated working and multi-agency working and how these can be overcome	Page 275	
1.5	How and why referrals are made between agencies Do you have any examples from your own practice?	Page 275	
1.6	The assessment frameworks that are used in own UK Home Nation Could you discuss the main aims of the Common Assessment Framework (CAF)?	Page 275	

Your tutor or assessor may need to observe your competence in your placement or work setting.

AC	What can you do now?	Assessment task	✓
2.1 2.2	Select and demonstrate the use of appropriate communication methods for different circumstances Do you have examples from your own practice to discuss with your assessor?	Page 279	
2.3	Prepare reports that are accurate, legible, concise and meet legal requirements Do you have actual examples to show your assessor?	Page 279	
3.1	Demonstrate own contribution to the development or implementation of processes and procedures for recording, storing and sharing information	Page 283	
3.2	Demonstrate how to maintain secure recording and storage systems for both paper-based and electronic information	Page 283	
3.3	Analyse the potential tension between maintaining confidentiality with the need to disclose information: • where abuse of a child or young person is suspected • when it is suspected that a crime has been/may be committed Could you discuss this with your assessor?	Page 283	

11 | Understand how to support positive outcomes for children and young people (CYP 3.7)

AC	What you need to know
1.1	The social, economic and cultural factors that will impact on the lives of children and young people
1.2	The importance and impact of poverty on outcomes and life chances for children and young people
1.3	The role of children and young people's personal choices and experiences on their outcomes and life chances
2.1	The positive outcomes expected for children and young people that practitioners should be striving to achieve
2.2	The importance of designing services around the needs of children and young people
2.3	The importance of active participation of children and young people in decisions affecting their lives
2.4	How to support children and young people according to their age, needs and abilities to make personal choices and experiences that have a positive impact on their lives
3.1	The potential impact of disability on the outcomes and life chances of children and young people
3.2	The importance of positive attitudes towards disability and specific requirements
3.3	The social and medical models of disability and the impact of each on practice

3.4	The different types of support that are available for disabled children and young people and those with specific requirements
4.1	The meaning of equality, diversity and inclusion in the context of positive outcomes for children and young people
4.2	The ways in which services for children, young people and their carers take account of and promote equality, diversity and inclusion to promote positive outcomes

There is no practical assessment for this unit, but your tutor or assessor may question you about some of the following points.

What you need to do

Show that you understand how social, economic and cultural factors might affect the life chances of the children or young people in your care and how you include children and young people in some of the decisions that might affect them

Show how you enable all children and young people in your care to achieve the five positive outcomes of Every Child Matters.

Show how you apply your knowledge of special educational needs to make sure that all children in your care receive equal opportunities to reach their potential

Show your understanding of the importance of equality, diversity and inclusion and promote positive outcomes for children and young people

This unit is designed to develop your working practice, which is relevant to every chapter of this book, but has particular links to other mandatory units.

CYP 3.1	Understand child and young person development
EYMP 4	Professional practice in early years settings
CYPOP 6	Support disabled children and young people and those with specific requirements

Some of your learning will be repeated in these units and will give you the chance to review your knowledge and understanding.

Understand how the social, economic and cultural environment can impact on the outcomes and life chances of children and young people

Your assessment criteria:

1.1 Describe the social, economic and cultural factors that will impact on the lives of children and young people

Key terms

Addiction: dependent on something that is habit-forming

Bereavement: the death or loss of a loved one

Cultural: beliefs and habits of family, race or religion

Economic: financial situation

Ethnic: belonging to a group of people with the same set of beliefs, often different from the majority

Poverty: having little or no money or possessions

Religious: showing belief in a god

Social: relationships with others

What are the factors that can affect children and young people's lives?

The environment around a child or young person can seriously affect their development. Factors in the environment are grouped into three categories: social, economic and cultural. Figure 11.1, opposite, summarises some of the influences on children and young people and what effect they may have.

Figure 11.1 Influences and effects of the social, economic and cultural environment

Social factors affecting development	How might these impact on the lives of children and young people?
• Poor housing • Addictions • Offending and anti-social behaviour • Bereavement and loss	The social environment can sometimes affect development negatively. Cramped, damp or cold conditions will not promote good health and can impact on development. If children and young people are influenced by others with addictions or anti-social behaviour, they are likely to suffer from neglect, poverty and low self-esteem. If there has been bereavement in the family, or if someone is in prison, other family members may become depressed, which can also lead to neglect.
Economic/poverty factors affecting development	**How might these impact on the lives of children and young people?**
• Poor health • Disability • Addictions • Lone parents	Research has shown that living in poverty has the largest negative effect on a child's or young person's development. If a family is poor then there might not be enough food, clothing or shelter. Look at Figure 11.2 (overleaf) to see how everything in a child's life depends on the basic needs. If a parent is in poor health, has a disability, is addicted to illegal substances or is a lone parent this can affect a family's income, as these things can make it more difficult to find or to remain in employment.
Cultural factors affecting development	**How might these impact on the lives of children and young people?**
• Personal choice • Community • Educational • Religious beliefs • Ethnic beliefs • Family expectations	Families all bring up their children differently. A family's religious or ethnic beliefs, their race or colour can vary from those of the people around them and this can lead to feeling different, isolated or rejected. If family expectations are very high this might put pressure on children and young people but if they are too low this might prevent children and young people from achieving their full potential. If children and young people are influenced by underachievement, they are less likely to achieve themselves.

Over to you!

Think about what you like and what you believe in. How do your beliefs influence the way you feel and behave? Discuss your ideas with others in your group and make a list of the differences.

The impact of poverty

In 1943 Abraham Maslow proposed the hierarchy of needs, shown in Figure 11.2. He described normal human development as dependent on basic needs, which must be met in order to progress up each level of the hierarchy. Poverty can affect negatively all the basic needs, so if children and young people do not have enough food, clean water, clothing or warmth all other developmental needs can be affected. Parents who struggle to feed their children and keep them safe may not have the resources, information or time to provide stimulating experiences. Research has shown that children may fail to develop normally if they are rarely spoken to, exposed to few toys or do not have opportunities to explore and experiment. These children therefore, despite their genetic potential, are automatically at a disadvantage because the poverty they live in has such a profound effect.

Your assessment criteria:

1.2 Explain the importance and impact of poverty on outcomes and life chances for children and young people

Key terms

Poverty trap: a situation that prevents people from improving their situation, e.g. if an increase in income from getting a job results in a loss of benefits so that they are no better off

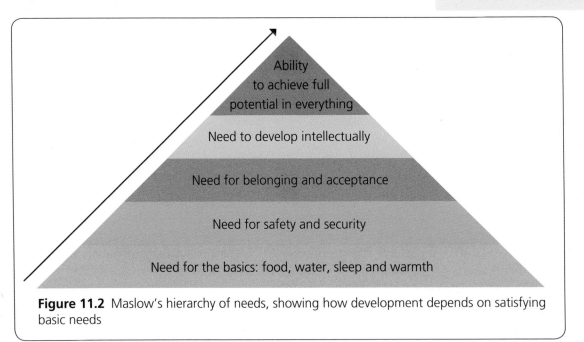

Figure 11.2 Maslow's hierarchy of needs, showing how development depends on satisfying basic needs

Circumstances leading to poverty

Different circumstances might lead to a family living in poverty, as shown in Figure 11.3. These situations often overlap and this makes getting out of the poverty trap very difficult. Even today, in the 21st century, there are very many children and young people living in poverty in Britain.

Over to you!

How do you think not having enough food or clothes might affect your life?

▶ *Look at Figure 11.2 and, starting at the bottom, make a list of how poverty might affect everything in your life.*

▶ *Compare your list with those of others in your group.*

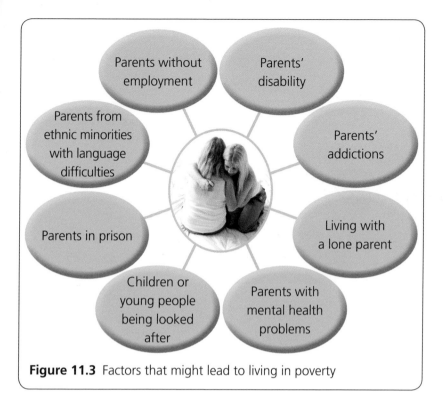

Figure 11.3 Factors that might lead to living in poverty

Case study

Emily is aged 14 and lives with her mum and two younger brothers in a high-rise flat. Emily's mum is a lone parent and suffers from depression much of the time, so Emily often has to care for her two younger brothers before and after school. Sometimes she stays at home because she is worried about her mum. The family survives on benefits and there is not enough money for any luxuries for Emily or her brothers.

1. Explain how Emily's living conditions might affect her health and hygiene.

2. Describe the factors that might contribute to Emily feeling depressed.

3. What factors might influence Emily's opportunities for finding long-term well-paid employment in the future?

Keep your notes as evidence towards your assessment.

Your assessment criteria:

1.3 Explain the role of children and young people's personal choices and experiences on their outcomes and life chances

The importance of personal choice

To provide a consistent approach to the development of children and young people there are several regulatory documents that give basic guidance for best practice. Two of these are *The United Nations Convention on the Rights of the Child (1989)* and, in England, *The Early Years Foundation Stage (EYFS) (2008)*

1. *The United Nations Convention on the Rights of the Child (1989),* for the first time put emphasis on children and young people having a say in the choices that affect them. When children and young people contribute to the decisions about their lives they experience increased self-esteem. More importantly, only when a child or young person is asked what they want is it possible for anyone else to know. Article 13 of *The United Nations Convention on the Rights of the Child* states that:

   'The child shall have the right to freedom of expression: this right shall include freedom to seek, receive and impart information and ideas of all kinds, regardless of frontiers, either orally, in writing or in print, in the form of art, or through any other media of the child's choice' (www.unicef.org/crc/)

2. *The Early Years Foundation Stage (EYFS) (2008)* places a strong emphasis on a mixture of child-led and adult-led experiences. If adults notice what a child does spontaneously (child-led) and their stages of development, they can provide appropriate activities and resources (adult-led). By using appropriate questioning and setting problems for children, adults can encourage children to show their preferences, even at a very young age.

   'As well as leading activities … you should support and extend all children's development and learning by being an active listener … Whatever children bring is an indication of their current interest and should be supported.' (EYFS)

The influences on personal choice

In some cases children and young people become influenced by others who might have a negative effect on their choices. Peer-group pressure, in particular, can negatively affect children and young people. Imagine a young teenager who does not spend much time at home and becomes part of a street gang. In order to stay part of the gang they will have to conform to the gang's norms of behaviour. On the other hand, a compliant child or young person whose parents are over ambitious can also suffer from not being allowed to make decisions about their own future. It is important to understand how children and young people can contribute actively to their own development by making personal choices, and also how the role of the practitioner supports and influences decision-making.

Over to you!

▶ Do you think children and young people should have a say in what happens to them? How much say do you have in your own life?

▶ Have you ever felt under pressure to conform to values of your peer group that were different from your own?

▶ In your placement or work setting, think about how you encourage children or young people to make choices.

▶ Compare your ideas with those of others in the group.

Knowledge Assessment Task   1.1   1.2   1.3

1. Design and produce an illustrated poster to describe how social, economic (including poverty) and cultural factors can affect a child's or young person's development. Include two examples of negative influences and two examples of positive influences that might affect children and young people.

2. Write a report to explain the impact of poverty and how children and young people's personal choices and experiences can affect their outcomes and life chances.

Keep your poster and report as evidence towards your assessment.

What are positive outcomes for children and young people and how can they be promoted by practitioners?

Children and young people all grow up in different environments but the quality of the experiences offered in settings and by other services can contribute significantly towards positive outcomes for all children.

The *Every Child Matters (ECM) (2003)* Famework was produced as a result of a review of services for children and young people. It had two main findings.

1. It identified five positive outcomes that children and young people should be supported to achieve.

    1   Be healthy.
    2   Stay safe.
    3   Enjoy and achieve.
    4   Make a positive contribution.
    5   Achieve economic wellbeing.

2. It highlighted the need for all services (such as social care, health, education, police, integrated children's services) to work together with children and young people to share information.

Every local authority has a duty to ensure that all children and young people in their care achieve the five positive outcomes and that there is good communication between the different services helping to look after children. This is achieved through the **Children's Trust** and the **Children's Plan**.

Key terms

Children's Plan: originally a governmental vision for change to make England the best place in the world for children and young people to grow up

Children's Trust: local authority department to promote children's health and wellbeing

Using the Early Years Foundation Stage (EYFS)

If you are working with children under five years of age in England, the EYFS will help you to promote the five positive outcomes for children. It outlines four main themes for the five positive outcomes.

1. *A unique child* – every child is a competent learner from birth who can be resilient, capable, confident and self-assured.

2. *Positive relationships* – children learn to be strong and independent from a base of loving and secure relationships with parents and/or a key person.

3. *Enabling environments* – the environment plays a key role in supporting and extending children's development and learning. Children need daily access to a safe and stimulating outdoor play space.

4. *Learning and development* – children learn and develop in different ways and at different rates and all areas of learning and development are equally important and interconnected.

These themes are described fully in Chapter 13, page 332. It is important to remember that this framework offers guidance for all adults working with children under five years of age and is very closely linked to the five outcomes.

Your assessment criteria:

2.2 Explain the importance of designing services around the needs of children and young people

2.3 Explain the importance of active participation of children and young people in decisions affecting their lives

2.4 Explain how to support children and young people according to their age, needs and abilities to make personal choices and experiences that have a positive impact on their lives

How do you design services around the needs of children and young people?

Designing services to benefit children and young people effectively must include knowing their opinions, their interests and their stages of development. Without these, services cannot be targeted and will become too general. Active participation by children and young people in discussing their own futures will help adults working with them cater more sensitively for their needs and wants, which will help children and young people develop confidence or independence in making their own choices.

How do you promote active participation of children and young people in decisions affecting their lives?

Children at the age of three can usually start to express clearly what they want or need. However, there are particular challenges in understanding the likes and dislikes of younger children and it requires greater sensitivity from the adult to understand how they think and feel.

To encourage children and young people to participate in choices that affect them, adults need to:

▶ understand how important this is

▶ be willing and able to ask questions

▶ listen to children and young people

▶ allow plenty of time

▶ work with children and young people to share their experiences and ideas

▶ be well organised and plan carefully.

How do you support personal choices and experiences that have a positive impact?

Some of the ways in which practitioners can help those in their care to make personal choices and experiences that have a positive impact on their lives are shown in Figure 11.4. The support provided will vary according to the age and individual needs of the child or young person.

Over to you!

▶ How do you let other people know what you need or want?

▶ Think about the children or young people in your placement or work setting. How would you find out about what they need or want?

▶ Discuss this with others in your group and make a list of the difficulties you might need to overcome to do this well.

Be healthy

- Promote healthy eating
- Promote physical exercise
- Minimise the chances of smoking and substance abuse

Stay safe

- Practice strict safeguarding procedures
- Complete risk assessments
- Work with other professionals
- Work with parents

Enjoy and achieve

- Understand children's and young people's interests
- Know their stage of development
- Provide a stimulating environment based on their needs, interests and stage of development

Make a positive contribution

- Ensure good behaviour management
- Model good team work
- Develop good communication skills
- Provide an inclusive environment

Achieve economic wellbeing

- Provide good education
- Provide suitable training
- Provide advice and access to employment opportunities

Figure 11.4 Supporting personal choices and experiences that have a positive impact

How do you provide support according to age, needs and abilities?

Once you start to find out about the interests and the stages of development of the children or young people you are working with, you can start to support personal choices and experiences to meet their needs. Figure 11.5 shows some of the ways you can do this.

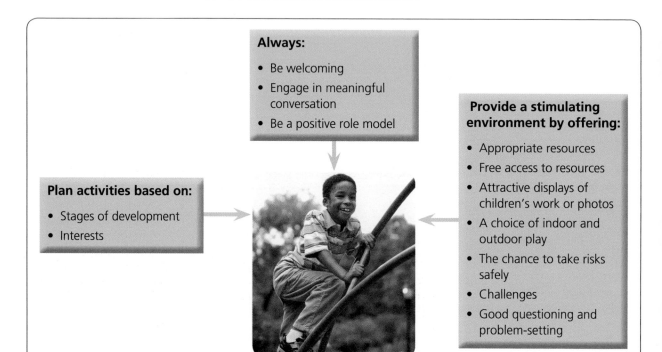

Always:

- Be welcoming
- Engage in meaningful conversation
- Be a positive role model

Provide a stimulating environment by offering:

- Appropriate resources
- Free access to resources
- Attractive displays of children's work or photos
- A choice of indoor and outdoor play
- The chance to take risks safely
- Challenges
- Good questioning and problem-setting

Plan activities based on:

- Stages of development
- Interests

Figure 11.5 Providing for the needs of children and young people

Case study

Stephen is three years old and attends Raindrops nursery school. His family is new to the area and he has only been at the nursery school for three weeks and has not settled well. He often talks about his pet dog and seems to be happiest playing outside. He likes to have stories read to him and he also likes the company of adults.

1. Imagine that you are Stephen's key person at Raindrops nursery school. Plan an activity for Stephen, using the information in the case study that might help him to settle when he comes to nursery tomorrow morning. Include the following information:
   ▶ why you have chosen the activity
   ▶ where the activity will take place
   ▶ what resources you would use.
2. How could you find out more about Stephen's interests and how to help him settle?
3. What might you notice as Stephen starts to make his own choices?

Your assessment criteria:

2.1 Identify the positive outcomes for children and young people that practitioners should be striving to achieve

2.2 Explain the importance of designing services around the needs of children and young people

2.3 Explain the importance of active participation of children and young people in decisions affecting their lives

2.4 Explain how to support children and young people according to their age, needs and abilities to make personal choices and have experiences that have a positive impact on their lives

Knowledge Assessment Task

2.1 **2.2** **2.3** **2.4**

1. Create an illustrated information leaflet for students that:
   ▶ highlights the five positive outcomes that practitioners aim to help children and young people achieve
   ▶ explains the importance of designing services around the needs of children and young people.
2. Write a reflective account giving examples from your placement or work setting to show how you have:
   ▶ encouraged the active participation of children or young people in decisions affecting their lives
   ▶ supported children or young people to make positive choices according to their age, needs and abilities.

Keep your leaflet and reflective account as evidence towards your assessment.

Key terms

Additional needs: when a child needs more help than normal to access or achieve something

Disability: a condition that makes routine tasks more difficult than normal

Impairment: some part of a child's body or mind that is diminished in strength, quality or utility

What is disability?

So far this unit has considered some of the different factors in a child's or a young person's environment that can promote or prevent positive outcomes and life chances. This section will consider the importance of a positive environment in promoting the five outcomes for children and young people who have an impairment or additional needs.

Disability occurs if a child or young person has an impairment that has a 'substantial and long-term adverse effect on their ability to perform normal day-to-day tasks' (Equality Act 2010). The term 'special educational needs' is often used to describe the additional needs of a person with a disability. Some people argue that all children have their own special educational needs. Practitioners need knowledge, sensitivity and understanding in order to work effectively with the child or young person.

The impact of disability and the importance of positive attitudes

If the child or young person does not experience positive surroundings the impact of disability might be quite negative, as shown in Figure 11.6. If you consider a child or young person who feels humiliation, isolation or anger because of the attitudes of others, you will realise that this could prevent them from being accepted as part of a group. This in turn could have an impact on their confidence, self-esteem and intellectual achievement.

Over to you!

Consider the five positive outcomes for children and young people. How do you think having a disability might prevent someone from achieving them?

If other children, young people or adults:

- Ignore
- Tease
- Pamper
- Underestimate ability

The child or young person could experience:

- Humiliation
- Sadness
- Isolation
- Frustration
- Anger
- Underachievement

Figure 11.6 How surroundings might impact on children and young people with a disability

Types of impairment

Different groups of impairments can lead to disability, as shown in Figure 11.7. It is important to remember that many of these will overlap and some can lead to other problems as well. Impairments can:

▶ be permanent (e.g. blindness) or temporary (e.g. broken leg)

▶ be easily recognisable (e.g. **Down's syndrome**) or difficult to detect (e.g. **Asperger's syndrome**)

▶ affect all areas of learning (e.g. **global learning delay**) or only one (e.g. **dyspraxia**)

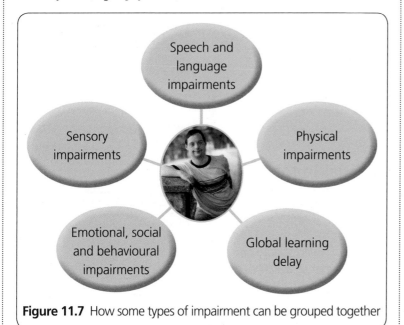

Figure 11.7 How some types of impairment can be grouped together

Specific requirements

Some children and young people have additional needs such as English as an additional language (EAL) or special dietary requirements. These do not indicate impairments or a disability but will also require an environment that is adapted to their particular needs.

Key terms

Asperger's syndrome: an autistic spectrum disorder causing difficulties in social interaction

Down's syndrome: a chromosomal disorder which causes distinct facial characteristics and learning difficulties

Dyspraxia: a disability that affects body movements and co-ordination

Global learning delay: a delay, generally in all areas of learning and development

How do the social and medical models of disability impact on practice?

There are two different ways of looking at the idea of impairment leading to disability.

1. *The medical model of disability* – this model views disability as an illness and considers that the practitioner's job is to make the child or young person better or more normal. It is a view that focuses on what the child cannot do, rather than what they can do.

2. *The social model of disability* – this model views disability as being caused by people and the environment around the disabled person. It is a view that focuses on the responsibility of society to provide a supportive environment for disabled people that enables them to achieve their full potential.

Your assessment criteria:

3.3 Explain the social and medical models of disability and the impact of each on practice

3.4 Explain the different types of support that are available for disabled children and young people and those with specific requirements

Case study

Peter is five years of age and has attention deficit hyperactivity disorder (ADHD). He finds it difficult to concentrate and cannot sit still for long. He is occasionally very angry, shouts at adults and hits other children. His condition affects his behaviour and learning in school and his teachers often become angry and frustrated with him.

1. In working with Peter, how might your practice be influenced by:
   a) the medical model of disability?
   b) the social model of disability?
2. Which model shows more respect for Peter and caters more for his needs?

The medical model

What types of support are available for children and young people who are disabled?

Services for children or young people who are disabled should be designed to meet their individual needs. Some types of available support are outlined in Figure 11.8

The social model

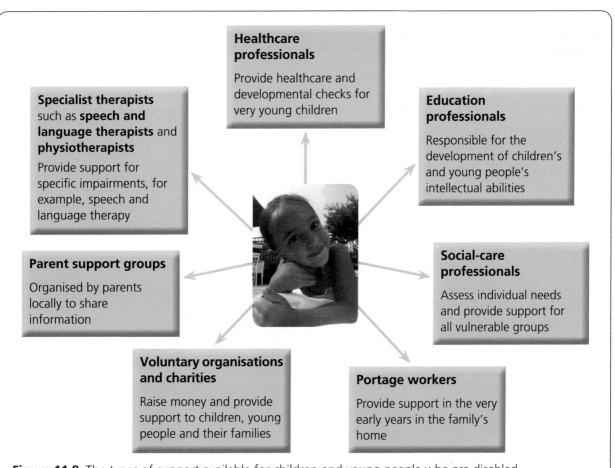

Figure 11.8 The types of support available for children and young people who are disabled

The following text appears within the figure:

Healthcare professionals

Provide healthcare and developmental checks for very young children

Specialist therapists such as **speech and language therapists** and **physiotherapists**

Provide support for specific impairments, for example, speech and language therapy

Education professionals

Responsible for the development of children's and young people's intellectual abilities

Parent support groups

Organised by parents locally to share information

Social-care professionals

Assess individual needs and provide support for all vulnerable groups

Voluntary organisations and charities

Raise money and provide support to children, young people and their families

Portage workers

Provide support in the very early years in the family's home

Knowledge Assessment Task   3.1   3.2   3.3   3.4

1 Investigate one particular disability. Imagine you were looking after a child or young person with this disability. Prepare a talk about the child or young person and how you might cater for their needs. You must include:

  ▶ the name of the disability and a brief description of its characteristics

  ▶ the age of the child or young person you are describing

  ▶ the potential impact of this disability on the child or young person's outcomes and life chances

  ▶ why positive attitudes towards disability are important and how you would promote positive attitudes in others towards the child or young person in your care.

Write a brief account that explains:

▶ both the medical and social models of disability and the impact of each on your own practice

▶ the different types of support available for children and young people with disabilities or specific requirements.

Keep your notes as evidence towards your assessment.

What is meant by diversity and inclusion?

Every child or young person has different abilities and individual interests, and comes from a family with different beliefs. This is referred to as **diversity**. **Inclusion** is the idea that all children or young people's abilities, interests and family backgrounds must be respected and catered for if they are to achieve their potential.

The meaning of equality

Every child in your care deserves to achieve their potential and it is your responsibility to ensure that they receive opportunities through your provision of care and education. This is the basis of **equality**. Equality does not mean that every child or young person is equal or that they should be treated equally. It does means that every child must be provided with equal opportunities to achieve and that everyone's needs must be treated with equal respect. In order to do this you need to know:

▶ what children and young people are capable of doing

▶ what they are interested in

▶ how to promote their development

▶ how to cater for any impairment or additional need they may have.

Your assessment criteria:

4.1 Explain the meaning of equality, diversity and inclusion in the context of positive outcomes for children and young people

Key terms

Diversity: the quality of being different

Equality: the quality of being the same in value or status

Inclusion: the idea that all people must be respected and treated equally

Looking again at Maslow's hierarchy of needs (page 290). Children and young people who are not treated with respect will not develop a strong sense of belonging to the groups they are part of and this can have serious implications for their future development and wellbeing.

Case study

Andrew is aged 12 and is normally an active boy with good physical development who loves playing outside. He attends an out-of-school club each evening from 3.30 to 6pm. Recently he broke his leg and is now attending the club but is using a wheelchair.

1. How might Andrew be affected by his current situation?

2. Give some examples of activities suitable for children aged 12 at the out-of-school club, to ensure that Andrew is included and his physical development is continued, despite his circumstances.

3. How can the club organisers make sure that their approach to all the children is inclusive and that every child or young person has their needs taken into account?

Over to you!

Make a list of all the different needs you have experienced with children or young people in your placement or work setting, for example:

▶ *physical or sensory impairments*

▶ *learning difficulties*

▶ *allergies or medical conditions*

▶ *English as an alternative language.*

How does your workplace cater for these special needs?

How could you improve the provision?

Your assessment criteria:

4.2 Compare, giving examples, ways in which services for children, young people and their carers take account of and promote equality, diversity and inclusion to promote positive outcomes

Promoting equality, diversity and inclusion

There are many practical ways in which your respect for the different needs of children and young people can be shown, as outlined in Figure 11.9.

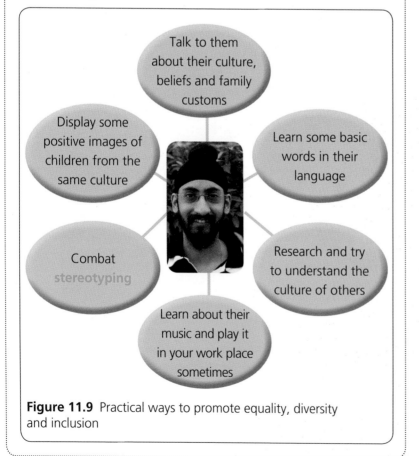

Figure 11.9 Practical ways to promote equality, diversity and inclusion

Key terms

Stereotyping: believing that all people within the same racial, ethnic or cultural group will act alike and share the same beliefs and attitudes

Stereotyping, prejudice and discrimination

When caring for children and young people you need to be aware of the dangers of stereotyping, prejudice and discrimination. One way to understand these ideas is to use a fictional scenario.

Imagine you are a visitor to Britain from a country where the food is very different. You are given a red apple and a green apple. When you try them you find the red apple is sour and rotten but the green apple is sweet and juicy. From then on, without trying any others, you consider all red apples are sour and rotten (stereotyping), you will not eat a red apple again because you hate them all (prejudice) and you even cut down trees that are growing red apples (discrimination) so that they can no longer be grown. This pattern, shown in Figure 11.10, can sometimes be seen in our work with children and young people and you must ensure that you do not form any stereotypes that can lead to prejudice or discrimination.

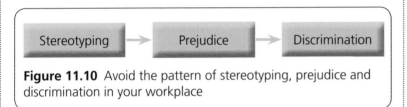

Stereotyping → Prejudice → Discrimination

Figure 11.10 Avoid the pattern of stereotyping, prejudice and discrimination in your workplace

Key terms

Discrimination: unfair treatment of a person or group on the basis of prejudice

Prejudice: a prejudgement such as a preconceived belief, opinion or judgement made without making certain of the facts

Knowledge Assessment Task   4.1   4.2

Create an outline for a media campaign to address issues around stereotyping, prejudice and discrimination, focusing on a particular group of children or young people, for example, disabled, gypsy, Roma or travellers, or racial minorities.

Your campaign could include an information leaflet, poster, webpage and TV advertisement and should include the following information:

1. an explanation of the meaning of equality, diversity and inclusion

2. examples of how services can take account of and promote equality, diversity and inclusion for this group to promote positive outcomes for children and young people.

Keep your notes and campaign material as evidence towards your assessment.

Are you ready for assessment?

AC	What do you know now?	Assessment task	✓
1.1	The social, economic and cultural factors that will impact on the lives of children and young people	Page 293	
1.2	The importance and impact of poverty on outcomes and life chances for children and young people	Page 293	
1.3	The role of children and young people's personal choices and experiences on their outcomes and life chances	Page 293	
2.1	The positive outcomes expected for children and young people that practitioners should be striving to achieve	Page 299	
2.2	The importance of designing services around the needs of children and young people	Page 299	
2.3	The importance of active participation of children and young people in decisions affecting their lives	Page 299	
2.4	How to support children and young people according to their age, needs and abilities to make personal choices and experiences that have a positive impact on their lives	Page 299	
3.1	The potential impact of disability on the outcomes and life chances of children and young people	Page 303	
3.2	The importance of positive attitudes towards disability and specific requirements	Page 303	
3.3	The social and medical models of disability and the impact of each on practice	Page 303	
3.4	The different types of support that are available for disabled children and young people and those with specific requirements	Page 303	
4.1	The meaning of equality, diversity and inclusion in the context of positive outcomes for children and young people	Page 307	
4.2	The ways in which services for children, young people and their carers take account of and promote equality, diversity and inclusion to promote positive outcomes	Page 307	

There is no practical assessment for this unit, but your tutor or assessor may question you about some of the following points.

What can you do now?

Understand the factors that might affect the development of the children in your care. Understand how you include children and young people in some of the decisions that might affect them

Do you have any specific examples from your practice to share with your assessor?

Show how you enable all children and young people in your care to achieve the five positive outcomes of Every Child Matters

In practice, show your support for children and young people in making positive choices.

Could you discuss this with your assessor?

Show how you apply your knowledge of special educational needs to make sure that all children in your care receive equal opportunities to reach their potential

Show a positive attitude towards minority groups of children or young people, making sure they are not stereotypical and you do not show prejudice.

Do you have any specific examples from your practice to share with your assessor?

12 | Context and principles for early years provision (EYMP 1)

Assessment of this unit

This unit is about the current frameworks for children's care and education used in the UK and how these have been influenced by some alternative philosophies of early years education. As part of this unit you have to create an environment in your workplace to support children's learning and development. The unit also considers partnerships with parents and carers and multi-agency working.

The assessment of this unit is partly knowledge-based (things that you need to know about) and partly competence-based (things you need to be able to do in the real work environment or in your placement).

In order to complete this unit successfully, you will need to produce evidence of your knowledge as shown in the 'What you need to know' chart opposite, and evidence of your practical competence in the workplace, as shown in the 'What you need to do' chart, also opposite.

Your tutor or assessor will help you to prepare for your assessment and the tasks suggested in this chapter will help you to create the evidence that you need. Part of this unit is assessed as a practical assessment in your workplace.

CHAPTER 12

AC What you need to know

1.1	The legal status and principles of the relevant early years framework/s, and how national and local guidance materials are used in settings
1.2	How different approaches to work with children in the early years have influenced current provision in the UK
1.3	Why early years frameworks emphasise a personal and individual approach to learning and development
3.1	The partnership model of working with carers
3.2	Barriers to participation for carers and how they can be overcome
3.3	Strategies to support carers who may react positively or negatively to partnership opportunities
3.4	How effective multi-agency working operates within early years provision and benefits children and carers

AC What you need to do

2.1	Prepare an area within the work setting, explaining how the area supports and extends children's learning and development
2.2	Monitor how children use the prepared area and evaluate how effective it has been in: • extending children's learning and development • encouraging high expectations of their achievement
2.3	Explain how the environment meets the needs of individual children

This unit also links to some of the other mandatory units:

EYMP 2	Promote learning and development in the early years
EYMP 3	Promote children's welfare and wellbeing in the early years
EYMP 4	Professional practice in early years settings
CYP 3.2	Promote child and young person development

Some of your learning from this unit will be repeated in these units and will therefore give you the chance to review your knowledge and understanding.

What are the purposes and principles of current early years frameworks?

Your assessment criteria:

1.1 Explain the legal status and principles of the relevant early years framework/s, and how national and local guidance materials are used in settings

In 1966 the government in England started to fund early years provision and since then there has been a variety of curricular guidance, culminating in the Early Years Foundation Stage 2008 (EYFS). A review by Dame Clare Tickell, published in March 2011, is summarised in Chapter 13, page 351. It is a legal requirement for all registered settings that receive government funding to adhere to the principles in the EYFS. Northern Ireland, Scotland and Wales have their own guidance and each of these frameworks is outlined in this chapter. All the tasks will help you to prepare for your assessment, whichever country you live in.

England

In line with the Every Child Matters (2006) (ECM) document, the EYFS gives guidance on how to provide an effective early years environment for children's care, learning and development. The EYFS guidance has two main sections: one covers the statutory welfare requirements, described in Chapter 14, page 360, and the other describes the learning and development guidance. The latter is divided into four themes, each with its own principle and four commitments, which link to the ECM outcomes, as shown in Figures 12.1, 12.2, 12.3 and 12.4.

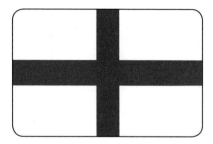

Figure 12.1 A unique child

EYFS theme	Principle	Commitments	ECM outcomes
A unique child	Every child is a competent learner from birth who can be resilient, capable, confident and self-assured.	1.1 Child development 1.2 Inclusive practice 1.3 Keeping safe 1.4 Health and wellbeing	• Make a positive contribution • Stay safe • Be healthy

The emphasis of this theme is the individuality of every child. It requires practitioners to understand child development and to show respect for all children and their families, making adaptations to the environment where necessary. It also focuses on the need to keep children physically and mentally safe and healthy.

'Meeting the individual needs of all children lies at the heart of the EYFS.'

(EYFS Practice Guidance, 2008, www.dcsf.gov.uk)

Figure 12.2 Positive relationships

EYFS theme	Principle	Commitments	ECM outcomes
Positive relationships	Children learn to be strong and independent from a base of loving and secure relationships with parents and/or a key person.	2.1 Respecting each other 2.2 Parents as partners 2.3 Supporting learning 2.4 Key person	• Make a positive contribution • Stay safe

The second theme concentrates on the importance of relationships with children and other people who can help to promote positive outcomes for children and their families. Positive relationships with children, their parents, other staff, other professionals and the local authority are all important and will contribute to an environment promoting children's life chances. The **key person** role is crucial to developing children's sense of belonging and sense of self-worth.

Key terms

Key person: the practitioner with particular responsibility for getting to know the child and his or her family

Case study

Emma is a 2½-year-old girl in your care and you are worried about her wellbeing. Until recently, Emma has been happy to attend nursery, leaving her mum easily in the mornings and happy to see her again in the afternoon. However, over the last two weeks, Emma has shown less confidence in leaving her mum and has not settled well for much of her time with you.

In pairs, role-play a discussion between the key person and Emma's mum about how Emma's confidence has changed recently. Make sure that respect is shown for Mum, Emma and the key person and that the concerns for Emma's wellbeing are made clear. Discuss whether there are any circumstances at home or elsewhere that might be disturbing Emma.

At the end of your discussion, describe to each other how it felt to be the key person or Emma's mum.

England *continued*

This theme, summarised in Figure 12.3, stresses the importance of the environment in helping children to achieve the positive outcomes. Everything that a child experiences is important in shaping their development, and it is the practitioner's responsibility to make the environment comfortable, attractive, stimulating and specific to all children's needs and interests.

As part of the child's environment you have a very important role, getting to know each child, catering for their needs and working with others who also know and work with the child. The role of a key person involves making careful observations of the children's development and interests (see Figure 12.4) and these will contribute to planning for the child's future development. The importance of this role cannot be overestimated.

Your assessment criteria:

1.1 Explain the legal status and principles of the relevant early years framework/s, and how national and local guidance materials are used in settings

Figure 12.3 Enabling environments

EYFS theme	Principle	Commitments	ECM outcomes
Enabling environments	The environment plays a key role in supporting and extending children's learning and development.	3.1 Observation, assessment and planning 3.2 Supporting every child 3.3 The learning environment 3.4 The wider context	• Enjoy and achieve • Make a positive contribution

Figure 12.4 Learning and development

EYFS theme	Principle	Commitments	ECM outcomes
Learning and development	Children learn and develop in different ways and at different rates, and all areas of learning and development are equally important and inter-connected.	4.1 Play and exploration 4.2 Active learning 4.3 Creativity and critical thinking 4.4 Areas of learning and development	• Enjoy and achieve

This theme discusses the opportunities for learning and development that should be provided for children. There is an emphasis on learning through play, through being active and through playing outdoors. One requirement in this theme is that children's thinking skills are developed. There are six areas of learning, as shown in Figure 12.5.

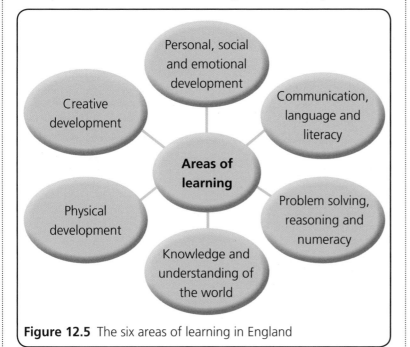

Figure 12.5 The six areas of learning in England

The EYFS gives guidance for practitioners on how to cater for children at different stages of development within each of these six areas of learning as children make progress towards the **early learning goals** at the end of the reception year. It also gives ideas about what to look out for when observing children, and it provides ideas for activities when planning the children's next steps.

See Chapter 13, page 332 for a summary of the review of March 2011, with recommendations for changes in the EYFS.

Key terms

Early learning goals: the expectations for children's learning and development for most children to reach by the end of their reception year at school

Over to you!

Make a sketch of the room you work in and label the different areas.

If you work with children aged from 18 months to pre-school:

▶ *What areas of the room do the children access most?*

▶ *What might this tell you about the children?*

▶ *What might this tell you about the set-up of the room?*

If you work with children under 18 months of age:

▶ *How and when are the different areas in your room used?*

▶ *How do the children make choices about what they play with or where they go?*

▶ *How might the environment be improved?*

Share your experiences with others in the group.

Northern Ireland (www.deni.gov.uk)

'Children who have a high-quality pre-school experience are better prepared for primary school and learn more quickly.'

(EPPNQ 2004)

The document *Our Children and Young People – Our Pledge – A Ten Year Strategy* sets the following high-level outcomes for children in Northern Ireland:

▶ being healthy

▶ enjoying, learning and achieving

▶ living in safety and with stability

▶ experiencing economic and environmental wellbeing

▶ contributing positively to community and society

▶ living in a society that respects their rights.

In line with this, the *Curriculum Guidance for Pre-school Education* emphasises the need for learning through play, the importance of the home environment, the need for children to be able to explore their environment and the need to cater for each child's individual needs. There are six areas of learning, as summarised in Figure 12.6.

The guidance states that the curriculum should:

▶ provide equality of opportunity

▶ be planned, purposeful and flexible

▶ provide challenge and stimulation through enjoyable activities

▶ promote active learning

▶ be broad and balanced.

'I want to see every child have the best possible start in life.'

(Outcomes from the review of pre-school education in Northern Ireland, DfES 2006)

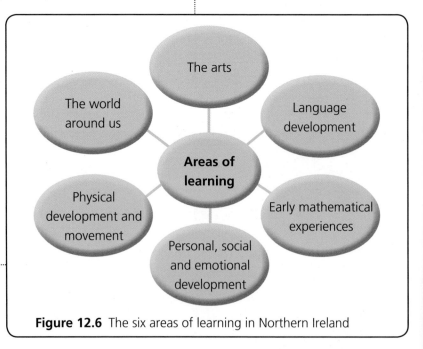

Figure 12.6 The six areas of learning in Northern Ireland

Scotland

'Care and wellbeing of children is the concern of everybody.'

(For Scotland's Children Report, 2001, www.tls.gov.uk)

The framework in Scotland consists of the *Curriculum for Excellence* which provides guidance for all children aged from 3 to 18 years old and 'Pre-birth to Three', published in December 2010.

There are three guiding principles for staff.

▶ Relationships: *'Relationships are influential. They provide the basis for young children's development and learning.'*

▶ Responsive care: *'Responsive care means knowing and accepting each child and respecting each child as an individual.'*

▶ Respect: *'Each child is an individual, a person who has the right to be responded to and treated with genuine respect at all times.'*

The *Curriculum for Excellence* is tied in closely to the *United Nations Convention on the Rights of the Child* and its purpose is summarised in four ideas:

▶ successful learners

▶ confident individuals

▶ responsible citizens

▶ effective contributors.

There is an emphasis on play, learning social relationships, emotional and physical wellbeing and the importance of early intervention for children with difficulties.

There are eight areas of experience, as summarised in Figure 12.7.

It is recognised that: *'the home learning environment in the early years is the largest factor in attainment and achievement at age 10'.*

(*Millennium Cohort Study*, a multidisciplinary research project started in 2000/1)

Over to you!

Maintaining confidentiality at all times, talk to a partner about one child in your care, whose needs you have identified.

▶ *How did you identify this child's needs?*

▶ *How did you cater for them?*

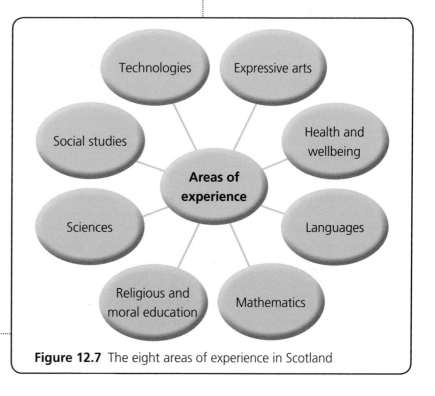

Figure 12.7 The eight areas of experience in Scotland

Wales

'All children and young people must be provided with an education that develops their personality and talents to the full.'

(www.foundationphasewales.com)

In August 2008 the Welsh Assembly started to introduce the Foundation Phase for Children's Learning for three- to seven-year olds and by August 2010 it had become a legal requirement for all those in receipt of government funding. Personal and social development, wellbeing and cultural diversity are considered to be at the heart of the Foundation Phase and should be emphasised throughout a child's experiences. There are seven areas of learning in the Foundation Phase, which provides the educational programme and lists the outcomes that children are expected to reach, as summarised in Figure 12.8.

The Foundation Phase contributes to the Curriculum Cymreig by developing children's understanding of the unique Welsh cultural identity so that children can understand Welsh heritage, literature and arts as well as the language. All settings and schools have to implement a Welsh-language educational programme in the Foundation Phase.

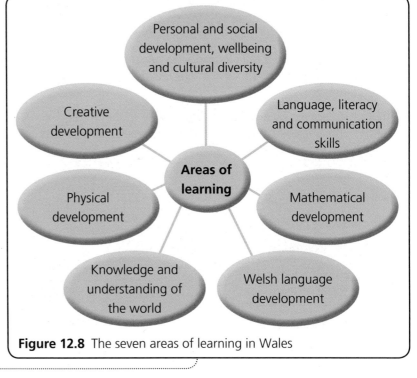

Figure 12.8 The seven areas of learning in Wales

Knowledge Assessment Task   1.1   1.3

Look carefully at the relevant guidance for the country you are working in.

Give a brief description of the guidance to help other pre-school workers understand it and explain its legal status. Say why you think it is important to have such guidance, what principles it is based on and how it is used in your setting.

Write a paragraph about each of the following points, referring to the guidance of your country and say how these are evident in your practice:

▶ children learning actively through play
▶ the importance of the home learning environment
▶ treating all children and families with respect
▶ the importance of a personal and individual approach to learning and development.

Keep your written work as evidence towards your assessment.

How have different approaches influenced early years provision?

Some of the pioneers of early years education are listed below, with brief descriptions of their influences in the modern curriculum.

Maria Montessori

Maria Montessori (1870–1952)

Maria Montessori was an Italian doctor working with orphaned children in Rome. The main features of a Montessori environment are:

▶ resources are made from natural materials

▶ resources have a specific educational value

▶ there is an emphasis on using real things found in the home

▶ children have a high level of choice in their activities

▶ adults are observers of children and preparers of the environment

▶ the environment is uncluttered and uses neutral calming colours.

Influences can be seen in the modern curricula as the emphasis has become focused on children's interests and stages of development, and in encouraging children to choose what they want to do. Many settings now are adopting calm environments to provide less stressful learning spaces.

Your assessment criteria:

1.2 Explain how different approaches to work with children in the early years have influenced current provision in the UK

Over to you!

▶ *In a small group, discuss what you see as the advantages and disadvantages of having curriculum guidance.*

▶ *Do you prefer to work with guidance or without it?*

Rudolph Steiner

Rudolph Steiner was an Austrian philosopher who started the first Steiner school in 1918. In Steiner settings there is a focus on:

- following the rhythms of nature

- using natural materials

- children being part of family daily routines, especially outdoors

- strong parental participation

- adults as important role models, sharing the lead in play.

Modern day curricula reflect the Steiner principles of outdoor play and the mixture of child-led and adult-led provision. The importance of parents' contributions is now a priority and there is more emphasis on natural materials, especially for use with children under two years of age.

High/Scope

The High/Scope early years approach was developed in America in the 1960s. It places a high importance on children:

- taking responsibility for their decisions

- planning, doing and reviewing their own work

- resolving their own conflicts

- gaining confidence by reporting back to their peers

- being active learners.

The strong link here with the current curriculum is the focus on children developing independence and confidence.

Reggio Emilia

This is another Italian approach to early years education with the following characteristics:

- a strong partnership with the parents

- children directing their own learning

- adults providing a richly resourced environment for children to express themselves as they choose

- children having free access to outdoor and indoor resources

- project work based on real-life situations.

'Our image of the child is rich in potential, strong, powerful, competent and, most of all, connected to adults and other children.'

(Malaguzzi, 1993)

Your assessment criteria:

1.2 Explain how different approaches to work with children in the early years have influenced current provision in the UK

Rudolph Steiner (1861–1925)

Links to the EYFS can be seen in the emphasis on the partnership with parents, the need to let children direct their own learning and the importance of a stimulating environment, especially recommending the use of the outdoors.

Common core 2010

After the death of Victoria Climbié in 2000, the Every Child Matters document was published, with five positive outcomes and recommendations that everyone working with children or young people should be communicating with each other. At the same time, the common core of principles was published and has been reviewed as recently as 2010. It is a set of principles for everyone working with children to focus on:

▶ effective communication and engagement with children, young people and families

▶ child and young person development

▶ safeguarding and promoting the welfare of the child or young person

▶ supporting transitions

▶ multi-agency and integrated working

▶ information sharing.

A personal approach

One of the over-riding principles in all the curricula discussed above is that children should be given opportunities to develop their own interests at their own rate. The most effective way for this to happen is for the adults caring for children to learn as much as they can about them. Only if we strive to know every child well and cater for their individual needs will we be able to provide a truly inclusive environment.

Over to you!

▶ *In a small group, discuss what you mean by 'a personal approach'.*

▶ *Can you think of times in your own education when a personal approach has affected you positively?*

Knowledge Assessment Task   **1.2**

Produce an information leaflet for new learners in your setting, which highlights how different approaches to working with children in the early years have influenced current provision in the UK.

Illustrate your leaflet with suitable images and keep your written work as evidence towards your assessment.

What makes a good learning environment for children?

From the descriptions of the various frameworks, it is clear that there are certain principles that are important to them all. This shows that the following factors are essential in an environment for children:

▶ carefully prepared activities and resources to extend children's learning, which are based on close observations of their interests and stages of development

▶ opportunities for children to learn through play

▶ opportunities for children to make their own choices about what they play with

▶ opportunities for children to play indoors and outdoors

▶ meaningful interaction with responsive adults

▶ opportunities for children to play on their own, in small groups and in large groups.

Babies

As well as all of the above, babies need a greater emphasis on sensory development as this is how they learn about their environment (see Figure 12.9).

Three- to five-year-olds

Older children have different requirements as they become more independent, so it can be difficult to balance adult-led and child-led play. Sensitive staff notice children's interests and stages of development and respond to their lead. These children need a carefully prepared environment with at least the following opportunities, best arranged in different parts of the nursery, some on tables and some on the floor, some indoors and some outdoors:

▶ role-play

▶ construction

▶ small world

▶ mark making

▶ craft corner

▶ sand, water and play dough

▶ book corner

▶ some ICT and resources that encourage exploration.

It is important that planned activities support and encourage all six areas of learning within the EYFS and are based on the children's interests and stages of development. Children also show preferences for the way they learn, sometimes called schemas.

Your assessment criteria:

2.1 Prepare an area within the work setting, explaining how the area supports and extends children's learning and development

Over to you!

How do you like to learn?

▶ *Do you prefer to listen, to write notes, watch demonstrations or take part in activities?*

▶ *Do you have any other preferences?*

Compare your own learning styles with others in your group.

Key terms

Schema: an organised pattern of thought or behaviour that temporarily influences the way a child plays

Movement – babies have a good sense of movement at birth and like to be active. Provide rocking chairs and plenty of opportunities for babies to start to sit up, crawl and walk when they are ready.

Smell – very well developed at birth and helps the baby to develop a sense of place and security.

Taste – this is closely aligned to smell and can be extended by providing a wide variety of foods for snacks.

Sight – the sense of sight is also not well developed at birth and babies gradually develop the ability to focus their vision and see further distances. The most important stimulation for a baby's vision is a familiar human face, but mobiles and other attractive toys will encourage the baby to explore with their eyes.

Touch – this is fairly well developed at birth and can be extended using treasure baskets, a variety of surfaces, materials and temperatures.

Sound – this is less well developed at birth and can be extended by introducing musical instruments, songs, musical toys and the human voice in conversation. Quiet times are also important so as not to overload the child's environment.

Figure 12.9 How to develop all the senses in young babies

Outdoors

Many activities that can be experienced indoors can also be experienced outdoors. However, there are activities that are better carried out outside, so practitioners should make the most of being outdoors and supporting activities such as noticing the weather, digging, den-making, studying the natural world, designing and using technology, planting and growing, hide and seek and channelling water.

Routines

Another important part of the environment is the daily routine. A child starts to feel confident in their surroundings when there is a familiar set of adults and a familiar shape to the day, although it is also important for children to learn to be flexible in responding to change. The existing routines must provide security but must also be tailored to individual needs.

Over to you!

Consider the following routines in your workplace:

▶ *snack*
▶ *indoor/outdoor play times*
▶ *clearing up*
▶ *hand washing*
▶ *toileting.*

   1. *Do they provide children with a secure and familiar environment?*
   2. *Do they allow for differences in children's individual needs?*
   3. *How might you change any of them?*

Monitoring use of activities

The effectiveness of a prepared environment can be monitored in different ways. In order to do this, you need to observe the area carefully. You could make notes on:

▶ who uses the environment

▶ how the resources are used by the children

▶ what language the children use and what questions they ask

▶ whether the children learn anything new.

Figure 12.10 lists the different techniques you can use to record your observations, and their advantages and disadvantages.

Figure 12.10 Different recording techniques

Method	Advantages	Disadvantages
Pen and paper	Cheap and easy to access	Slow and inaccurate
Digital camera	Easily processed and easy to use	Doesn't capture language and requires live batteries
Video recorder	Captures actions and voices	More conspicuous and means you are behind a lens more of the time Can take longer to set up
Voice recorder	Captures language	Sometimes unclear which child is talking and requires live batteries

Your assessment criteria:

2.1 Prepare an area within the work setting, explaining how the area supports and extends children's learning and development

2.2 Monitor how children use the prepared area and evaluate how effective it has been in:
• extending children's learning and development
• encouraging high expectations of their achievement

2.3 Explain how the environment meets the needs of individual children

Practical Assessment Task

Choose an area in your workplace to introduce some new ideas for the children. Prepare the chosen environment, using resources to extend the children's learning and development. Use the questions below as a guide.

1. Is the area to be used by all children or a small group of children?

2. Is it for free play or is it for an adult-led group activity?

3. Will it be indoors or outdoors?

4. What resources will you provide?

5. How will you know whether it is supporting and extending the children's learning?

6. What will be the role of the adult?

7. How will you cater for individual children's needs?

8. How will you monitor the children's use of the area or their progress?

9. How will you show your high expectations for the children?

10. How will you report back your findings to your room supervisor?

Once you have prepared an area for the children and monitored the effectiveness of it, you should write a reflective account that:

▶ includes a sketch of the area

▶ describes the resources you chose and why

▶ explains how the environment met the individual needs of the children

▶ explains how children's learning was extended and how you encouraged high expectations of the children's achievement

▶ describes how you monitored the use of the area.

Keep your reflective account to help you with your assessment. Your evidence for this task must be based on your practice in a real work environment and must be presented in a format that is acceptable to your assessor.

Why is it important to work closely with others?

'Children learn to be strong and independent from a base of loving and secure relationships with parents and/or a key person.' (EYFS principle)

Over the past few years, greater recognition has been given to the importance of parents' influence on their child's development, so much so that it is now a standard principle for those working with children to believe that parents are the first and most important educators of their children. Therefore working in close partnership with parents and carers is essential.

Partnership model – ideals and problems

Knowing children well is important to becoming able to provide a truly inclusive environment for them. In an ideal world all practitioners would work very closely with the parents or carers of their key children to share ideas, concerns, developments or problems. The more we know about a child, the more their personal interests can be planned and catered for by the setting and the child's parents or carers. Unfortunately, this ideal is not always possible, however hard we try.

Your assessment criteria:

3.1 Explain the partnership model of working with carers

3.2 Review barriers to participation for carers and explain ways in which they can be overcome

3.3 Explain strategies to support carers who may react positively or negatively to partnership opportunities

3.4 Explain how effective multi-agency working operates within early years provision and benefits children and carers

Effective multi-agency working

Since the Laming report, which produced the Every Child Matters document in 2003, there has been a strong emphasis on working together with other agencies, as well as parents, for the same reasons as above. If a team of people is working with the child, it can only be of benefit to them if this group of people works together. When this team consists of different specialists from different agencies, this is called multi-agency working. All records about a child can be kept in one place by completing a **common assessment framework** (CAF) to increase information sharing. There is more information about multi-agency working in Chapter 10, page 268. All of this is summarised in Figure 12.14, overleaf. Figure 12.13, below, represents diagrammatically how all adults working with the child should try to communicate with each other as well as with the child.

There is more information about multi-agency working in Chapter 10, page 268.

Key terms

Common assessment framework: an assessment shared by all members of a multi-agency team working with a child or young person

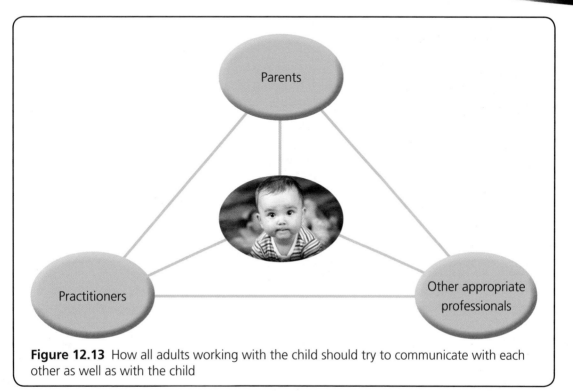

Figure 12.13 How all adults working with the child should try to communicate with each other as well as with the child

Knowledge Assessment Task   3.1   3.2   3.3   3.4

Mr and Mrs Burgess have just moved into the area and have a two-year-old son called Tim who has hearing difficulties. They want him to attend a pre-school three days each week. Unfortunately, they had a bad experience in the past when they didn't feel welcome at a nursery. They felt that the previous staff had ignored their requests for help with Tim's hearing difficulties and are now nervous about how to trust any setting. Mr Burgess works away from home a lot and Mrs Burgess does not speak fluent English. Answer these questions about what should happen when they visit the setting.

1. What would you tell Mr and Mrs Burgess about the model of partnership that exists in the setting?

2. What do you think might be the barriers to working closely with Mr and Mrs Burgess?

3. How could you try to overcome these barriers?

4. What strategies would you employ to encourage Mr and Mrs Burgess to overcome their fears about working in partnership with the setting?

5. How would you reassure Mr and Mrs Burgess and explain that effective multi-agency working will support them and Tim's individual needs?

Your assessment criteria:

3.1 Explain the partnership model of working with carers

3.2 Review barriers to participation for carers and explain ways in which they can be overcome

3.3 Explain strategies to support carers who may react positively or negatively to partnership opportunities

3.4 Explain how effective multi-agency working operates within early years provision and benefits children and carers

---

Figure 12.14 Different strategies for practitioners to work closely with parents and carers

Strategies for working together	Effects for parents	Barriers to working well with parents	How barriers might be overcome
Open door policy	Feeling welcome Chance to experience what is happening in the nursery and to talk to staff Talking daily about their child	Parents are in a hurry when dropping off and picking up Staff are split between talking to parents and caring for the children Lack of private space for discussion Parents staying longer than is beneficial for the child Too many parents in the room at the same time	Find time to have a few words with each parent when they arrive. Make home link books for parents and staff to share information. Offer contact by phone or email if privacy is difficult. Establish a time each day for parents to leave.

continued...

Strategies for working together	Effects for parents	Barriers to working well with parents	How barriers might be overcome
Sharing observations and planning with the parents	Opportunities to talk about their child's progress and contribute to suggestions for the future.	Parents lacking confidence to offer suggestions. Discrepancy between what the parents think is best for their child and what the professionals think.	Make time for discussions with parents about their child's progress and show them the child's records to help parents to overcome fear. Hold parents' evenings to show some aspect of the setting's programme so parents know what you are doing and why. Find as many opportunities as possible to explain fundamental principles to parents.
Invitations to parents to share sessions and their expertise	Parents will see how the setting operates and how their child benefits. Parents are often happy to share a special hobby, a national celebration or their work, adding to the richness of the children's environment.	Not all parents have spare time during the day.	Make a variety of times available for meetings with parents, some in the evenings. Home visits can be helpful but time consuming. Communication via telephone or email can keep parents informed if they cannot visit during the day.
Ask the parents for help and advice or offer them time to discuss the needs of their child, especially for children with English as an additional language (EAL) or special educational needs (SEN)	The information parents have about their child's SEN or language is invaluable and will help you to provide the best inclusive environment.	Parents might know little about the SEN, especially if the diagnosis is new. Parents may have disabilities or learning difficulties. Parents may not speak much English themselves.	Provide information for families to help them understand SEN. Create opportunities for parents with SEN themselves to access your support and the setting. Provide translations for letters and notices in appropriate languages. Arrange for other speakers of the same language to act as translators.

Are you ready for assessment?

AC	What do you know now?	Assessment task	✓
1.1	The legal status and principles of the relevant early years framework/s, and how guidance materials are used in settings	Page 318	
1.2	How different approaches to work with children in the early years have affected current provision in the UK	Page 321	
1.3	Why early years frameworks emphasise a personal and individual approach to learning and development	Page 318	
3.1	The partnership model of working with carers	Page 328	
3.2	Barriers to working with carers, and how they can be overcome	Page 328	
3.3	The strategies to support carers who respond positively or negatively to partnership opportunities	Page 328	
3.4	How effective multi-agency working operates within early years provision and benefits children and carers	Page 328	

Your tutor or assessor may want to observe you actually doing this in your placement or work setting.

AC	What can you do now?	Assessment task	✓
2.1	Prepare an area in the work setting and explain how it supports and extends children's learning and development	Page 325	
2.2	Monitor how children use the prepared area, and evaluate how effective it has been in extending children's learning and development and encouraging high expectations of their achievement	Page 325	
2.3	Explain how the environment meets the needs of individual children	Page 325	

13 | Promote learning and development in the early years (EYMP 2)

Assessment of this unit

This unit is about promoting children's learning and development in the early years. It covers the requirements of the relevant early years frameworks and explores some of the ways in which practitioners can promote learning and development through engaging with children and planning activities. This unit also examines the importance of reflecting on professional practice for practitioners working in the early years.

The assessment of this unit includes both knowledge (things that you need to know about) and competence (things you need to be able to do in the real work environment).

In order to complete this unit successfully, you will need to produce evidence of your knowledge and competence. The chart opposite explain what you need to know and do, alongside the relevant assessment criteria.

Your tutor or assessor will help you to prepare for your assessment and the tasks suggested in this chapter will help you to create the evidence you need.

CHAPTER 13

AC   What you need to know

1.1	Each of the areas of learning and development and how these are interdependent
1.2 1.3	The documented outcomes for children that form part of the relevant early years framework and how these documented outcomes are assessed and recorded.

AC   What you need to do

2.1	Use different sources to plan work for an individual child or group of children
2.2	Engage effectively with children to encourage the child's participation and involvement in planning their own learning and development activities
2.3	Support the planning cycle for children's learning and development
3.1	Explain how practitioners promote children's learning within the relevant early years framework
3.2	Prepare, set out and support activities and experiences that encourage learning and development in each area of the relevant early years framework
4.1	Work alongside children, engaging with them in order to support their learning and development
4.2	Explain the importance of engaging with a child to support sustained shared thinking
4.3	Use language that is accurate and appropriate in order to support and extend children's learning when undertaking activities
5.1	Reflect on own practice in supporting learning and development of children in their early years
5.2	Demonstrate how to use reflection to make changes in own practice

This unit links with some of the other mandatory units:

SHC 32	Engage in personal development in health, social care or children's and young people's settings
CYP 3.2	Promote child and young person development
CYP 3.7	Understand how to support positive outcomes for children and young people
EYMP 1	Context and principles for early years provision
EYMP 5	Support children's speech, language and communication

Some of your learning will be repeated in these units and will give you the chance to review your knowledge and understanding.

Your assessment criteria:

1.1 Explain each of the areas of learning and development and how these are interdependent

Statutory Framework for the Early Years Foundation Stage

May 2008

Setting the Standards for Learning, Development and Care for children from birth to five

Every Child Matters
Change For Children

STATUTORY FRAMEWORK

department for
children, schools and families

What are the relevant early years frameworks?

The four nations within the United Kingdom have all developed their own early years frameworks and these have been discussed in Chapter 12, page 310.

In summary, they are:

England – The Early Years Foundation Stage (EYFS)
www.education.gov.uk

N. Ireland – The Curriculum Guidance for Pre-school Education
www.deni.gov.uk

Scotland – The Curriculum for Excellence www.tls.gov.uk

Wales – The Foundation Phase www.foundationphasewales.com

The focus of this chapter is the Early Years Foundation Stage, but the requirements should be related to the early years framework for the relevant country in which you live.

The Early Years Foundation Stage

The Early Years Foundation Stage (EYFS) was introduced in England in September 2008. This framework is built around four main themes (see Chapter 12, page 310); it sets out the welfare and learning and development standards that must be met by providers of education and care for children from birth to five years of age.

The welfare requirements of the EYFS are statutory and include important regulations about safeguarding and promoting children's welfare (see Chapter 14, page 360). The learning and development standards are based on the principles of children learning through play. They make recommendations for planning and organising children's learning and development, based on the following six key areas of learning.

1. *Personal, social and emotional development*, for example, how children develop confidence, independence and social skills for getting along with others

2. *Communication, language and literacy*, for example, how children learn to speak, listen, read and write

3. *Problem-solving, reasoning and numeracy*, for example, how children learn to use numbers, work things out and develop logical thinking

4. *Knowledge and understanding of the world*, for example, how children learn about the world around them, science and technology, nature and different cultures

5. *Physical development*, for example, how children learn to move and co-ordinate their bodies and use equipment with their hands

6. *Creative development*, for example, how children learn to use their imagination and represent their ideas creatively through music, art, dance and other forms of play

The EYFS highlights the importance of practitioners using observations when planning activities to meet children's individual needs and interests.

Key terms

Logical thinking: the ability to think and work things out, using reasoning

Over to you!

Investigate the relevant early years framework for the country you live in.

Examine the detailed guidance that is included for each of the areas of learning.

The six areas of learning

The Practice Guidance for the Early Years Foundation Stage provides support for practitioners and divides each area of learning into different aspects, as summarised in Figure 13.1.

Figure 13.1 The six areas of learning

Area of learning	Aspects	Example of requirements
1. Personal, social and emotional development (PSED)	Dispositions and attitudes Self-confidence and self-esteem Making relationships Behaviour and self-control Self-care Sense of community	*'Children must be provided with experiences and support, which will help them to develop a positive sense of themselves and of others; respect for others; social skills; and a positive disposition to learn.'*
2. Communication, language and literacy (CLL)	Language for communication Language for thinking Linking sounds and letters Reading Writing Handwriting	*'Children's learning and competence in communicating, speaking and listening, being read to and beginning to read and write must be supported and extended.'*
3. Problem-solving, reasoning and numeracy (PSRN)	Numbers as labels and for counting Calculating Shape, space and measures	*'Children must be supported in developing their understanding of PSRN in a broad range of contexts in which they can explore, enjoy, learn, practise and talk about their developing understanding.'*
4. Knowledge and understanding of the world (KUW)	Exploration and investigation Designing and making ICT Time Place Communities	*'Children must be supported in developing the knowledge, skills and understanding that help them to make sense of the world. Their learning must be supported through offering opportunities for them to use a range of tools safely; encounter creatures, plants, people and objects in their natural environments and in real-life situations; undertake practical 'experiments'; and work with a range of materials.'*

continued...

Area of learning	Aspects	Example of requirements
5. Physical development (PD)	Movement and space Health and bodily awareness Using equipment and materials	*'The physical development of babies and young children must be encouraged through the provision of opportunities for them to be active and interactive and to improve their skills of co-ordination, control, manipulation and movement… They must be supported in developing an understanding of the importance of physical activity and making healthy choices in relation to food.'*
6. Creative development (CD)	Being creative – responding to experiences, expressing and communicating ideas Exploring media and materials Creating music and dance	*'Children's creativity must be extended by the provision of support for their curiosity, exploration and play. They must be provided with opportunities to explore and share their thoughts, ideas and feelings, for example, through a variety of art, music, movement, dance, imaginative and role-play activities, mathematics and design and technology.'*

All six areas of learning are **interdependent** and it is important for practitioners to use a **holistic** approach when observing children and using the EYFS Framework.

Key terms

Holistic: emphasising the importance of the whole child

Interdependent: connected and dependent on each other

Case study

Jamal is four years old and attends a local day nursery every morning. Jamal's key person observes him regularly when he is playing and, in a recent observation, recorded the following information.

Jamal is playing outside in the sand. He is digging with the big spade and making a pile of sand on the edge of the sand pit. When the pile of sand is quite high, he starts to dig a tunnel through the middle. The sand keeps breaking up around the edges of the tunnel, making it collapse. Jamal calls out to another child to come and help him and, together, they compress the sand and work on the tunnel until it is big enough to push the toy dumper truck through to the other side. Jamal then pushes the dumper truck over to the garden and loads it up with stones. He tells his friend that he is making a delivery from the quarry and pushes it back to the sand pit. Together, they dig another space in the sand to put the stones from the garden. Jamal tells his friend that the stones have come from the desert and they are going to make a special building.

1. Which of the six areas of learning from the EYFS can you identify in this play scenario?

2. Explain how the areas of learning and development are interdependent in this example.

Documenting outcomes

One of the aims of the EYFS is to provide high-quality early years education to support young children's learning and development. In order to achieve this, practitioners need to gather information and use ongoing observations to monitor and assess the progress of individual children. Within the EYFS, children's learning and development are reviewed and documented, using the **Early Years Foundation Stage Profile (EYFS Profile)**. This document provides a record of children's progress in each of the six areas of learning and the **eProfile** programme provides an electronic means of supporting practitioners to do this.

The EYFS Profile has 13 assessment scales, representing the different aspects within the six areas of learning. Each assessment scale has nine levels for assessing children's progress towards the final outcomes, which are called **Early Learning Goals (ELGs)**.

The example in Figure 13.2 shows the scale for 'numbers as labels and for counting', which is one aspect of problem-solving, reasoning and numeracy. Levels 1–3 describe children who are still working towards the ELGs, levels 4–8 describe children who have achieved the ELGs and level 9 describes children who are beyond the ELGs for that area.

Your assessment criteria:

1.1 Explain each of the areas of learning and development and how these are interdependent

1.2 Describe the documented outcomes for children that form part of the relevant early years framework

1.3 Explain how the documented outcomes are assessed and recorded

Key terms

Early Years Foundation Stage Profile (EYFS Profile): the regulatory and quality framework for the provision of learning, development and care for children between birth and the academic year in which they turn five

eProfile: an electronic means of building a record of assessment outcomes throughout the Reception Year to support the making of final judgements for the EYFS profile

Early Learning Goals (ELGs): targets for learning and development, which describe the expectations for children's achievement by the end of the EYFS

The National Strategies
Early Years

Progress Matters: Reviewing and enhancing young children's development

Professional development meetings 1 and 2

department for
children, schools and families

Numbers as labels and for counting (EYFS Profile)

1. Says some number names in familiar contexts, such as nursery rhymes.
2. Counts reliably up to three everyday objects.
3. Counts reliably up to six everyday objects.
4. Says number names in order.
5. Recognises numerals 1 to 9.
6. Counts reliably up to 10 everyday objects.
7. Orders numbers, up to 10.
8. Uses developing mathematical ideas and methods to solve practical problems.
9. Recognises, counts, orders, writes and uses numbers up to 20.

Figure 13.2 An example of a scale from the EYFS Profile

Documenting outcomes (*continued*)

Children's progress towards or achievement of the ELGs has to be assessed when they complete the EYFS, which will usually be at the end of their Reception Year, at about the age of five.

> *This must be completed in the final term of the year in which the child reaches the age of five and no later than 30 June in that term.*

(EYFS statutory framework)

This summary will usually be completed by the Reception class teacher and can then be used to support and extend children's learning as they move into Key Stage 1. The example in Figure 13.3 shows the ELGs for Problem-Solving, Reasoning and Numeracy (PSRN).

Your assessment criteria:

1.1 Explain each of the areas of learning and development and how these are interdependent

1.2 Describe the documented outcomes for children that form part of the relevant early years framework

1.3 Explain how the documented outcomes are assessed and recorded

Problem Solving, Reasoning and Numeracy (ELGs)

By the end of the EYFS, children should:

- Say and use number names in order in familiar contexts.
- Count reliably up to 10 everyday objects.
- Recognise the numerals 1 to 9.
- Use developing mathematical ideas and methods to solve practical problems.
- In practical activities and discussion, begin to use the vocabulary involved in adding and subtracting.
- Use language such as 'more' or 'less' to compare two numbers.
- Find one more or one less than a number from one to 10.
- Begin to relate addition to combining two groups of objects and subtraction to 'taking away'.
- Use language such as 'greater', 'smaller', 'heavier' or 'lighter' to compare quantities.
- Talk about, recognise and recreate simple patterns.
- Use language such as 'circle' or 'bigger' to describe the shape and size of solids and flat shapes.
- Use everyday words to describe position.

Figure 13.3 An example of Early Learning Goals (ELGs)

The requirements clearly state that any judgements about children's learning and development must be based on actual observations, predominantly from **child-initiated activities**. It is also important to remember that all children are different and their progress will vary a great deal, depending on their individual needs. For example, children with special educational needs (SEN) may require an alternative approach to assessment and this should be discussed with their parents or carers.

Key terms

Child-initiated activities: activities that are chosen and directed by children themselves, following their own ideas and individual interests

Over to you!

Investigate and find more information about monitoring children's progress within the EYFS in the document 'Progress Matters' (http:// nationalstrategies.standards.dcsf.gov.uk/earlyyears).

Knowledge Assessment Task   1.1   1.2   1.3

Investigate the relevant early years framework for the country where you live.

Write a report that explains:

- ▶ each of the areas of learning and how these are interdependent
- ▶ the documented outcomes for children
- ▶ how the documented outcomes are assessed and recorded.

Keep your report as evidence towards your assessment.

What different sources can inform planning?

The EYFS emphasises the importance of knowing and understanding each child as a unique individual, in order to plan and provide the best possible experiences in their early years. This knowledge about a child should come from a variety of different sources, some of which are listed here.

The child's interests and enthusiasms

▶ What play choices does the child make?

▶ What is the child really interested in?

▶ What does the child like/dislike?

Observations and assessments

▶ How does the child interact with others?

▶ How does the child respond to different situations and routines?

▶ What can the child do?

▶ How does the child like to learn?

▶ What individual needs does the child have?

Information from parents and carers

▶ What do parents tell you about their child?

Information from colleagues and other professionals

▶ What can professional partners, (such as health visitors or speech and language therapists) contribute to the picture?

The child's own views

▶ How are the child's views sought and taken into account?

Engaging with children to plan learning and development activities

Simply gathering information about a child is not enough. Practitioners need to make sure that the information is used effectively, to plan experiences and activities that encourage and extend children's learning and development. An important part of this process involves engaging effectively with children in order to find out about their real interests and needs. This includes not only observing children but also actively seeking out their own views and opinions. Encouraging children to participate in the planning process can be challenging, particularly with very young children or children with limited communication skills. However, it is important for practitioners to use different methods, such as visual prompts, pictures, photographs or symbols, to help children express their needs.

One system that actively encourages children's participation is the Mosaic approach. This technique uses a variety of methods to gather information from the child's own perspective, including stories, drawings and photographs taken by the child.

The HighScope approach in early education actively involves children in the planning process. When using the 'plan-do-review' process, children are given the opportunity to create and express their own goals, generate their own learning experiences and reflect on the process.

> **Key terms**
>
> **HighScope:** an educational approach that emphasises active participatory learning and encourages children to engage in hands-on experiences
>
> **Mosaic approach:** a framework for listening to children and young people, which combines the traditional research tools of observation and interviewing with participatory methods, including the use of cameras, map-making and child-led tours

Over to you!

▶ *Investigate the HighScope approach (www.high-scope.org.uk).*

▶ *Make notes about some of the different ways in which children are encouraged to participate in planning their own activities and reflecting on the process.*

The planning cycle

Effective planning to support children's learning and development is based on observation and assessment. Analysing observations helps practitioners to identify children's needs, and make decisions about the next steps, to encourage learning and development. This is often referred to as the observe–assess–plan–review cycle, as outlined in Figure 13.4.

The EYFS Framework clearly states that observation must be used as a basis for planning children's learning and development. It is also a legal requirement for practitioners to carry out observational assessment and plan experiences appropriate to each child's stage of development as they progress towards the early learning goals.

Planning is an active, continuous process. Practitioners need to be flexible in their approach and constantly aware of children's changing needs. Many settings use wipe-clean whiteboards to outline planning ideas for individual children or record on sticky notes their spontaneous ideas to use in future planning.

Your assessment criteria:

2.1 Use different sources to plan work for an individual child or group of children

2.2 Engage effectively with children to encourage the child's participation and involvement in planning their own learning and development activities

2.3 Support the planning cycle for children's learning and development

Observation
Look, listen and note

Review
How did it go?
Any improvements?

The Child

Assessment
Analyse and evaluate observations to identify child's needs

Planning
What next? Activities, experiences resoureces, environment

Figure 13.4 The planning cycle

Case study

Sophie is 11 months old and is sitting next to a treasure basket, exploring the contents.

The treasure basket is filled with a range of natural materials, including large pinecones, large shells, soft brushes, shiny objects and other natural materials.

Jess, who is Sophie's key person, makes the following observation notes.

> *Sophie sits sturdily and reaches for objects, using both hands independently. She spends a long time exploring a shiny spoon, puts it in her mouth, looks at it intently and waves it around.*
>
> *Sophie seems to enjoy exploring the mirror; she looks at her reflection, licks the mirror and laughs at Jess. Sophie is fully engaged with the treasure basket for 10 minutes.*

1. How could Jess use this information to plan the next steps for Sophie's learning and development?

2. What resources, activities or experiences might Jess provide for Sophie?

3. What factors (including the six areas of learning from the EYFS) should Jess consider when reviewing her plans for Sophie?

Practical Assessment Task

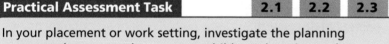 2.1 2.2 2.3

In your placement or work setting, investigate the planning processes that are used to promote children's learning and development. Talk to staff in the setting and make notes on their responses to the following questions.

▸ What different sources are used to gather information about individual children?

▸ How do the staff engage with children to encourage participation in the planning process?

▸ How is the planning cycle used to promote children's learning and development?

Keep your notes, along with examples of planning documents from the setting, as evidence towards your assessment.

Key terms

Child-initiated activities: activities that are chosen and directed by children themselves, following their own ideas and individual interests

Continuous provision: resources, toys and play materials that are always available for the children

How can practitioners promote children's learning?

In addition to observation, assessment and planning, there are many other ways in which practitioners can promote children's learning in the early years. Some of these ways are outlined in Figures 13.5 and 13.6. Providing a wide range of resources as **continuous provision** enables children to make their own decisions and choices in **child-initiated activities**. Some settings use continuous provision planning sheets to provide a basis for play activities, which children can then adapt or change themselves. Observing children's play and individual interests will help practitioners to suggest ideas for developing and enriching children's play. An example of a continuous provision planning sheet is shown in Figure 13.5.

Basic provision:	Key learning opportunities	Assessment points
	Continuous planning **Domestic role-play**	
Enrichment ideas	Adult role	

Figure 13.5 An example of a continuous planning sheet

Figure 13.6 Ways to promote children's learning in the early years

Ways to promote learning	How can this be done?	Example
'Tuning in' to children	Following children's interests and stage of development	Planning activities to develop a child's interest (e.g. in dinosaurs); making sure activities and resources are age-appropriate
Sensitive intervention	Recognising **play cues** Understanding when to join in children's play and when to hold back and observe	Responding to a child's request (e.g. for you to 'be the witch' in a play session) Staying on the sidelines when a group of children are developing their play ideas together
Supporting, facilitating, modelling and coaching	Providing advice, help, resources, praise and encouragement Demonstrating how to do something	Making suggestions (e.g. that using wet sand might help to build a sturdier sandcastle – and by providing some water!) Providing practical help (e.g. helping a child to operate a new digital camera)
Providing a balance of child-initiated and **adult-led** activities (both in and out of doors)	Making sure that resources and activities are available as continuous provision, for children to choose and direct their own plays Suggesting and directing children in exciting activities, based on their individual needs and interests	Providing resources (e.g. a selection of cardboard boxes outdoors for children to explore, investigate and develop their own play ideas) Playing a matching game about farm animals, following on from one child's visit to the city farm

Key terms

Adult-led activities: activities chosen and planned by adults for children to carry out

Play cues: clues given out by children as to when adult intervention is appropriate and when it is not

Preparing, setting out and supporting activities

In order to support and promote children's learning, practitioners need to use their knowledge of child development and be constantly aware of what stage a child is at and what the next step would be. This will involve not only planning activities and experiences but also adjusting resources, changing routines or rearranging the environment. For example, a practitioner may provide a range of different bags and boxes for a toddler who is fascinated by putting things in and out of containers, or change the location of the sand tray so that more children can use it.

In preparing activities it is important for practitioners to:

▶ focus on children's individual needs and interests, based on observation

▶ consider health and safety issues, for example, how many children will be able to play safely

▶ take into account the specific needs of particular children, for example, the need for specialised equipment or resources

▶ remember the simplicity of **open-ended resources**, for example, a bag of assorted fabric or a pile of big wooden blocks

▶ provide activities and experiences for all areas of learning.

In setting out activities, practitioners need to consider:

▶ the location of activities, for example, in or out of doors, space considerations and access

▶ the variety and amount of resources provided, for example, the number of bikes outside, the different colours of paint, paper or card

▶ the scope for children to use their imagination, creativity and problem-solving skills, for example, designating the role-play area as a 'magic space' for children to develop their own play ideas, rather than specifically as a shop, hairdressers or hospital.

In supporting activities, practitioners need to:

▶ observe children's interest and participation in the activity

▶ intervene sensitively, observing children's play cues

▶ use praise and encouragement to build confidence, credit effort and support achievement

▶ model language and behaviour, for example, introducing new vocabulary and reinforcing appropriate behaviour

▶ use questions and reflection to sustain and develop children's interest

▶ observe how resources are used and enhance the provision if necessary, for example, by adding extra materials.

Your assessment criteria:

3.1 Explain how practitioners promote children's learning within the relevant early years framework

3.2 Prepare, set out and support activities and experiences that encourage learning and development in each area of the relevant early years framework

Key terms

Open-ended resources: resources that may be put to various and different uses

This preparation and support is important in encouraging children's learning and development for each of the six areas of learning in the EYFS.

Figure 13.7 Encouraging children's learning and development in the EYFS

Area of learning	Some factors to consider
Personal, social and emotional development (PSED)	Opportunities for children to make choices; activities to encourage social interaction and for children to express their feelings; praise and encouragement to build confidence and self-esteem
Communication, language and literacy (CLL)	Opportunities for children to share books, stories, songs and rhymes; activities to encourage mark-making with different tools; modelling good communication, listening, reading and writing
Problem-solving, reasoning and numeracy (PSRN)	Opportunities for children to explore, experiment and work things out; activities to encourage matching, sorting, making patterns, weighing, measuring and counting; using mathematical language such as 'bigger than'
Knowledge and understanding of the world (KUW)	Opportunities for children to experience nature, engage with technology and encounter new ideas; activities to encourage exploration, such as treasure baskets; providing a variety of resources for children to investigate
Physical development (PD)	Opportunities for children to move around and play outdoors; activities to encourage children to use a variety of appropriate tools with their hands, such as rattles, scissors, crayons or glue sticks; supporting physical movement with other activities, for example, action rhymes
Creative development (CD)	Opportunities for children to use all their senses, such as touching different materials, hearing a variety of music and sounds; activities to encourage children to dance, sing, make music and engage in different art projects; focusing on the creative process rather than the end product

Over to you!

Look at Figure 13.7 and use it to complete this task.

▶ Make a list of some of the activities you have supported for children in your placement or work setting.
▶ Think about how these activities have encouraged children's learning and development in each of the six areas of learning.
▶ Share your ideas with others in the group.

Case study

Aaron is three years old and he attends Busy Bears nursery every morning.

He can walk up and down stairs confidently (two feet to a step), jump with both feet together and kick a football with accuracy. He uses a fist-like grasp to make marks with a chunky crayon, feeds himself with a spoon and fork and enjoys imaginative play. He has a wide-ranging vocabulary and uses simple sentences in conversation. Aaron enjoys the company of other children, particularly in outdoor play, and he loves to do things for himself. Olga is Aaron's key person and she carries out regular observations on Aaron to monitor his learning and development.

Recent observations have shown that Aaron enjoys playing outside; he has been investigating lengths of drainpipe and pouring water through them. He also enjoys climbing on the logs in the garden and has made a den with some of the other children. Inside, Aaron loves to play with the trains; he also creates imaginary stories involving lots of different characters.

1. What might you identify as Aaron's individual interests?

2. Give three examples of activities or experiences you might plan for Aaron, based on this information.

3. Describe how one of your chosen activities or experiences would encourage Aaron's learning and development across all six areas of learning within the EYFS.

4. What factors would you consider in preparing, setting out and supporting this chosen activity for Aaron?

Your assessment criteria:

3.1 Explain how practitioners promote children's learning within the relevant early years framework

3.2 Prepare, set out and support activities and experiences that encourage learning and development in each area of the relevant early years framework

Review of the Early Years Foundation Stage

In March 2011, the Early Years Foundation Stage (EYFS) was reviewed by Dame Clare Tickell. Some of her recommendations for changes to the EYFS include:

1. increasing the six areas of learning and development to seven and dividing these into two groups, called 'prime' areas and 'specific' areas

The three prime areas are:

▶ Personal, Social and Emotional development (PSED)

▶ Communication and Language (CL)

▶ Physical Development (PD).

The four specific areas are:

▶ Literacy (L)

▶ Mathematics (M)

▶ Understanding the World (UW)

▶ Expressive Arts and Design (EAD).

2. reducing the number of Early Learning Goals (ELGs)

3. introducing a simpler assessment scale for the EYFS Profile, with three sections to show whether children's skills are 'emerging', 'expected' or 'exceeding' the ELGs

4. clearer links between the ELGs and the Key Stage 1 curriculum.

The Tickell review also recommends that:

▶ more needs to be done to involve parents in their children's early learning

▶ the government should continue to develop early years as a graduate-led profession.

Practical Assessment Task   3.1   3.2

In your placement or work setting, think about how you promote children's learning and development across all the relevant areas of learning. Make notes about specific examples of activities and experiences that you have prepared, set up and supported with children, which you could discuss with your assessor.

Think about the factors you considered in encouraging children's learning and development.

Your assessor will need to assess your competence in the real work environment but your notes will help you to collect the evidence that you need.

How can practitioners engage with children to support their learning and development?

Engaging with children means showing a genuine interest in them and the things that they like to do. Adults can engage with children to support learning and development in a variety of different ways, including:

▶ following the child's lead and not dominating the situation, for example, in play

▶ using positive communication, both verbal and non-verbal, and being enthusiastic

▶ intervening sensitively and being aware of the child's needs, mood and level of interest.

Sustained shared thinking

Sustained shared thinking is a process that involves adults encouraging children to use language and explore ideas. This is extremely important in helping children to process information, make connections in their learning and become critical thinkers. In order for sustained shared thinking to take place, children need to be very interested and actively engaged in what is happening. An example is given in the case study opposite.

Key terms

Sustained shared thinking: a process that involves adults encouraging children to use language and explore ideas

Children should be encouraged to use language and explore ideas in sustained, shared thinking.

Case study

Owen, aged four, is fascinated by a fly caught in a spider's web in the nursery garden.

Owen:	'Look…'
Practitioner:	'Ooh, the spider has caught a fly in its web.'
Owen:	'It's trapped.'
Practitioner:	'Yes, it's like a net, that's how the spider catches its food.'
Owen:	'It doesn't fall off.'
Practitioner:	'I wonder why.'
Owen:	'It's all tied up, it can't escape.'
Practitioner:	'Yes, it's all tangled up in the web and the spider will come and eat it.'
Owen:	'Where's the spider?'
Practitioner:	'Let's have a look shall we?' (*Takes out a magnifying glass and together they examine the web.*)
Owen:	There's the spider, on the edge.'
Practitioner:	'Yes, it's waiting to pounce!'
Owen:	'And eat the fly.'

1. Explain how the practitioner engaged with Owen here to support sustained shared thinking.

2. Give two examples of ways in which the practitioner could further extend Owen's understanding of this situation through play activities or experiences.

Using language to support children's learning

The importance of language is discussed in Chapter 16, page 420. The way practitioners use language has a significant impact on extending children's learning, including such factors as using language that is accurate and grammatically correct as well as language that promotes children's curiosity, problem-solving and understanding of concepts. Some of these factors are summarised in Figure 13.8. The importance of language is discussed further in Chapter 16, page 420.

Figure 13.8 Using language to support children's learning

Language use	Example
Open-ended questions to promote and extend children's learning and understanding	'Why do you think that happened?' 'I wonder how this works?'
Descriptive language to extend children's vocabulary and understanding of sentence construction	'That's a beautiful, yellow sunflower.' 'We all had an exciting time at the funny pantomime.'
Mathematical language to support children's understanding of mathematical concepts (e.g. size, shape, measure, calculating, time)	Bigger, smaller, nearest, behind, inside, increase, take away, earlier, later, tomorrow, yesterday
Correct language (accurate, grammatically correct)	Using plurals, past and future tense correctly: 'Two feet, three mice'; 'I went, we bought'; 'I am going to'; 'We will'
Correct vocabulary (using the right words to name and describe things)	Names of animals, plants, countries, different foods and even different kinds of dinosaurs!

Your assessment criteria:

4.1 Work alongside children, engaging with them in order to support their learning and development

4.2 Explain the importance of engaging with a child to support sustained shared thinking

4.3 Use language that is accurate and appropriate in order to support and extend children's learning when undertaking activities

Over to you!

- *Think about the dialect spoken in your region and how specific words are pronounced, for example, 'ain't' (isn't it) or 'dunt' (doesn't it).*

- *Discuss different examples with others in the group and compare experiences of children's dialects from your placement or work setting.*

- *You may have experience of different languages being spoken in the setting, for example, Gaelic or Welsh.*

Effective interactions with children across the EYFS involve all of the following approaches.

- *Tuning in*: to evidence of children's thinking; listening and observing

- *Showing genuine interest*: giving undivided attention and affirmation

- *Respecting children's own decisions and choices*: helping children to follow things through and learn from their mistakes

- *Inviting children to elaborate*: being enthusiastic and asking appropriate questions

- *Supporting sequencing of ideas*: helping children to organise their ideas

- *Recapping*: re-running children's thinking with them ('So, you think that…')

- *Clarifying ideas*: helping to clarify meaning ('So, you are telling me that this will happen if I do that?')

- *Reminding*: helping children to hold on to their thoughts

- *Offering your own experience*: ('I really like to listen to music, it makes me feel happy.')

- *Suggesting* ('You might like to try it this way…')

- *Using encouragement* ('You have really worked hard on building that…')

- *Offering an alternative viewpoint*: gently challenging thinking ('Maybe… perhaps…')

- *Speculating*: considering other possibilities ('Do you think…?')

- *Modelling thinking* ('After work I need to take my dog to the vet, take my books back to the library and buy some food for supper. I wonder what I should do first…')

Practical Assessment Task

Think about the different ways in which you engage with children in your placement or work setting.

- How do you support sustained shared thinking?
- How do you use language to extend children's learning?

Make notes about some specific examples that you could discuss with your assessor.

Keep your notes as evidence towards your assessment.

Your assessor will need to assess your competence in the real work environment, but your notes will help you.

Why is it important to reflect on your own practice in supporting children's learning?

The importance of professional reflection has been discussed in Chapter 2, page 4. In this unit, reflective practice is considered in the context of supporting and promoting children's learning and development and how it can be a valuable way to:

▶ review the effectiveness of your practice in supporting children's learning

▶ think about how your practice could be improved, and make changes if necessary

▶ continually improve the quality of your practice and of the early years provision.

The reflective process

The process of reflection generally consists of different stages that encourage the assessment of a situation. In your own practice, this could be expressed as questions to ask yourself, for example:

▶ What did I do? What happened?

▶ What went well? What didn't go so well?

▶ What could have been improved?

▶ What will I do differently next time?

Here is an example of a reflection from a practitioner engaged in sand play with Scott (aged three years).

What went well: How my practice supported Scott's learning

▶ *I supported Scott's learning by providing wet and dry sand to enable him to explore the different textures and a variety of play. This also helped him to understand the principle of cause and effect when adding water to make wet sand.*

▶ *I provided equipment for both wet and dry sand, for example, buckets, spades, waterwheels, containers and funnels of varying sizes. This made sure that a variety of resources were available for him to choose from, which helped his decision-making skills.*

▶ *I praised and encouraged Scott with language, facial expressions, touch, gestures and Makaton signs to role-model a variety of ways of communicating and to support his own understanding of the language I used.*

Your assessment criteria:

5.1 Reflect on own practice in supporting learning and development of children in their early years

5.2 Demonstrate how to use reflection to make changes in own practice

▶ I repeated and extended Scott's own language to promote understanding and to build on his language skills and vocabulary.

▶ I asked open-ended questions to encourage Scott to use more vocabulary.

What I could have improved

I could have:

▶ encouraged Scott to use all the different-sized containers

▶ provided some alternative resources, such as shells or stones, to add a different dimension to Scott's play

▶ asked Scott what else we could use, to give him a further opportunity to choose and make decisions

▶ used more words to extend Scott's vocabulary, such as 'spinning' and 'turning'.

Using reflection to make changes

The reflective process enables you to analyse your practice and think about changes or improvements you could make. This might relate to your own interactions with children, for example, your verbal or non-verbal communication and use of language, or it may include the provision of more resources, making changes to the planning or adapting the layout in the setting. Reflection is a continuous process and a very important part of professional practice in early years.

Practical Assessment Task   `5.1`   `5.2`

Use the table below as a model to create your own record of reflective practice. Use your chart to record examples of your own effectiveness in supporting children's learning and development. Identify changes you could make to your own practice and make a note of the help you need from others.

Reflection on practice	Evidence	How could I improve?	Things I need help with
Do you observe what children are interested in and what they can do?			
Do you use this information to plan activities and experiences for children?			
Do you prepare, set out and support activities and experiences to encourage children's learning and development?			
Do you engage with children and support sustained shared thinking?			
Do you use language that is accurate and appropriate to support and extend children's learning?			

Are you ready for assessment?

AC	What do you know now?	Assessment task	✓
1.1	Each of the areas of learning and development and how these are interdependent	Page 341	
1.2 1.3	The documented outcomes for children that form part of the relevant early years framework and how these documented outcomes are assessed and recorded	Page 341	

AC	What can you do now?	Assessment task	✓
2.1	Use different sources to plan work for an individual child or group of children Do you have actual examples from your practice that you could discuss with your assessor?	Page 345	
2.2	Engage effectively with children to encourage the child's participation and involvement in planning their own learning and development activities	Page 345	
2.3	Support the planning cycle for children's learning and development Do you have any examples of planning documents that are used in your setting?	Page 345	
3.1	Explain how practitioners promote children's learning within the relevant early years framework Could you discuss this with your assessor?	Page 351	
3.2	Prepare, set out and support activities and experiences that encourage learning and development in each area of the relevant early years framework	Page 351	
4.1	Work alongside children, engaging with them in order to support their learning and development	Page 355	
4.2	Explain the importance of engaging with a child to support sustained shared thinking Do you have actual examples from your practice that you could discuss with your assessor?	Page 355	
4.3	Use language that is accurate and appropriate in order to support and extend children's learning when undertaking activities	Page 355	
5.1	Reflect on own practice in supporting learning and development of children in their early years Could you discuss this with your assessor?	Page 357	
5.2	Demonstrate how to use reflection to make changes in own practice Do you have any examples of this?	Page 357	

14 | Promote children's welfare and wellbeing in the early years (EYMP 3)

Assessment of this unit

This unit describes the regulations that should be followed to ensure that children's welfare and wellbeing are promoted. It includes the basic requirements for a hygienic environment as well as basic nutritional needs and the promotion of health.

The assessment of this unit is partly knowledge-based (things that you need to know about) and partly competence-based (things you need to be able to do in the real work environment or in your placement).

In order to complete this unit successfully, you will need to produce evidence of your knowledge, as shown in the 'What you need to know' chart below, and evidence of your practical competence in the workplace, as shown in the 'What you need to do' chart opposite.

Your tutor or assessor will help you to prepare for your assessment and the tasks suggested in this chapter will help you to create the evidence that you need. Part of this unit will be assessed as a practical assessment in your work setting or placement.

AC	What you need to know
1.1	The welfare requirements and guidance of the relevant early years framework
1.2	The lines of reporting and responsibility within the work setting
3.1	How to promote children's health and wellbeing in an early years work setting
3.2	The roles of key health professionals and sources of professional advice in promoting positive health and wellbeing for early years children and their families and carers
5.1	How to identify balanced meals, snacks and drinks for children in their early years, following current government guidance on nutritional needs
5.2	Why it is important to follow carers' instructions in respect of their child's food allergies or intolerances
5.3	The dietary requirements of different cultural or religious groups
5.4	How to describe methods of educating children and adults in effective food management

CHAPTER 14

AC   What you need to do

2.1   Demonstrate safe supervision of children whilst allowing the child to explore and manage risk and challenge

2.2   Explain systems for supporting children's safety when:
- receiving children into the setting
- ensuring their safety on departure
- during off-site visits

2.3   Demonstrate and evaluate how the environment, both inside and outside, and equipment and materials are checked and used to ensure safety

2.4   Explain, giving examples, why minimum requirements for space and staff ratios are necessary for children's safety

4.1   Demonstrate how equipment and each area of the setting are kept clean and hygienic

4.2   Demonstrate and evaluate measures taken in the setting to prevent cross-infection

4.3   Explain how to prepare and store food, formula and breast milk safely according to health and safety guidelines

6.1   Demonstrate how to support children's personal care routines, showing respect to the child and using opportunities to encourage learning and development

6.2   Explain the regulations concerning management of medicines and how these are interpreted in the work setting

6.3   Explain how to protect yourself when lifting and handling children and equipment in the work setting

---

This unit also links to some of the other mandatory units:

EYMP 1   Context and principles for early years provision

CYP 3.3   Understand how to safeguard the wellbeing of children and young people

EYMP 5   Support children's speech, language and communication

Some of your learning from this unit will be repeated in these units and will therefore give you the chance to review your knowledge and understanding.

Why are welfare requirements important?

As an early years practitioner, it is your responsibility to ensure that children in your care are kept clean and safe. Children's welfare and wellbeing are dependent on a clean and hygienic environment. If these basic needs are not met, children's learning and development can be affected. The welfare requirements make sure that settings abide by strict codes of practice relating to children's health and safety.

Welfare requirements

In England, welfare requirements apply to all types of early years childcare provision and it is a **statutory duty** to comply with them. They can be found in the Statutory Framework for the Early Years Foundation Stage. The opening sentence states: *'Every child deserves the best possible start in life and support to fulfil their potential.'* Care of children to ensure that they achieve their potential starts with the quality of the environment.

The details in this chapter refer to the English requirements. If you live and work in another country within the UK, you must make sure that you learn about the regulations relevant to you as you work through the chapter. However, the general principles here are relevant to all countries within the UK.

Key terms

Statutory duty: legal requirement

Over to you!

▶ *Make sure you have a copy of the welfare requirements relevant to your workplace.*

▶ *Why do you think a legal document like this is necessary?*

Being able to play safely is an important part of children's welfare

Within the Statutory Framework in England there are five main sections, called the general welfare requirements, which are outlined in Figure 14.1. The rest of this chapter will be looking more closely at some aspects of the 'Safeguarding and promoting children's welfare' section and the 'Suitable premises, environment and equipment' section, which all practitioners need to know about and practise.

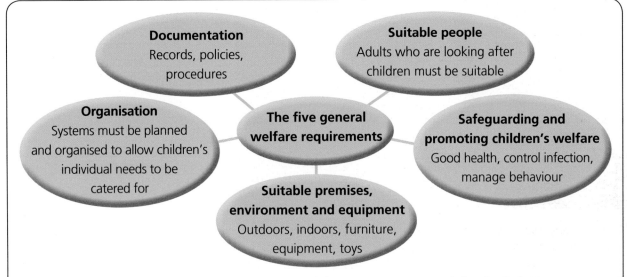

Figure 14.1 The five general welfare requirements of the Statutory Framework for the Early Years Foundation Stage

Lines of reporting

It is important to know the lines of reporting in your setting because you might be unsure of something and need to ask about it, or you might suspect that things are not being done as they should be. The lines of reporting tend to vary according to the size of the setting. In small settings you might go straight to the supervisor or manager with any kind of problem. In larger settings there are usually members of staff allocated to specific roles, such as the special educational needs co-ordinator (SENCo) or the health and safety officer. Practitioners must know the roles and responsibilities of different staff in the setting and should know who to report any concerns to.

Knowledge Assessment Task

Using the relevant welfare requirements for your setting, make a poster for the staffroom to explain the requirements and guidance of the main sections.

Make a flow chart to highlight the staff responsibilities in your setting and explain the lines of reporting and responsibility.

Keep your work as evidence towards your assessment.

How do we make sure children are safe in the setting?

This section looks at the welfare requirements relating to children's safety. Young children are very vulnerable and rely on adults to keep them safe. It is the responsibility of every member of staff to be aware of these requirements and to take an active part in ensuring that they are complied with.

Safe supervision and risk management

Supervision of children does not just mean making sure they are safe; it can also mean encouraging them to be more adventurous, to help them to learn more about themselves and their abilities. The quality and sensitivity of staff interaction and their responses to children are fundamental.

There must be a balance between making sure children are safe and allowing them to take risks. A recent trend has taken health and safety concerns to an extreme and children have been stopped from doing many things in case they hurt themselves. The climate is now becoming more realistic and it is recognised that if we don't allow young children to learn how to measure risk for themselves, they will grow up lacking this vital skill. The compromise is to provide opportunities that challenge children, having first completed a risk assessment that has highlighted any dangers to identify how they will be managed.

When completing risk assessments, it is sensible to consider the risk benefits as well as the dangers. A risk assessment must be a tool that allows adults and children to manage risk in the setting, not a reason to prevent children from experiencing new environments.

Case study

Liam and Enzo are three-year-old boys attending a private nursery school every morning. You have noticed that they both like playing outside, especially with water, but recently, as the days have been getting cooler, some staff have been saying, *'We're not going to take the children out, as they'll get colds,'* and *'We must stop the boys playing with water, as they get their sleeves wet.'*

1. What might be the underlying reasons why some staff are saying these things?

2. Write a balanced risk assessment that will help the staff manage the risks that might be present without over-protecting the children.

3. How can the children be included in the risk management and in making decisions about their environment?

4. Why is it important for the boys to continue to play outside?

5. What would you say to the worried staff to convince them that the boys should still go outside?

Systems for supporting safety

There are some situations that can be dangerous if sufficient consideration is not given to how they are managed. Figure 14.2 outlines three situations when careful supervision is essential.

Figure 14.2 Situations when careful supervision is essential

Situation	Possible dangers	Possible solutions
1. When children arrive at the setting	• No record is kept of which children are on the premises. • Correct staffing ratios are not maintained. • Children find it difficult to leave their parents.	• A member of staff is on duty at the door to welcome and record arrivals. • Parents sign their children in on arrival. • Staff mark the arrival of their key children by welcoming them into the setting.
2. When children leave the setting	• The record of who is in the setting is not kept up to date. • Children can leave the building or premises unseen. • Children may leave with the wrong adult.	• A member of staff opens and closes the door for children and parents to leave. • Staff or parents sign the children out. • A strict procedure is in place so that all staff know who will be taking the children away from the setting.
3. During off-site visits	• Lost children • First aid needs • Emergencies • Extreme weather conditions	• Parents' emergency telephone numbers and first-aid kit are carried at all times. • Risk management document is completed. • Strict procedures are in place for lost children. • High adult/child ratios might be necessary. • Carry extra money. • Make sure all children have suitable protective clothing.

Environment and equipment checks

Assessing the safety of the environment should be a daily habit. The whole of the setting, including resources, furniture, outdoor environment, bathrooms and playroom need to be thoroughly checked on a regular basis to make sure it is safe for the children to use.

However, this is not enough. Each day there must be a visual check of some aspects of the provision to ensure that health and safety issues are addressed. Some settings create a system whereby the children are part of this daily check, using a clipboard and photographs of different areas of the setting.

Particular attention must be given to unusual weather conditions and any new challenges or equipment available for the children to use.

Space and staff ratio requirements

Young children need supervision, which includes making sure they are safe as well as encouraging them to try new challenges. In order to complete this in an efficient way there are minimum requirements for staff ratios for children. Figure 14.3 shows the standards in the English welfare requirements. The younger the children are, the more space they require and the higher the staff ratio.

Your assessment criteria:

2.1 Demonstrate safe supervision of children whilst allowing the child to explore and manage risk and challenge

2.2 Explain systems for supporting children's safety when receiving children into the setting, ensuring their safety on departure and during off-site visits

2.3 Demonstrate and evaluate how the environment, both inside and outside, and equipment and materials are checked and used to ensure safety

2.4 Explain, giving examples, why minimum requirements for space and staff ratios are necessary for children's safety

---

Practical Assessment Task   2.1 2.2 2.3 2.4

To prepare for the practical assessment of this section, you need to make sure that you can demonstrate or talk about:

▶ how you have made sure children stay safe while allowing them to explore and take risks in their play

▶ risk assessment checklists that you have used for part of your work, inside and outside, at the setting, including safety of the environment and equipment

▶ how your setting ensures children's safety at the start and end of a session and during off-site visits

▶ a list of things you would take with you if you were taking children on a trip out of the setting, and why these are important

▶ an understanding of the use of space and the staffing qualifications and ratios in the room in which you work, and why these are necessary.

Your evidence must be based on your practice in a real work environment and must be in a format that is acceptable to your assessor.

Over to you!

If you were in charge of your setting, what daily checks would you want your staff to make on the indoor and outdoor environment? Which of these could the children do themselves? Create a checklist that staff or children could use to show that inspection checks were made on a daily basis.

Key terms

EYPS: early years professional status

PVI: private, voluntary and independent settings

QTS: qualified teacher status

Figure 14.3 Space and staff ratios in the English welfare requirements

Age of children Space requirement	Staff ratio	Additional requirements
Under two years 3.5m² per child	At least one member of staff to three children	One member of staff must hold a Level 3 qualification. Half of all other staff must hold a Level 2 qualification. Half the staff must have training in the care of babies.
Aged two years 2.5m² per child	At least one member of staff to four children	One member of staff must hold a Level 3 qualification. Half of all other staff must hold a Level 2 qualification.
Aged three years and over 2.3m² per child With a person holding **QTS** or **EYPS** present **PVI** or independent schools	At least one adult to 13 children	One other member of staff must hold a Level 3 qualification.
Aged three years and over Without a person holding QTS or EYPS present PVI or independent schools	At least one adult to eight children	One other member of staff must hold a Level 3 qualification. Half of all other staff must hold a Level 2 qualification.
Aged three years and over With a person holding QTS present Maintained nursery class	At least one adult to 13 children	At least one other member of staff must hold a Level 2 qualification.
Aged four years and over Reception classes	At least one teacher to 30 children	
Children with childminders	A maximum of six children under eight years old A maximum of three children under five years old Usually no more than one under two years old	If a child minder employs or works with another child minder, then the numbers on the left apply to both child minders.

Why is it important to promote positive health and wellbeing for children?

The health and wellbeing of children is the responsibility of all adults who care for a child. This is one of the reasons why the staff in the setting should build a good partnership with the children's parents. Positive health and wellbeing are extremely important for children's learning and development (see Chapter 11, page 286). In this context, health refers to the physical state of the children and wellbeing refers to their mental state.

How to promote health and wellbeing

In order to promote health and wellbeing, staff must ensure that children's basic needs are met. (See also Chapter 11, page 286) Those basic needs are summarised in Figure 14.4.

Your assessment criteria:

3.1 Explain how to promote children's health and wellbeing in an early years work setting

Getting enough sleep is important for healthy development

Over to you!

Make a list of the different ways that your setting provides:

▶ *food and water for the children*

▶ *opportunities for exercise, both indoors and outdoors*

▶ *routines to promote good hygiene habits.*

Share your experiences with others in the group.

Figure 14.4 Children's basic needs

Factors		Details
Basic physical needs	Food	Children need high quality, balanced nutrition to meet their growth and developmental needs (see page 376).
	Water	Dehydration in children is a common problem. Ideally, children should be given free access to fresh drinking water at all times, particularly in hot weather.
	Light	Outdoor light is important because sunshine is necessary for the production of vitamin D, which prevents a condition called rickets in children. Light also helps the production of serotonin, which promotes happiness. Experiencing daily light patterns also helps to establish a healthy sleep routine.
	Rest and sleep	The importance of sleep is not yet fully understood, but children who do not get enough sleep become irritable and lack concentration, possibly leading to poor memory function and unstable emotions. Children who do not get enough sleep do not grow properly and can become obese. Settings should have a separate sleeping area for children under two years old.
	Warmth	Indoor rooms should be at temperatures of 18–21°C. Sensible clothing is essential for children's temperature control, as their self-regulating mechanisms are still developing. Hats should be worn in cold weather in winter and in hot sun in summer. Waterproof clothing should be available so that children can play outdoors whatever the weather.
	Fresh air	Fresh air provides children with more oxygen and reduces the spread of infection. Children who spend time outdoors get fewer colds than those who spend a lot of time indoors.
	Exercise	Exercise is important for the development of the heart and other muscles and for lung capacity. Children may lack exercise because adults worry about traffic or stranger danger, but this is likely to contribute to the number of children being overweight and unfit. As described under light, exercise stimulates the production of serotonin, promoting mental wellbeing.
Health and hygiene needs	Hygiene	Children need to be clean and to develop good hygiene habits to prevent illness and infection (see page 372).
	Security	Children need a secure environment to gain confidence in their surroundings and ultimately in themselves. This security can come from being with familiar adults with whom they form strong attachments (see page 370) and by following a familiar daily routine.
	Love and affection	Once a child's basic needs are catered for and they have an hygienic and secure environment, they will only thrive if they receive love and affection. The mental health this promotes will compliment the physical health achieved if all the factors above are in place, leading to the best possible environment for children to begin to learn.

Attachment

In the 1950s John Bowlby developed his theory of attachment describing the emotional relationship between children and adults. He believed that a child's secure attachment to their mother is essential for mental health and subsequent development. He believed that 60 per cent of attachments between mothers and their children were secure, a figure that has been confirmed by scientists today. Insecure attachments can result in children displaying separation anxiety when leaving their parents, and can ultimately lead to poor life chances (see Chapter 5, page 144).

It is possible for children to have secure attachments to more than one adult. When we look after children in our settings we must be committed to form close, secure attachments to the children in our care. This responsibility is so important that staff are often given the role of being a key person to a child.

The key person role involves getting to know the child as well as possible and building up a strong positive relationship with the child's parents or carers. The handover time on arrival and departure is crucial in order to guarantee that a child's health and wellbeing are maximised.

Key health professionals

There are many other professionals who might have an input into the care and development of the children in your setting. To know the child well, it is essential to have a good relationship with other professionals and be prepared to signpost parents to the person who can help them. The work of some key professionals is outlined below.

▶ *General practitioners* are doctors based in a surgery or health centre and have a responsibility for the general health of registered patients in their local community.

▶ *Health visitors* work from health centres and visit families in their own homes. They have a responsibility for the health and development of children under the age of five.

▶ *Family outreach workers* are usually based at children's centres and provide support for vulnerable children and families in their own homes.

Your assessment criteria:

3.1 Explain how to promote children's health and wellbeing in an early years work setting

3.2 Describe the roles of key health professionals and sources of professional advice in promoting positive health and wellbeing for early years children and their families and carers

Forming secure attachments with adults is necessary for stable and healthy emotional development

▶ *Paediatricians* are based in hospitals and specialise in all childhood health problems.

▶ *Educational psychologists* provide assessment and support for children with special educational needs, including behavioural difficulties.

▶ *Speech and language therapists* provide assessment and support for children with speech, language or communication difficulties (SLCD).

▶ *Physiotherapists* provide assessment and support for children with movement or coordination difficulties.

▶ *Dieticians* provide advice about nutrition.

▶ *Ophthalmologists* and *opticians* provide assessment and support for children with visual problems.

Paediatricians specilise in childhood health issues

Case study

Emma works in a very large day nursery in an urban area of a large city. Three children from the same family attend the setting: Sally is eight months old, William is two years old and Jessica is four years old. Their mother recently returned to work and is always in a hurry when she drops off the children, and she generally appears stressed. Emma has some concerns about each of the children.

▶ William is having difficulty settling when he arrives each morning and staff are worried that he has a language delay.

▶ Sally always has a runny nose, finds it difficult to sleep during the day and is difficult to comfort.

▶ Jessica is very energetic and becomes irritable and impatient when she has been inside the building for a long time.

1. Why is it important for Emma to discuss her concerns with the children's mother?

2. Describe how other professionals may be able to support the health and wellbeing of these children.

Knowledge Assessment Task   3.1   3.2

Create an information leaflet or webpage for new learners in your setting which:

▶ explains the importance of promoting positive health and wellbeing for children

▶ describes the roles of key health professionals and sources of professional advice in promoting positive health and wellbeing for children and their families.

Keep your written work as evidence towards your assessment.

Why is hygiene important in the early years setting?

Young children are vulnerable to infection and good hygiene is essential to protect them from illness and promote good health. In a setting where there are groups of very young children together, the prevention of cross-infection is important as these children are still developing their immune system, and infection can easily spread from one child to another. This section examines the importance of a clean environment, ways to prevent cross-infection and the safe storage of food and milk.

Cleanliness of equipment and the setting

The environment contains many different kinds of organism and some of these are harmful to the health of young children. The word 'germs' refers to different type of harmful organisms such as bacteria and viruses, which can spread rapidly if the environment is not clean and hygienic.

Some areas and equipment in the setting need special attention in order to maintain a clean and hygienic environment, as outlined in Figure 14.5.

Figure 14.5 Ways to maintain a clean and hygienic environment

Areas and equipment	Ways to keep them clean and hygienic
Floors	Clean spillages immediately and mop or vacuum daily.
Tables and work surfaces	Disinfect at least once a day and after the presence of food.
Toys and play equipment	Clean and disinfect on a regular basis.
Feeding equipment	Clean thoroughly after each use.
Soft toys and dressing-up clothes	Machine wash on a regular basis.
Waste bins	Empty frequently and disinfect daily.
Fridges and cupboards	Disinfect on a weekly basis.
Nappy changing areas	Disinfect after each nappy change.
Outdoor environment	Check daily for animal faeces.

Measures taken to prevent cross-infection

Germs are spread in different ways and it is important to understand how to prevent infection spreading from one child to another.

Airborne or droplet (breathing in): many germs are spread through the air. When someone coughs or sneezes, their germs spray

Your assessment criteria:

4.1 Demonstrate how equipment and each area of the setting are kept clean and hygienic

4.2 Demonstrate and evaluate measures taken in the setting to prevent cross-infection

Key terms

Bacteria: unicellular microorganisms, occurring everywhere; some are harmful and some are helpful

Cross-infection: when infection is spread from one child to another

out into the air around them and can easily infect other people. Measures that help to prevent this include:

▶ making sure the setting is well-ventilated and keeping windows slightly open if possible

▶ encouraging children to cover their mouths or use tissues when they cough or sneeze, and have tissues available throughout the setting for children to help themselves

▶ making 'tissue tables' with mirrors, tissues, hand-washing bowls, baby wipes, antibacterial liquid or soap and paper towels for children to access freely. Encourage children to dispose of their tissues appropriately.

Ingested (swallowed): some germs can be spread through touching them and putting them into our mouths. Measures that help to prevent this include:

▶ keeping surfaces and toys clean and disinfected

▶ encouraging children in good hand-washing procedures – after using the toilet, before and after eating, after coughing or sneezing or after playing outdoors

▶ making sure food is hygienically prepared.

Through the skin: sometimes germs can move directly from one person to another through cuts or grazes to the skin. This can be minimised by:

▶ covering our own cuts with a plaster or suitable dressing

▶ wearing disposable gloves when dealing with children's cuts and grazes, treating them promptly and covering them with a suitable dressing.

Another very important way of preventing cross-infection in the workplace is for the setting to have a clear and effective health and hygiene policy. This should include information for parents about the importance of not bringing their child to the setting if the child is ill.

When dealing with more serious diseases, guidance from the Department of Health should always be followed. There is a published list of notifiable diseases, their incubation times and the recommended isolation period. It is important for practitioners to be familiar with different diseases and to understand the policies and procedures in the setting.

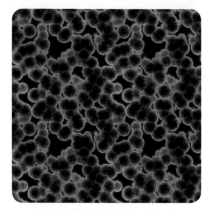

Bacteria seen through a microscope

Key terms

Incubation time: the time between exposure to an organism and when symptoms and signs are first apparent

Immune system: a system in the body that can destroy or neutralise various germs, poisons and other foreign substances

Isolation period: the time when a disease is infectious and children should not mix with others

Notifiable disease: a disease that is required by law to be reported to government authorities

Organism: a living thing that has the ability to act or function independently

Virus: a small contagious organism that can replicate only inside the cells of other organisms

Over to you!

Think about the routine cleaning procedures in your placement or work setting. What special precautions are taken for babies and toddlers? Share your experiences with others in the group.

Food storage

Many germs live on and in the food we eat. Some are very dangerous and, if allowed to multiply, can result in food poisoning. This can be extremely serious for young children and in some cases can even be fatal. Some foods are more likely to harbour germs than others, including raw meat and fish, fruit and vegetables. Practitioners involved in preparing snacks or meals for children should have attended basic food hygiene training.

The spread of infection can be minimised by taking the following precautions.

- Wash your hands well before starting to prepare food.
- Wear an apron and keep long hair tied back.
- Avoid coughing or sneezing near food.
- Buy fresh food from a reputable provider.
- Wash fruit and vegetables before using them for snacks or meals.
- Don't use food after its use-by date.
- Don't refreeze food after it has been thawed.
- Store food in the fridge at 0–5°C if it needs to be kept cold.
- Wrap food with plastic film or tin foil once opened.
- Use separate implements and boards when preparing raw meat, fish and poultry.
- Cook all raw meat, fish and poultry thoroughly before serving them.
- Keep raw food separate from cooked food.
- Cover cuts with plasters or gloves.
- Wash all kitchen linen thoroughly and often.
- Wash and disinfect surfaces after food preparation.

Preparing and storing formula milk

The Department of Health recommends that formula milk should be freshly made up each time it is required, rather than made up in advance and stored. This is important in preventing infection as warm milk is an ideal breeding ground for bacteria. If facilities for making up the formula milk are not available, for example, when going on an outing, then it is a good idea to take a flask of hot water and make up the milk when it is required. The bottles used for formula milk need cleaning thoroughly and sterilising after each feed. Never store any left over formula milk for use later.

Many foods need to be stored in a fridge to stay fresh

Storing breast milk

Sometimes parents bring in breast milk that has been expressed for the baby to drink during the day. This milk can be stored in the fridge for up to five days or in the freezer compartment of a fridge for up to two weeks. Breast milk that has been frozen should be thoroughly defrosted before use and any leftover milk should be thrown away.

Practical Assessment Task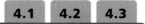

This section must be assessed in your placement or workplace. Before assessment, make sure you are able to demonstrate the required skills as listed in the table below.

Your evidence must be based on your practice in a real work environment and must be in a format that is acceptable to your assessor.

4.1 Demonstrate how equipment and each area of the setting are kept clean and hygienic	Be competent in keeping the following areas of the setting clean. Be able to talk about how and why cleanliness is necessary in each area: • toys and equipment • bathroom • nappy changing tables • kitchen • surfaces, tables and floors.
4.2 Demonstrate and evaluate measures taken in the setting to prevent cross-infection	Understand the meaning of 'cross-infection'. Know how germs can be passed from one person/child to another. Know how to prevent cross-infection in each case. Be able to discuss how well your setting manages to control cross-infection. Discuss if any improvements could be made.
4.3 Explain how to prepare and store food, formula and breast milk safely according to health and safety guidelines	Be able to demonstrate your knowledge of good practice in preparing and storing food. Be able to prepare children's snacks to demonstrate your understanding practically. Recognise the potential dangers and how to prevent them. Know how to make up and store formula milk. Understand the need for sterilisation and how to manage using formula milk when you are away from the setting. Know the most recent guidelines for storing breast milk.

Understand how to ensure children in their early years receive high quality, balanced nutrition to meet their growth and development needs

Why is balanced nutrition important?

Children should always be encouraged to eat healthy food and establish sensible eating patterns. Healthy eating habits can be developed from a very young age and are very important in preventing **obesity** and controlling other related health problems, such as **diabetes**.

Balanced nutrition is important for young children who are growing quickly and have high energy levels and requirements. It supports good dental health and can establish life-long healthy eating habits.

Childhood obesity is a concern of modern times with many factors being blamed for its increase.

- ▶ Watching television and playing computer games reduce the time spent doing physical exercise.

- ▶ There is parental fear about the safety of children outdoors, either from strangers or traffic.

- ▶ There is poor understanding about the nature of a well-balanced diet.

- ▶ There are high levels of advertising of unhealthy foods through the media.

- ▶ Families living in poverty find some healthier foods expensive.

A balanced diet for children

All people need to follow a balanced diet of food and drink in order to stay healthy. A balanced diet is a diet containing the correct quantities of different types of foods that contain different **nutrients**. The types of food needed are illustrated in Figure 14.6.

Figure 14.6 Types of food and drink that make up a balanced diet

Type of food or drink	Nutrients
Meat, fish, eggs, dairy products, beans	Provide protein for muscle development and strength.
Fresh vegetables and fruit	Provide vitamins and minerals for normal general development, protection from disease and roughage (fibre) for good digestion.
Bread, pasta, potatoes, rice	Provide carbohydrates for energy.
Butter, oils and meat	Provide fat for energy and for digesting some vitamins.
Water	Replaces the water lost through excretion.

Key terms

Diabetes: a condition characterised by a high blood sugar (glucose) level as a result of the body not producing enough insulin

Nutrients: substances an organism needs to live and grow well, which must be taken in from its environment

Obesity: weighing more than 20% (for men) or 25% (for women) over ideal weight as determined by height and build

Unbalanced diets

Children's diets can become unbalanced because they:

▶ eat or drink too many sugary foods, which can lead to obesity and tooth decay

▶ eat lots of ready meals that contain high levels of salt, which can cause raised blood pressure, even in children

▶ eat insufficient vegetables or fruit, which means they do not have adequate protection against disease or do not show normal development

▶ eat insufficient protein, which means their muscles do not develop strength

▶ eat too many fatty foods, which can lead to obesity

▶ are not given free access to drinking water, which can lead to dehydration.

Figure 14.7 shows the relative proportions of the different foods that children should be eating. When providing snacks and meals for children, we need to make sure they are getting the correct proportions of different food types that make up a balanced diet.

It is important to confirm the contents of packaged food by checking the ingredients on the label. The main factors to look out for are the fat and salt content, and the **calorific content** of the food which tells you how much energy it will provide.

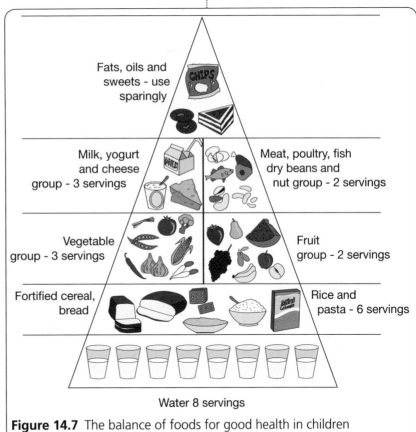

Figure 14.7 The balance of foods for good health in children

Fats, oils and sweets - use sparingly

Milk, yogurt and cheese group - 3 servings

Meat, poultry, fish dry beans and nut group - 2 servings

Vegetable group - 3 servings

Fruit group - 2 servings

Fortified cereal, bread

Rice and pasta - 6 servings

Water 8 servings

Key terms

Calorific content: the number of calories or units of energy contained in a substance

Case study

At Little Ducklings nursery, the children receive snacks provided by the setting in the morning and afternoon and the children have free access to fresh drinking water at all times. If the children stay for lunch, the parents are asked to provide a packed lunch.

Two children from the same family consistently bring lunch boxes with the following items:

▶ a packet of crisps

▶ a fizzy drink

▶ a chocolate bar

▶ a small packet of biscuits

▶ a jam sandwich.

1. What are the major types of food represented in these boxes?
2. What types of foods are missing?
3. If the children continue with this lunchtime diet, what might be the consequences?
4. What foods might you suggest the parents include instead?

Your assessment criteria:

5.1 Identify balanced meals, snacks and drinks for children in their early years, following current government guidance on nutritional needs

Food conditions, allergies and intolerances

Parents may tell you about their children's special dietary requirements and these should always be carefully recorded. Food allergies and intolerances can lead to short- or long-term problems for children and in some cases can even be fatal. Some examples of food conditions, allergies and intolerances and the special care required are highlighted in Figure 14.8.

Figure 14.8 Food conditions, allergies and intolerances which require special care

Condition, allergy or intolerance	Requirements	Dangers
Diabetes: this is a condition that means children cannot digest sugars properly. As all carbohydrates are changed to sugar in the body, these children will therefore not be getting energy from their food.	Children with diabetes need daily injections of insulin to help them digest sugar. They also need a carefully controlled diet, which the parents will tell you about. Snacks and meals should not contain excessive sugar.	Children may take in too few carbohydrates and can become unconscious. If this happens, make sure they receive something sugary immediately, such as a sugary drink, glucose sweets or chocolate. (The parents will usually tell you what is best to use.)
Peanut allergy: this can produce various levels of reaction in any of the following symptoms: • swelling or puffiness around the eyes or lips • redness of the face or neck • itching • difficulty in breathing.	If the parents tell you that their child has a peanut allergy, you must make sure that nothing containing peanuts is present in the setting. Notices in the food preparation room and letters to all parents asking for no foods containing peanuts to be put in any children's lunch boxes are a minimum requirement.	If children experience a very severe reaction to eating or coming into contact with peanuts or peanut products, they can die after going into a condition called anaphylactic shock (anaphylaxis). You can receive special training on how to use an EpiPen, which gives the child a shot of adrenalin.
Coeliac disease: this condition is caused by an allergy to gluten, which is contained in wheat, rye, barley and oats. It causes short-term discomfort in the abdomen, but has more serious long-term consequences, as food cannot be digested correctly.	These children should not be given any foods containing gluten. Packages are well-labelled nowadays, so always check the ingredients before giving a commercial product to a child.	This condition is not life threatening. However, gluten is present in many foods, which you might not expect, so be careful. Gluten-free products are available, so children should not be excluded from taking part in cooking activities.
Food intolerances: children can be intolerant to different foods such as dairy products or those containing gluten.	Avoid giving children foods they have an intolerance for and make sure all staff providing food are well informed of children's dietary requirements.	Most food intolerances are not life threatening, but can lead to diarrhoea, vomiting or abdominal discomfort.

Cultural or religious dietary requirements

As well as food allergies, there are other circumstances when children's diets may need to differ from those of others.

▶ **Vegetarian** households do not eat meat or poultry and some do not eat fish either. Vegetarian diets are healthy, but you must listen carefully to the parents about how they would like you to provide a balanced diet for their child.

▶ **Vegan** diets are more restrictive and no animal products are eaten at all. Vegan diets are not recommended for children.

▶ **Muslim** families do not eat pork. Other meats and fish have to be prepared according to dietary laws. All food that is allowed to be eaten by Muslims is called **halal**.

▶ **Jewish** families also do not eat pork and they do not eat shellfish either. Their food is also prepared according to dietary laws and is called **kosher**.

▶ **Hindu** families do not eat beef and are mainly vegetarian, although some Hindu communities do eat fish and some meat.

Muslim and Jewish families observe a fasting time each year although young children are not expected to fast.

Effective food management

With the recent concerns about children's weight problems, it is essential to teach children to manage their food intake. Too much food and insufficient exercise can lead to obesity, but an obsession with children's weight can also lead to children being undernourished and therefore underweight. Children need a well-balanced diet to meet their growth and development needs (see page 376).

Your assessment criteria:

5.1 Identify balanced meals, snacks and drinks for children in their early years, following current government guidance on nutritional needs

5.2 Recognise why it is important to follow carers' instructions in respect of their child's food allergies or intolerances

5.3 Identify the dietary requirements of different cultural or religious groups

5.4 Describe methods of educating children and adults in effective food management

Key terms

Halal: any object or action that is permissible to use or engage in, according to Islamic law

Hindu: a person who adheres to Hinduism

Jewish: relating to Jews or their culture or religion

Kosher: food that fulfils the requirements of Jewish dietary law

Muslim: a believer in or follower of Islam

Vegan: someone who eats no animal or dairy products at all

If parents know approximately how much children should weigh, they can keep a check on this. It is not unusual for children to have preferences for foods but it is always a good idea to put a little of everything on a child's plate. Fussy eating is not usually healthy and can be perpetuated by adults offering too many choices to children when they are eating. If children are becoming fussy, try to present a variety of foods in different ways so they get used to different tastes and different textures. If possible, let children choose how much food they want to put on their plates.

If children are not following a healthy diet or eat too little or too much or are noticeably underweight or overweight, a visit to the doctor is a sensible recommendation.

Key terms

Vegetarian: someone who follows a plant-based diet, with or without dairy products and eggs

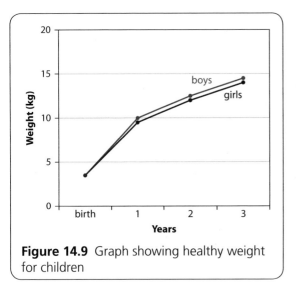

Figure 14.9 Graph showing healthy weight for children

Figure 14.10 Healthy weight and height by age and gender

Sex	Age	Weight (kg)	Height (cm)
Girls	Birth	3.5	50
	1 year	9.5	74
	2 years	12	85
	3 years	14	95
Boys	Birth	3.5	52
	1 year	10	75
	2 years	12.5	87
	3 years	14.5	96

Knowledge Assessment Task   5.1 5.2 5.3 5.4

Imagine that you are the cook in a multicultural early years setting, including children from the Muslim community. All the children receive cooked meals for lunch and one Muslim child in the pre-school room has a nut allergy.

1. Create menus (Monday to Friday) for the children's morning and afternoon snacks and lunches, making sure they are receiving a balanced diet.

2. Identify how you would follow government guidelines on nutritional needs for the children.

3. Describe why it is important to follow carers' instructions relating to food allergies and intolerances.

4. Identify the dietary requirements of different cultural or religious groups.

5. Describe how you might educate children and adults in effective food management.

Keep your work as evidence towards your assessment.

Over to you!

Health visitors will use percentile charts and graphs to monitor children's growth. Using the percentile charts at your placement or work setting, plot the growth of some of the children you work with.

Over to you!

▶ *What different eating habits are you aware of within your peer group?*

▶ *Discuss where these originate and how some might be dangerous for very young children.*

Be able to provide physical care for children

Why is physical care important?

Physical care is very important for the basic needs of all children. Good general hygiene, keeping clean and taking care of children's skin, hair and teeth are all part of personal care routines. Young children will develop independence through learning how to wash themselves, go to the toilet and brush their own teeth. These regular routines will help them to establish good hygiene habits for life.

As well as providing a balanced diet for children, practitioners have to provide physical care for children. This section discusses some of the most common types of physical care for children. It is important for children's self-esteem that they are encouraged and enabled to take responsibility for their own physical care as soon as possible.

Supporting children's physical care routines

The main aspects of physical care routines are summarised in Figure 14.11 (opposite).

Independence and self-care

It is important to balance the need to help a child with the need for them to become independent, and practitioners need to use sensitive encouragement, particularly with tasks such as:

- dressing and undressing
- using aprons
- toileting
- choosing resources, both indoors and outdoors
- eating, preparing a snack, laying and clearing the table
- hand washing
- risk monitoring
- tidying up.

Your assessment criteria:

6.1 Demonstrate how to support children's personal care routines, showing respect to the child and using opportunities to encourage learning and development

Figure 14.11 The main aspects of physical care routines

Hand washing	Children should be taught to wash their hands before and after eating, after using the toilet, before preparing food and after playing outside. Do not presume that children know how to wash their hands well; be ready to show them how to use running warm water, soap and paper towels.
Toileting	This is a sensitive topic and should always be handled with respect, following the policies of the setting. As soon as possible, it is important that children are allowed to go to the toilet by themselves; however, young children may need help with wiping their bottoms and deal with their clothing. If there is any problem with this, a discussion with the parents is sensible.
Skin care	The most important factor here is that children are not exposed to too strong sunlight as sunburn can lead to skin cancer later in life in extreme cases. Sun cream provided by the parent should be applied and sun hats used whenever children are outside on a sunny day.
Hair and teeth	Children can be taught about the need to keep their bodies clean, particularly their hair and teeth. You can ask parents to bring in toothbrushes so that children can learn to brush their own teeth, but do not presume that children will know how to do this and give help and guidance if necessary.
Nappy changing	Nappies should be changed whenever necessary for the individual child in order to maintain comfort and prevent nappy rash. Parents may provide special cream to use.
Dressing and undressing	At every opportunity, such as playing outside, visiting the toilet or using dressing-up clothes, encourage children to start to dress and undress themselves (even though it may be quicker to dress the children yourself). Being able to dress themselves will boost children's self-esteem.

Over to you!

► Talk to the members of your group about how easy or how difficult you find it to help children with putting on their coats or shoes.

► How do you balance the child's need to develop independence with your need to get everyone dressed in as short a time as possible?

Managing medicines

There may be circumstances in a setting when a child is well enough to attend but needs to take prescribed medication or when they routinely need prescribed medicine. Figure 14.12 highlights some situations you might experience.

Figure 14.12 Situations that require administering medication

Condition	Treatment	Comments
Diabetes	Children might need insulin injections or emergency sugar supplies.	Parents might show you how to inject or come into the setting to do the injection themselves. Always keep sugar supplies available.
Asthma	Parents will provide an asthma inhaler and will tell you exactly when and how much to use.	Asthma inhalers often look the same so make sure each one is clearly labelled with the child's name, out of reach but to hand for emergencies.
Anaphylactic shock (anaphylaxis)	Injection of adrenalin via an EpiPen	You can receive special training on how to use an EpiPen.
Some infections	Prescribed antibiotics	Follow the instructions carefully, using a timer to remind you if necessary.

Some rules regarding administering prescribed medication

▶ Always follow the setting's policy and procedure for administering medicines.

▶ Obtain written information from parents about what the child is taking and why, when to take it and how much to give.

▶ Always record accurately how much medicine has been given, when it was given and who gave it.

▶ Keep medicines in their original box, well labelled, out of the reach of children and in the fridge if necessary.

Lifting and handling children and equipment

When working with children under five years old, it's likely that you will have to lift them up sometimes. If heavy things are not lifted correctly, you can damage your back. Lifting and manual handling training is regularly offered under health and safety law.

Your setting will have a policy and procedure for manual handling and it is important that this is always followed.

Your assessment criteria:

6.1 Demonstrate how to support children's personal care routines, showing respect to the child and using opportunities to encourage learning and development

6.2 Explain the regulations concerning management of medicines and how these are interpreted in the work setting

6.3 Explain how to protect yourself when lifting and handling children and equipment in the work setting

Over to you!

▶ *Talk to a partner about the different medication procedures you have been asked to adhere to in your placement or work setting so far.*

▶ *How are these recorded in your setting? Is the system effective?*

Good habits when lifting

ALWAYS:

▶ think carefully before lifting or moving anything heavy

▶ ask someone for assistance if you think something might be too heavy

▶ reduce the weight of the equipment if possible, for example, by taking some things out of the box

▶ bend your knees, place your feet apart and lift using your leg muscles but keeping your back straight when you are lifting anything from the floor.

NEVER:

▶ lift anything heavy with your back bent

▶ twist or turn while you are lifting anything heavy.

| Practical Assessment Task | 6.1 | 6.2 | 6.3 |

Be ready to demonstrate the following in your placement or work setting:

1. how to support children in eating, dressing, washing their hands and using the toilet while helping to develop their independence and self-respect

2. that you can confidently discuss the medicine management policy and procedure in the setting

3. how to lift a child or a piece of heavy equipment in order to protect yourself.

Your evidence for this task must be based on your practice in a real work environment and must be in a format that is acceptable to your assessor.

Are you ready for assessment?

AC	What do you know now?	Assessment task	✓
1.1	The welfare requirements and guidance of the relevant early years framework	Page 363	
1.2	The lines of reporting and responsibility within the work setting	Page 363	
3.1	How to promote children's health and wellbeing in an early years work setting	Page 371	
3.2	The roles of key health professionals and sources of professional advice in promoting positive health and wellbeing for early years children and their families and carers	Page 371	
5.1	How to identify balanced meals, snacks and drinks for children in their early years, following current government guidance on nutritional needs	Page 381	
5.2	Why it is important to follow carers' instructions in respect of their child's food allergies or intolerances	Page 381	
5.3	The dietary requirements of different cultural or religious groups	Page 381	
5.4	How to describe methods of educating children and adults in effective food management	Page 381	

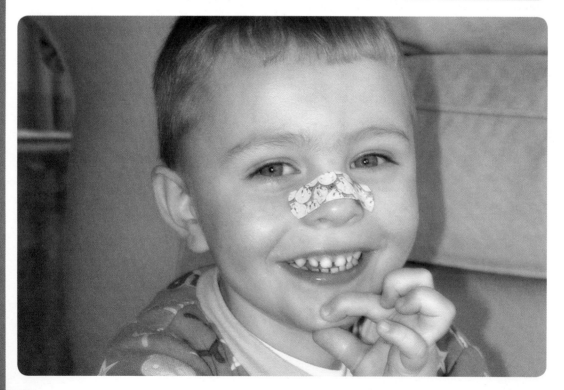

Your tutor or assessor may want to observe you actually doing this in your placement or work setting.

AC	What can you do now?	Assessment task	✓
2.1	Demonstrate safe supervision of children whilst allowing the child to explore and manage risk and challenge	Page 366	
2.2	Explain systems for supporting children's safety when: • receiving children into the setting • ensuring their safety on departure • during off-site visits	Page 366	
2.3	Demonstrate and evaluate how the environment, both inside and outside, and equipment and materials are checked and used to ensure safety	Page 366	
2.4	Explain, giving examples, why minimum requirements for space and staff ratios are necessary for children's safety	Page 366	
4.1	Demonstrate how equipment and each area of the setting are kept clean and hygienic	Page 375	
4.2	Demonstrate and evaluate measures taken in the setting to prevent cross-infection	Page 375	
4.3	Explain how to prepare and store food, formula and breast milk safely according to health and safety guidelines	Page 375	
6.1	Demonstrate how to support children's personal care routines, showing respect to the child and using opportunities to encourage learning and development	Page 385	
6.2	Explain the regulations concerning management of medicines and how these are interpreted in the work setting	Page 385	
6.3	Explain how to protect yourself when lifting and handling children and equipment in the work setting	Page 385	

15 | Professional practice in early years settings (EYMP 4)

Assessment of this unit

This unit describes the competence required to apply principles and values in everyday work. It begins with a description of the present climate in early years provision, and considers the nature of professional practice, the need to reflect and review and the importance of evidence-based practice. The unit requires a focused approach to the development of strategies to aid professional development, especially in challenging areas.

The assessment of this unit is partly knowledge-based (things that you need to know about) and partly competence-based (things you need to be able to do in the real work environment or in your placement).

In order to complete this unit successfully, you will need to produce evidence of your knowledge, as shown in the 'What you need to know' chart opposite, and evidence of your practical competence in the workplace, as shown in the 'What you need to do' chart, also opposite.

Your tutor or assessor will help you to prepare for your assessment and the tasks suggested in this chapter will help you to create the evidence you that need. Part of this unit is assessed as a practical assessment in your workplace.

CHAPTER 15

AC   What you need to know

1.1	How the range of early years settings reflects the scope and purpose of the sector
2.1	The current policies, frameworks and influences on the early years
2.2	The impact of the current policies, frameworks and influences on the early years sector
2.3	What is meant by evidence-based practice and examples of how this has influenced work with children in their early years
3.1	The meaning of diversity, inclusion and participation
3.2	The importance of anti-discriminatory/anti-bias practice and examples of how it is applied in practice with children and carers
3.3	How the active participation of the children in decisions affecting their lives promotes the achievement of positive outcomes

AC   What you need to do

4.1	Explain the importance of reviewing your own practice as part of being an effective practitioner
4.2	Undertake a reflective analysis of your own practice
4.3	Develop strategies to deal with areas of difficulty and challenges encountered in professional practice in your early years setting

This unit also links to some of the other mandatory units:

CYP 3.7	Understand how to support positive outcomes for children and young people
EYMP 1	Context and principles for early years provision
EYMP 3	Promote children's welfare and wellbeing in the early years

Some of your learning from this unit will be repeated in these units and will therefore give you the chance to review your knowledge and understanding.

The importance now placed on the early years sector and its value in child development means that there is a greater responsibility for staff to become well educated and demonstrate a professional attitude in the workplace. The new early years professional status is raising the standards of work in the early years and, as a result, the quality of provision is gradually rising.

Your assessment criteria:

1.1 Explain how the range of early years settings reflects the scope and purpose of the sector

What is the scope and purpose of the early years sector?

It is only recently, since the publication of specific research, that the early years sector has been given greater status. With the rise in universally better education for women and expectations for women's futures in employment, childcare issues have become more important, as they were during the Second World War when women had to go out to work. Nowadays, many women have jobs to contribute to the family income, and therefore the need for a wide range of childcare options has reappeared.

While these social changes have been taking place, there has also been an expansion of research into the early years. All the current research into the importance of good early years care and education reveals how much of a difference high-quality early years provision has in promoting positive outcomes for children.

The purpose of the early years sector

As a result of the present social climate and academic evidence about the importance of good early years provision, the early years sector in Britain has developed a wide range of provision to cater for differing needs. The purpose of early years provision is to promote the positive outcomes for children as described in Every Child Matters (ECM) to raise the achievement and the life chances for all children (see Chapter 11, page 286).

The variety of provision reflects the differing needs of parents today, but all should be aiming to promote positive outcomes for children. Parents have a wide choice and they will need to consider factors such as:

▶ their need for full-time or sessional care

▶ whether they want to stay with their children or not

▶ whether they want their children to be in larger or smaller groups, or in a home-based setting

▶ their need for regular or intermittent care

▶ their preference for formal or informal care

▶ their ability to pay.

All provision varies according to the type of setting it belongs to. It is recommended that parents visit settings before they make their choices about where to send their children.

Funding

In an attempt to enable all parents to access high-quality early years care, the government in England provides funding to support free nursery places for all three and four-year-old children for 15 hours a week. In addition, there has been a trial to fund the most disadvantaged two-year-old children to attend settings and it is expected that this funding trial will be expanded in the near future.

The scope of the early years sector

Figure 15.1 shows the variety of types of setting available in Britain today. To cater for everyone's needs, they all differ considerably in how and when they are run.

Figure 15.1 The different types of childcare settings in Britain

Parent and toddler groups	These groups are sessional and take babies to two or three years. They are parent or voluntarily run, and parents stay with their children. They have very low charges.
Pre-school playgroups	These groups are sessional and take children to two or four years. They are committee run and are free for three- and four-year-olds and some 2-year-olds.
Crèches	These are sessional and take babies to four years. They are run by a private company. There may be charges or they may be provided free by an employer.
Nursery schools	These provide all-day or sessional provision and take children from three months to four years. They are usually privately owned. Parents are charged, but they do also accept the free entitlement.
Children's centres	These are sessional and take children from birth to four years. They are run by the local authority and parents stay with their children. There are no charges.
Nursery classes in schools	These are sessional and take children from two to four years. They are run by a state or private company. They are free for three- and four-year-olds and some two-year-olds in state schools and private schools.
Reception classes in schools	These operate school hours and take four- and five-year-olds. They are run by a state or private company. They are free in state schools, but there are charges in private schools.
Child minders	Child minders are sessional or run all day and take children from birth to four years. They are privately run. They charge parents, but some accept the free entitlement.

Over to you!

Did you attend any kind of early years provision as a child?

▶ *Do you remember anything about it?*

▶ *With a partner, discuss which type of setting you are working in and why parents might choose to use your setting and why they might not.*

Knowledge Assessment Task   1.1

Produce an illustrated information leaflet for new parents explaining the purpose of the early years sector and informing them of the range of provision that is available.

Keep your work as evidence towards your assessment.

What are the influences on the early years sector?

The fact that the early years of children's lives are the most important years of their education and development is slowly being recognised. The government has funded early years education since 1996 and is increasing its investment now to include more disadvantaged two-year-olds. This indicates how much importance is placed on this early learning stage.

Current policies

Our work with children is shaped and guided by legislative policies and two of the most important of these are described below.

1. In 1989, the General Assembly of the United Nations adopted the Convention on the Rights of the Child, which has been fundamental guidance for work with children since then. It sets out the agreed basic rights of all children in the countries that sign up to it. Article 2 states

   'The convention applies to everyone, whatever their nation, race, colour, sex, religion, abilities, opinion, wealth or social position'

   and this can be related to all five current outcomes for children to be found in the Every Child Matters document.

2. In October 2010, the Equality Act was introduced, which replaced seven other acts to deliver a simple discrimination law designed to protect individuals from unfair treatment and to promote a fair and more equal society. This law protects people from discrimination, harassment and victimisation to ensure that everyone has the same chances to do what they can.

There are many influences on the provision of childcare, including government policy and social trends. Some examples are given below.

Your assessment criteria:

2.1 Identify current policies, frameworks and influences on the early years

2.2 Explain the impact of current policies, frameworks and influences on the early years sector

2.3 Describe what is meant by evidence-based practice and give examples of how this has influenced work with children in their early years

Reading research papers and policy documents gives a thorough understanding of the evidence on which practice is based

Government policies such as The Social Inclusion and Anti-poverty Act 2009 (web2.gov.mb.ca/bills/39-3/b204e.php):

▶ aims to reduce the number of families receiving benefit by getting people back into work, in an attempt to reduce the level of child poverty in Britain – for young parents to be able to work there must be good childcare provision

▶ is attempting to enable all people, whatever their personal circumstances, to take advantage of available opportunities – this was the policy behind the introduction of Sure Start Children's Centres.

Social trends, such as women's higher expectations for careers and incomes and women as lone parents, have also had an influence on current thinking.

Frameworks

In Chapter 12, page 310, there is a full description of the early years frameworks used in the four countries in the UK. The regional governments of England, Northern Ireland, Scotland and Wales have all produced such frameworks to:

▶ provide a consistent care and educational environment for all children

▶ set standards

▶ illustrate good practice

▶ give guidance for new staff

▶ provide a training model for managers.

Over to you!

Research these two policy documents on the internet.

www.unicef.org/crc/
www.equalities.gov.uk/equality_act_2010.aspx

Case study

Sandi is 22, lives on her own and has two children, Ben who is four years old and Kelly who is 18 months old. Sandi lives in council accommodation but does not live near her parents and is not in contact with the fathers of her children. Her only income is from state benefits.

1. Describe how the government could be helping Sandi to get back into work.

2. Think about Sandi's circumstances and describe the barriers to her starting work again.

Other influences

Much of the government's change in thinking has been influenced by academic research. Three important research projects are:

1. Researching Effective Pedagogy in the Early Years (REPEY) 2002

2. Key Elements of Effective Practice (KEEP) 2005

3. Effective Provision in Pre-school Education (EPPE) 2006.

Together, these provide many recommendations. Overall, they emphasise that children benefit from attending high-quality pre-schools with highly qualified staff, that good staff interaction is important and that working closely with parents and other professionals is crucial.

Impact on the early years sector

As a result of social trends, the government's policies and research studies:

▶ the early years sector has gained in status

▶ a wider choice of settings has become available

▶ more money is being provided to support children, especially the youngest, most-disadvantaged children

▶ funding is being provided to increase the qualifications of the workforce

▶ children are receiving more effective care and education.

Already there is evidence to show that good-quality pre-school education has increased all children's life chances, but particularly those from disadvantaged backgrounds.

Tackling discriminatory behaviour

As an early years practitioner, you must be certain that you are not discriminating against any child. However, it is also your responsibility to ensure that the whole environment you are providing for the children is non-discriminatory and this might mean challenging others as well. To do this you must:

▶ challenge all discriminatory comments or gestures immediately

▶ reflect on your own prejudices and consider how to overcome them.

It is often too late to wait until someone displays a discriminatory attitude to do anything about it, and is also much more difficult to challenge discrimination than it is to try to prevent it. One of the most difficult actions of all is to recognise our own prejudices and to accept that we must try not to let them influence our practice.

Your assessment criteria:

2.1 Identify current policies, frameworks and influences on the early years

2.2 Explain the impact of current policies, frameworks and influences on the early years sector

2.3 Describe what is meant by evidence-based practice and give examples of how this has influenced work with children in their early years

Over to you!

Look at the national early years framework that is relevant to your setting. How does it meet the requirements of the points listed here?

Active participation

As we have already seen in Chapter 11 (page 286), if children are given a chance to participate in decisions about their lives and their experiences, then their positive life chances are increased. By listening to children we can:

▶ find out what they want and what they are interested in

▶ understand their motivations

▶ develop greater self-esteem and self-worth in children

▶ cater for their needs more effectively.

Evidence-based practice

The fact that early years care and education frameworks are based on the findings of the research projects mentioned above has been an important factor in convincing the government and the public of the importance of the early years. This is what is meant by evidence-based practice. The frameworks are based on the findings of acknowledged, stringent research projects.

Case study

Hayley is a first-year childcare student working in a day nursery. Her manager has suggested she needs to read about the main findings of the EPPE research project to help her understanding of the importance of good early years care and education. Hayley does not like reading reports, so she is not going to do so.

1. Why might Hayley's manager think it is a good idea to read research reports?

2. Look at the EPPE summary yourself and summarise what Hayley should learn from it.

3. Consider how you might persuade Hayley to do as her manager has asked.

Knowledge Assessment Task   **2.1**   **2.2**   **2.3**

Write an essay on what policies, frameworks and social changes have influenced the early years sector recently. Explain what you understand by evidence-based practice and give examples of how this has influenced working with children in their early years.

Keep your work as evidence towards your assessment.

Your assessment criteria:

3.1 Explain what is meant by diversity, inclusion and participation

3.2 Explain the importance of anti-discriminatory/ anti-bias practice, giving examples of how it is applied in practice with children and carers

3.3 Explain how the active participation of the children in decisions affecting their lives promotes the achievement of positive outcomes

Why are diversity, inclusion and participation important in early years settings?

Chapter 11, page 286, discusses **diversity** and **inclusion** in some detail. It explores the meaning and importance of these topics. This unit focuses on how you can support diversity and inclusion in your setting. It discusses the meaning of **participation**, referring to the way all children are enabled to take part in activities in the setting and take part in making choices about how the provision caters for them.

The importance of anti-discriminatory practice

Having seen how damaging stereotyping and discrimination can be to children's self-esteem, it must be high on our list of priorities to make sure that all children and families feel they are respected and valued. It is practitioners' attitudes and actions that can promote an **anti-discriminatory** environment which gives all children positive encouragement to be proud of themselves and their families. Figure 15.2 highlights some examples of how practitioners can achieve this.

Key terms

Anti-discriminatory: preventing discrimination

Diversity: identifiable differences between individuals or groups of individuals

Inclusion: the idea that all people should freely, openly and without pity accommodate all other people

Participation: the process where individuals are consulted about or have the opportunity to become actively involved in a project or programme of activity

Figure 15.2 How practitioners can promote an anti-discriminatory environment

Factor	How this can be achieved in the work setting
Prepare the environment to represent all the children who attend the setting in a positive light.	Place photos of all children who attend the setting around the room.
	Place positive images of children with disabilities, from other countries and from different religious backgrounds around the room.
	Provide books, toys and resources that are representative of all children attending the setting.
	Provide dual-language posters to help staff to know some of the children's vocabulary.
Introduce activities that encourage children to look positively at similarities and differences.	Hold discussions about acceptance of similarities and differences in a wide range of subjects to introduce those that are sensitive in the setting.
Deliberately introduce new and focused vocabulary to empower children to talk about their differences in a positive light.	Use books, posters, photographs or parents' knowledge and skills to introduce different vocabulary for food, clothing, customs or special educational needs that differ among the families attending the setting.
Challenge the pre-conceived ideas of many people about roles, beliefs, customs and habits within our society.	Provide images of a range of different people performing different tasks that might be contrary to the stereotypical view.
	Model positive attitudes and make sure children know that you do not have different stereotypical expectations for different children.
Answer children's questions about differences honestly and simply.	When children ask questions about differences, answer honestly and in simple terms.

Knowledge Assessment Task · 3.1 · 3.2 · 3.3

At St Monroe's nursery a member of staff witnesses a racial incident in the setting. Mrs Thomas, the mother of a white boy called Billy, says loudly to a junior member of staff that Billy mustn't share toys with Philip, an Afro-Caribbean boy, because Philip is 'dirty'.

1. Draft a letter to Mrs Thomas explaining the importance of anti-discriminatory practice and how it is applied at St Monroe's nursery.

2. Explain what is meant by 'diversity', 'inclusion' and 'participation' and say why this incident contravenes the setting's beliefs.

3. Explain how staff can make sure that Billy and Philip actively participate in making decisions about what happens in the setting and how this can promote positive outcomes for them.

Keep your work as evidence towards your assessment.

What is a reflective practitioner?

A reflective practitioner is one who can think critically about what they have done or said in their work (see Chapter 3, page 68). The best practitioners not only think carefully about their practice, but they also, most importantly, constructively criticise their own practice and find ways of improving it. Some practitioners find it very difficult to criticise themselves.

Sometimes your thinking will show you that you need some more training and the time to talk about this is during staff appraisals with your manager. These should be seen as supportive and helpful and you should use them to focus on your own needs. Once self-reflection is an established way of thinking, you will find that you apply it to all aspects of your life.

If you are truly reflective, you will always be looking for ways of improving your own practice, therefore the outcomes for the children in your care will be enhanced. Reflection must be a continuous process as it is the only sure way of improving the quality of your practice. For more about reflective practice, see Chapter 2, page 40.

Reflection on a specific incident

This is the easiest type of reflection as it is focused on something you can identify that has happened in the workplace. This can be quite a painful process if you remember something that did not go well but, even with situations that went well, there is a place for reflection as there is always room for improvement.

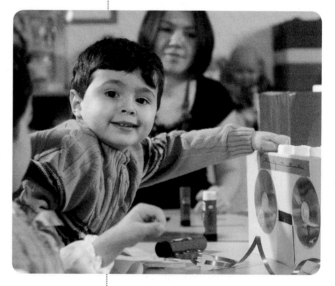

Every child will have their own special interests and enthusiasms and you should try hard to get to know all children as well as possible, but especially those who are your key children. Sometimes children might need special attention for the following reasons:

▶ shyness

▶ poor attention skills

▶ hearing difficulties

▶ global learning delay

Your assessment criteria:

4.1 Explain the importance of reviewing your own practice as part of being an effective practitioner

4.2 Undertake a reflective analysis of own practice

4.3 Develop strategies to deal with areas of difficulty and challenges encountered in professional practice in your early years setting

▶ English as an alternative language

▶ high intelligence

▶ unhappy to leave a parent in the mornings.

General reflection

It can be more difficult to question yourself generally about your practice. This requires an overview of how you perform in the workplace, and might be informed by asking your supervisor or your colleagues about how you are doing.

Strategies to deal with areas of difficulty

To some extent everyone finds challenging discrimination difficult. If you find something difficult, it is important to admit this to yourself and to try to learn how to overcome it.

You will know how you learn best. Some ways to deal with any difficulties you may be having might include:

▶ researching on the internet

▶ reading books

▶ speaking to your supervisor

▶ watching how others deal with similar situations

▶ asking questions of your peers

▶ practising your responses by looking at case studies

▶ critically reflecting on situations that you have encountered and considering how they might have been handled differently.

Over to you!

Write a brief outline of something you did with a child or a group of children recently in your placement or work setting.

▶ Describe what went well and what did not. Reflect on and describe how you could have improved what you did, even the parts that went well.

▶ With a partner, discuss how it feels to be critical of yourself.

Over to you!

Think carefully about a child in your setting who might have special requirements. Ask yourself the following questions:

▶ Do I really know what this child can do and is interested in?

▶ How have I made the provision more accessible for this child?

▶ What else could I do to promote positive outcomes for this child?

Share your thoughts with the group and ask others how they might cater for this child's needs.

Over to you!

Make a list of all the ways you have enabled individual children in your setting to make greater use of resources or to feel more welcome.

▶ What worked well?

▶ What could have worked better?

▶ What are your strengths?

▶ What do you need to develop in the future?

Practical Assessment Task   4.1   4.2   4.3

In preparing for your assessment, follow these steps.

1. Be able to discuss why it's important to be a reflective practitioner.

2. Be ready to discuss some specific examples of ways in which you have altered your own practice in the setting in order to accommodate the needs of individual children. You might want to take photographs or write a short diary to show your assessor.

3. From those specific examples, be prepared to discuss what went well and how you could have been more effective.

4. Prepare some specific examples of the strategies you have developed in order to handle difficult situations, for example, having to challenge cases of discrimination.

Your evidence for this task must be based on your practice in a real work environment and must be in a format that is acceptable to your assessor.

Are you ready for assessment?

AC	What do you know now?	Assessment task	✓
1.1	How the range of early years settings reflects the scope and purpose of the sector	Page 391	
2.1	The current policies, frameworks and influences on the early years	Page 395	
2.2	The impact of the current policies, frameworks and influences on the early years sector	Page 395	
2.3	What is meant by evidence-based practice and examples of how this has influenced work with children in their early years	Page 395	
3.1	The meaning of diversity, inclusion and participation	Page 397	
3.2	The importance of anti-discriminatory/ anti-bias practice and examples of how it is applied in practice with children and carers	Page 397	
3.3	How the active participation of the children in decisions affecting their lives promotes the achievement of positive outcomes	Page 397	

Your tutor or assessor may need to observe your competence in your placement or work setting.

AC	What can you do now?	Assessment task	✓
4.1	Explain the importance of reviewing your own practice as part of being an effective practitioner	Page 399	
4.2	Undertake a reflective analysis of your own practice	Page 399	
4.3	Develop strategies to deal with areas of difficulty and challenges encountered in professional practice in your early years setting	Page 399	

16 | Support children's speech, language and communication (EYMP 5)

Assessment of this unit

This unit is about supporting the development of children's speech, language and communication skills. It covers the importance of speech and language for children's overall development and explores some of the different ways in which adults can provide support through everyday activities and interactions with children.

The assessment of this unit includes both knowledge (things that you need to know about) and competence (things you need to be able to do in the real work environment).

In order to complete this unit successfully, you will need to produce evidence of your knowledge and competence. The charts below and opposite explain what you need to know and do, alongside the relevant assessment criteria.

Your tutor or assessor will help you to prepare for your assessment, and the tasks suggested in this chapter will help you to create the evidence you need.

AC	What you need to know
1.1	How to explain the terms 'speech', 'language', 'communication' and 'speech, language and communication needs'
1.2	How speech, language and communication skills support children's learning, behaviour and their emotional and social development
1.3	The potential impact of speech, language and communication difficulties on the overall development of a child, both currently and in the longer term
2.1 2.2	The ways in which adults can effectively support and extend the speech, language and communication development of children during the early years and the relevant positive effects of adult support for the children and their carers
2.3	How levels of speech and language development vary between children entering early years provision and need to be taken into account during settling in and planning

CHAPTER 16

AC What you need to do

3.1 Demonstrate methods of providing support, taking into account the age, specific needs, abilities, home language (where this is different from that of the setting) and interests of the children in own setting

3.2 Demonstrate in own practice how day-to-day activities within the setting can be used to encourage speech, language and communication development in young children

3.3 Demonstrate in own practice how to work with children to develop speech, language and communication in groups and on a one-to-one basis

3.4 Evaluate the effectiveness of speech, language and communication support for children in own setting

4.1 Explain the importance of the environment in supporting speech, language and communication development

4.2 Review evidence about the key factors that provide a supportive speech, language and communication environment

4.3 Demonstrate how settings use the environment to provide effective support for speech, language and communication for all children

---

This unit links with some of the other mandatory units:

SHC 31 Promote communication in health, social care or children's and young people's settings

CYP 3.1 Understand child and young person development

CYP 3.2 Promote child and young person development

CYP 3.5 Develop positive relationships with children, young people and others involved in their care

Some of your learning will be repeated in these units and will give you the chance to review your knowledge and understanding.

What is the importance of speech, language and communication for children's overall development?

Young children need to be able to communicate in order to express their ideas and feelings, to interact with others and develop friendships. Being able to communicate effectively underpins all other areas of development, but it is particularly important for children's learning and their emotional, social and behavioural development. If young children cannot communicate their needs or make themselves understood, then they will easily become frustrated and this can lead to negative behaviour patterns.

Speech, language and communication

The terms 'speech', 'language' and 'communication' are often used interchangeably, but it is important to understand exactly what each of these terms really means.

Speech refers only to actual spoken language, the vocalised form of human communication.

Language refers to a systematic way of communicating, using sounds or symbols. These can be spoken, written or signed and follow a series of rules, for example, the order of words in a sentence.

Communication refers to the complex two-way process of sending messages to others and receiving messages. This includes both speech and language and can be verbal (using spoken words) or non-verbal (using body language, signing, gestures or facial expressions).

Development of speech, language and communication is a very complex process; children need to learn a whole range of skills in order to become confident communicators. The progress that a child makes, from a gurgling baby to a fluent talker, is a complicated journey and children need consistent support from adults.

Speech, language and communication needs

It is very important for adults to provide stimulation and encouragement to support children's speech, language and communication needs. Providing a language-rich environment, with conversation, active listening, positive interactions and interesting activities, will help to meet children's speech, language and communication needs. However, some children may experience difficulties with their speech, language or communication development and their needs may be more specific. For example, some children may have difficulty in forming sounds or pronouncing specific words and they may need more individualised help and support. Children with a hearing impairment may need support with sign language and children who do not speak English as their first language may need more specialised, bilingual support. Children with speech, language and communication needs will have difficulties in communicating with others. They may not be able to express themselves effectively or they may have difficulties in understanding what is being said to them.

How do speech, language and communication skills support other areas of development?

Being able to communicate is the foundation for many other areas of children's development. Children need to be able to use and understand speech and language in order to learn. For example, being able to ask, 'What's that?' or, 'How do I do this?' and being able to understand the reply is an important part of children's learning. Speech, language and communication also support children's emotional and social development. For example, being able to express feelings such as, 'I'm scared,' or, 'I don't like that.' Being able to use positive body language in social situations is an important aspect of how children develop an awareness of themselves and make friendships with others.

Figure 16.1 (overleaf) shows some of the ways that speech, language and communication skills support other areas of children's development.

Over to you!

▶ Think about all the different ways in which you communicate with other people and how that affects:
  – your friendships
  – how you find out about things
  – how you express yourself and make yourself understood.
▶ Make a list of the problems you might experience if you had speech, language or communication difficulties.
▶ Share your ideas with those of others in the group.

Figure 16.1 Some ways that speech, language and communication skills support other areas

Area of development	Examples of how development is supported by speech, language and communication
Learning	Babies use sounds and facial expressions to communicate their needs and express themselves.
	Toddlers use words and gestures to make connections and develop their knowledge and understanding (e.g. 'All gone!').
	Pre-school children ask questions and make sense of the responses, they use words to express their ideas and develop their understanding.
Emotional	Babies use sounds and facial expressions to develop an attachment relationship with their main carers.
	Toddlers use words and body language to express their feelings (e.g. temper tantrums).
	Pre-school children use speech and language to express their feelings and exert their independence (e.g. 'I want to do it!').
Social and behavioural	Babies use sounds and facial expressions in responding to adult interactions (e.g. smiling, cooing and gurgling).
	Toddlers use words and gestures to interact with others; starting to understand the word 'no'.
	Pre-school children use speech and language to interact with others and develop friendships; understanding how the rules of behaviour are communicated (e.g. 'We don't hurt each other.').

Your assessment criteria:

1.1 Explain each of the terms:
- speech
- language
- communication
- speech, language and communication needs

1.2 Explain how speech, language and communication skills support each of the following areas in children's development:
- learning
- emotional
- behaviour
- social

1.3 Describe the potential impact of speech, language and communication difficulties on the overall development of a child, both currently and in the longer term

Case study

Evie is four years old and attends the Rainbow nursery every morning. She is becoming a fluent communicator, with a wide vocabulary, and she can use fairly long sentences in her conversations with both children and adults. Evie is very curious and asks lots of questions, such as, 'Why is the grass green?' and 'How does this work?' She enjoys learning new words and likes to use these in her conversations. Evie is very sociable and has lots of friends at nursery. She enjoys role-play and dressing up and often

continued...

makes up quite complicated imaginary games with other children. Evie's mum recently had a new baby boy and Evie is getting used to the idea of being a 'big sister' in the family.

1. Explain how Evie's speech, language and communication skills will help to support her learning at Rainbow nursery.

2. Explain how Evie's speech, language and communication skills could help her adjust to having a new baby brother in the family.

Speech, language and communication difficulties

Having examined how speech, language and communication support other areas of children's development, it is easy to see that children who have any kind of communication difficulties may also have other developmental problems. Speech, language and communication difficulties can affect children's development, both in the short term and over longer periods of time.

Short-term effects might include:

▶ difficulties in learning and understanding information

▶ difficulties in making friends

▶ problems with making themselves understood

▶ low levels of self-confidence and self-esteem

▶ problems with expressing their feelings, leading to frustration, anger or withdrawal.

Longer-term effects are more difficult to assess, but might include:

▶ failure to reach their full potential

▶ difficulties in making and sustaining relationships

▶ long-term problems with behaviour.

Knowledge Assessment Task   1.1   1.2   1.3

Create a leaflet for parents that explains the importance of speech, language and communication in children from birth to five years of age. The content should include:

▶ what is meant by speech, language and communication

▶ the speech, language and communication needs of young children

▶ how speech, language and communication skills support other areas of development

▶ the potential impact of speech, language and communication difficulties on children's overall development.

You can illustrate your leaflet with relevant images.

Keep your leaflet as evidence towards your assessment.

How can adults support and extend children's speech, language and communication development?

Your assessment criteria:

2.1 Explain the ways in which adults can effectively support and extend the speech, language and communication development of children during the early years

It is vitally important for adults to communicate with young children, right from birth, in order to support and extend their speech, language and communication development. This should include not only verbal communication but also positive body language, gestures and facial expressions. As children get older, it will also include using appropriate vocabulary, asking **open-ended questions**, providing interesting activities and working closely with parents and carers in order to support children's communication needs.

The importance of positive interaction

Interacting positively with young children is an extremely important way to support their speech, language and communication development. Using encouraging smiles, clear gestures and helpful body language are all valuable ways to develop children's understanding and extend their communication skills. Active listening is another way to support children's speech, language and communication. Being patient, showing genuine interest and responding appropriately, will all help children to gain confidence in developing their communication skills.

Some settings use **baby signing** as a way of supporting speech and language development with babies and toddlers. This technique involves a system of simple gestures that are taught to babies alongside the appropriate word, for example, putting your finger tips to your lips to represent the word 'food'. Some research has shown that this method can positively support language development in the very early years.

Language use

The words and level of language we use with young children are also important in supporting and extending their speech, language and communication development. Babies and very young children will respond more effectively to simple language, which focuses on key words and is reinforced with exaggerated gestures or facial expressions. The term **parentese** is often used to describe the 'sing-song' way that adults use to communicate with babies.

As children get older, they develop both **expressive** and **receptive language** skills. Expressive language refers to the actual words spoken, whereas receptive language refers to the child's understanding of language. Most toddlers will understand far more language than

Key terms

Baby signing: communicating with babies and toddlers, using simple gestures alongside the appropriate words

Expressive language: ability to communicate wants and needs; the ability to make oneself understood

Open-ended questions: questions that cannot be answered in one word, such as 'yes' or 'no'

Parentese: non-standard, sometimes 'sing-song' form of speech that adults use to communicate with babies and toddlers

Receptive language: understanding of speech sounds, sentences, grammatical structures, and implications of what someone says

the words they can actually speak so, for example, if you were to say to an average 18-month-old, '*Go into the kitchen and get your red shoes,*' they would understand and obey your request, even though they may actually be able to say only one or two recognisable words. At this stage, it is important to think about extending children's vocabulary and developing their language by using lots of repetition, adding descriptive words and expanding their sentences.

Over to you!

▶ *In your placement or work setting, think about all the different ways that you use positive interaction, body language and active listening to support and extend children's speech, language and communication development.*

▶ *Compare examples with others in the group.*

▶ *Investigate baby signing on the internet and try out some of the signs for yourself.*

Case study

Annie works in the toddler room at Little Teddies nursery and she is the key person for Jack, aged 18 months. A recent conversation between Jack and Annie went like this.

Jack: 'Car…'

Annie: 'Yes, it's a blue car.'

Jack: 'Brm brm…'

Annie: 'The car goes brm, brm.' (*Moves the toy car on the mat.*)

Jack: 'Dadda car…'

Annie: 'Your daddy has a blue car.' (*Points to the toy car.*)

Jack: 'Bu car…'

Annie: 'Yes your daddy has a blue car; clever boy, Jack.' (*Gives Jack a big smile and a hug.*)

1. Explain the ways in which Annie supported and extended Jack's speech, language and communication development in this conversation.

2. Give **two** examples of different ways that Annie could further develop Jack's communication skills in this conversation.

3. Explain why it is important for practitioners to support and extend children's speech, language and communication development in the early years.

Questions

Your assessment criteria:

2.1 Explain the ways in which adults can effectively support and extend the speech, language and communication development of children during the early years

2.2 Explain the relevant positive effects of adult support for the children and their carers

2.3 Explain how levels of speech and language development vary between children entering early years provision and need to be taken into account during settling in and planning

The use of questions can be effective in extending and supporting children's speech and language development. Questions encourage children to think about their responses and help to expand their use of vocabulary. Different types of question will prompt different responses; it is important to consider this when thinking about children's speech and language development. Some examples of questions are given in Figure 16.2.

Figure 16.2 Examples of open and closed questions

Type of question	Characteristics	Example	Comments
Closed	Short and simple; require a basic response or one-word answer	'What's that?' 'Did you like that' 'Can you do that?'	Useful for engaging very young children with limited language; can be helpful starting points in conversations; less useful for older children who need more opportunity to extend their language use and express themselves.
Open-ended	More searching; require a more detailed, considered response with more information	'Why do you think that happened?' 'I wonder how this works?'	Encourage children to think about their response and use a wider range of vocabulary; useful for children who are gaining confidence with speech and language.

Activities and experiences

The provision of different activities and experiences acts as a positive stimulus for children's speech and language development. For example, books, puppets, dressing up and outdoor play all give children the opportunity to communicate with each other, express their ideas, learn new words and develop their use of language. Going on an outing to the park or visiting new places, such as the local fire station, gives children something to talk about. This provides the opportunity for children to extend their vocabulary and develop their conversation skills.

Over to you!

▶ Think about the activities and experiences you provide for children in your placement or work setting.

▶ Make a list of some specific examples, such as painting, and record some of the ways that this encourages children's speech and language development.

▶ Share your ideas with others in the group.

Case study

Coleen works at the Little Ducklings nursery. Recently, she has been thinking about how she could improve the ways in which she supports the speech, language and communication with children in the setting.

In each of the following examples, make a list of the vocabulary Coleen could introduce and the questions she might ask with children engaged in these activities.

1. Playing with an 18-month old at the water tray with a selection of plastic boats and rubber ducks
2. Eating a snack of breadsticks, fruit and milk with a group of three-year-olds
3. Visiting the local park in the autumn with a group of four-year-olds

The importance of parents and carers

Parents and carers are children's most important teachers; their role in helping speech and language development is extremely significant. Most parents spend regular periods of time every day chatting with their child as they go about their daily activities. This has a considerable impact on children's speech, language and communication skills. It is important for staff in early years settings to acknowledge the role of parents and carers and actively promote parents as positive language partners for their children.

Many settings provide resources that can be taken home and used by parents with their children to encourage speech and language; examples include books, puppets and games for them to play together. Some settings also offer sessions for parents to learn more about how to encourage their children's speech and language development. This may be particularly important for children with individual speech, language or communication needs, or where parents may need to work together with a speech and language therapist or a bilingual support worker.

Positive effects of adult support

The positive effects of adult support for children's speech and language have been well documented. The **Every Child A Talker** programme, introduced by the government in 2008, has found that positive adult support for children's speech and language can help to:

► develop children's self-confidence

► increase children's self-esteem and enhance their wellbeing

► improve children's ability to interact socially with others

► develop children's ability to express their feelings and manage their behaviour

► enrich children's involvement in speaking and listening activities

► reduce the number of referrals for specialist speech, language and communication support.

Variation in levels of speech and language

Children in early years settings will have different levels of speech and language, which are dependent on a range of factors including:

► their age and stage of development

► the amount of stimulation and encouragement they have received

► their first language or language spoken at home

► individual speech, language or communication needs or specific difficulties.

Key terms

Every Child A Talker: a national project to develop the language and communication of children from birth to five years of age

When providing care and planning experiences for children in the setting, practitioners need to take these factors into account. This is particularly important at key times during the day, for example, during settling in or when there is a change in the routine and children are more likely to feel anxious and insecure. Practitioners need to be more aware of their interactions with children and the importance of non-verbal communication at these times; for example, using soothing sounds and sensitive body language with a child who has limited communication skills and is upset about leaving their parent when they arrive at the setting.

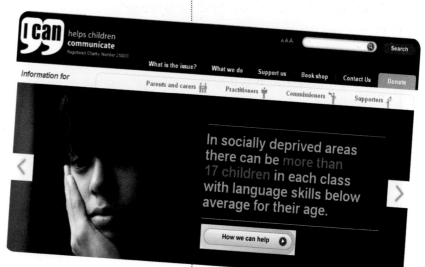

It is also important to consider how children's different levels of speech and language can be accommodated when planning activities and experiences in the setting, for example, by providing a range of activities that can be **differentiated** for children with varying levels of language ability or by using visual prompts, labels and symbols around the setting. It is also important to take into account how children are grouped according to their language needs and the role and responsibilities of the key person, see Chapter 9, page 256.

Key terms

Differentiated: varied or adjusted to suit the level of ability or understanding

Knowledge Assessment Task   2.1   2.2   2.3

Prepare a presentation that could be used to inform new students about supporting speech, language and communication with young children in your setting. Your presentation should cover:

▶ different ways in which adults can effectively support and extend the speech, language and communication development of children in the early years

▶ the positive effects of adult support, for both children and their carers

▶ how levels of speech and language development vary between children and the need to take this into account during settling in and planning in your setting.

You can use a slide show or other suitable format for your presentation. You should keep your notes as evidence towards your assessment.

Over to you!

▶ *Investigate the work of the organisations, listed below, that support children's speech and language development.*

ICAN: www.ican.org.uk/

The National Literary Trust: www. literacytrust.org.uk/talk_to_your_babyv

▶ *Make a list of the different ways in which these organisations provide support for:*

    – *parents and carers*

    – *staff working in settings.*

Be able to provide support for the speech, language and communication development of the children in own setting

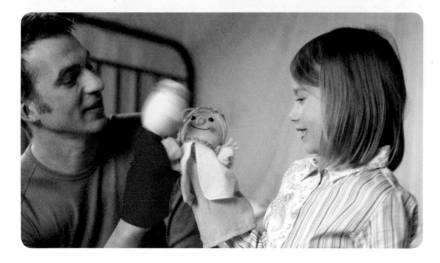

Your assessment criteria:

3.1 Demonstrate methods of providing support taking into account age, specific needs, abilities, home language (where this is different from that of the setting) and interests of children in own setting

How can adults provide support for children's speech, language and communication?

There are many aspects to consider when providing support for children's speech, language and communication needs. Adults should take into account factors such as children's age and stage of development, specific needs, abilities and interests as well as children's own home language.

Over to you!

Try this quiz and then check your answers on the student information sheet at:
www.literacytrust.org.uk/assets/0000/1060/SchoolResourceKit_Quiz.pdf

1. *When should you start talking to babies?*
   a. *From the moment they are born*
   b. *After six weeks*
   c. *When they smile at you*

2. *When does the majority of brain development occur in children?*
   a. *In the first four weeks*
   b. *From birth to age two*
   c. *When they start school*

3. *When do babies start to communicate?*
   a. *Before they start talking*
   b. *After they start talking*
   c. *As soon as they've said their first word*

4. *If a young child says something incorrectly, what should you do?*
   a. *Nod in agreement*
   b. *Say it back the right way*
   c. *Write down the correct word*

Key terms

Autistic spectrum disorder (ASD): a neuro-developmental disorder of varying degrees, characterised by inflexibility of thought and imagination, impaired social interaction and difficulties with communication

Some of the ways that adults can provide support are summarised in Figure 16.3.

Figure 16.3 How adults can provide support for children's speech, language and communication needs

Way to provide support	Importance	Examples
Adapting own language by emphasising key words, simplifying sentences or using exaggerated body language and facial expressions	This is particularly important with very young children, children whose first language is not English or children who have particular needs, such as those with **autistic spectrum disorder (ASD).**	'Well done Rashid' (using a thumbs up sign) 'All gone' (pointing to a toddler's empty bowl) 'Good sitting Jamie'
Scaffolding children's language by repeating, reinforcing and extending communication, taking care not to over-correct children's speech	This helps to cement children's understanding and use of language. Rephrasing, rather than correcting children's speech helps them to develop correct language patterns.	Child: 'Duck gets two feets' Adult: 'Yes, the duck has two feet; one … two.' Child: 'Mine' Adult: 'Yes, that's your pink teddy.' Baby: 'Dadada' Adult: 'Daddy; there's your daddy.' (with emphasis on the word daddy)
Active listening and giving children time to communicate **O**bserve **W**ait **L**isten	This helps children to process language and gives them time to respond and is particularly important for very young children or children whose first language is not English.	Child: 'What about that one … that one … that … ?' Adult: Focuses on the child, makes eye contact, smiles warmly and waits patiently without speaking Child: 'That one for my mummy.' Adult: 'Oh, the red one is for your mummy is it?'
Providing play activities that support children's individual interests and encourage children to use language and develop their communication skills	Play provides a wonderful medium for children to express themselves, learn new vocabulary, communicate with each other and develop friendships.	Role play, puppets, small-world play, constructive, creative, imaginary play, play with natural materials such as sand and water

Providing support in early years settings

There are many different ways in which practitioners can provide support for children's speech, language and communication in early years settings, for example, circle time or group time with the key person, talking to babies during nappy changing, encouraging conversations at snack time and reinforcing familiar language in daily routines. These will vary, according not only to the child's individual needs but also the routines, policies and procedures in the setting. Some of the ways that practitioners can provide support in settings are summarised in Figure 16.4.

Figure 16.4 Some ways to provide support for children's speech, language and communication

Professional practice	Importance
Using communication systems such as **Makaton** and the **Picture Exchange Communication System (PECS)**	This is particularly important for children with specific communication needs, for example, children with hearing impairment or children with autistic spectrum disorder (ASD).
Working with children on a one-to-one basis	This gives children individual, focused attention; they can communicate at their own pace and do not have to compete with other children.
Working with groups of children	This can facilitate communication between children and encourage social interaction; the group size should never be too large with young children.
Day-to-day activities such as personal care routines, snack time, choosing play activities, tidying up or home time	Daily routines can provide rich opportunities for reinforcing children's language, extending their vocabulary and developing their understanding through simple conversations, the use of open-ended questions and listening to children.

Key terms

Makaton: a system of communication that uses manual signs, graphic symbols and speech, used by individuals who have communication, language or learning difficulties

Picture Exchange Communication System (PECS): a system of communication that uses pictures and symbols, used by individuals with autistic spectrum disorder (ASD) and other communication difficulties

Evaluating practice

It is extremely important for anyone who works with young children constantly to evaluate the effectiveness of their practice. In terms of supporting children's speech, language and communication, there are several ways in which this can be achieved. Some settings use different methods of observing practitioners working with children in practical situations, for example:

▶ DVD or video recordings of staff communicating and interacting with children

▶ digital sound recordings of staff engaged in conversations with children, asking questions and scaffolding children's language.

These observations can then be used to review and reflect on the effectiveness of professional practice in supporting children's speech, language and communication. For example, how effectively staff:

▶ use positive non-verbal communication (body language, gestures and facial expressions)

▶ ask open-ended questions to encourage children to express themselves and develop their language use

▶ listen actively and give children time to respond

▶ adapt their own language to an appropriate level that meets children's individual needs

▶ use specific communication systems (such as Makaton) to support the communication needs of individual children.

Such observations can also be used to monitor children's progress in speech and language development, over a period of time, and to plan stimulating activities and experiences that will encourage the continued development of children's communication skills.

Your assessment criteria:

3.1 Demonstrate methods of providing support taking into account age, specific needs, abilities, home language (where this is different from that of the setting) and interests of children in own setting

3.2 Demonstrate how day-to-day activities within the setting can be used to encourage speech, language and communication development in young children

3.3 Demonstrate in own practice how to work with children to develop speech, language and communication in groups and on a one-to-one basis

3.4 Evaluate the effectiveness of speech, language and communication support for children in own setting

Practical Assessment Task   3.1 3.2 3.3 3.4

In your placement or work setting, think about the different ways in which you provide support for children's speech, language and communication through:

▶ day-to-day activities and routines
▶ play experiences
▶ working with children, both on a one-to-one basis and in groups.

Make notes about specific examples from your own practice that demonstrate your effectiveness in supporting speech, language and communication with individual children. For example, you may have encouraged a particular child in learning new vocabulary, or worked alongside a bilingual support assistant and learnt some words in different languages, or you might have supported a group of children in learning some basic Makaton gestures.

Keep your notes towards the evidence for your assessment.

Your tutor or assessor will need to assess your competence in a real work environment and you may also choose to show evidence or statements from colleagues, or observations you have carried out.

417

What is the importance of the environment in supporting children's speech, language and communication?

Children need to be surrounded by a language-rich environment that provides interesting activities, stimulating resources and a wide variety of experiences to support their speech, language and communication, both indoors and outdoors. This gives children the opportunity to develop their language use, learn new vocabulary and improve their conversational skills. It is important to think about balancing different factors within the environment. If children are constantly exposed to noise and activity, the atmosphere can become very chaotic and they may find it difficult to communicate effectively. Adults need to provide both excitement and inspiration, combined with a calm and relaxed environment, in order to support children's speech, language and communication needs.

Practical Assessment Task

▶ In your placement or work setting, investigate how the environment supports children's speech, language and communication. Look particularly at these areas.

- ▶ *The layout and how the space is organised: Are there small cosy spaces and areas where children can interact together both indoors and outdoors?*
- ▶ *The noise levels and quality of light: Is there a lot of background noise or music constantly playing? Are spaces well lit?*
- ▶ *The activities, toys and resources: Is there a variety of interesting experiences, both indoors and outdoors?*
- ▶ *Staff roles: Do staff interact with children positively to encourage communication? Do staff carry out observations to tune in to children's individual interests and communication needs? Do staff take part in training events?*
- ▶ *Involvement of parents and carers: How are parents involved in supporting children's communication in the setting?*

▶ Think about the importance of the environment in supporting children's speech, language and communication and the key factors that support this in your setting.

▶ Make notes about specific examples that you could discuss with your assessor and keep your notes to help you with your assessment.

Key factors for supporting the speech, language and communication environment

There are many different factors that can support the provision of an effective communication environment. Some of these are summarised in Figure 16.5.

Figure 16.5 Key factors for supporting the speech, language and communication environment

Key factor	How it supports an effective communication environment	Examples
The physical environment	Layout and organisation of the space; lighting; noise level; access to outdoor space	Creating small, cosy spaces for children to talk and interact with each other (both in and out of doors); minimising noise levels by reducing background noise and using fabric and soft furnishings; ensuring good lighting (particularly important for children with hearing or visual impairment)
Staff roles and responsibilities	Key person or language partner system; planning activities and routines; observation and monitoring; keeping up to date with staff training and development	Planning specific times to communicate with children, both individually and in groups (e.g. snack time); observing and recording children's language; attending specific courses (e.g. to learn Makaton or baby signing)
Activities, toys and resources	Providing resources and materials for child-initiated and adult-led activities; providing specific toys and activities to encourage and support communication	Books and stories, puppets, toy telephones, songs and rhymes, role play, digital recording equipment
Views of the child	Tuning in to children's specific needs and interests; allowing children to take the lead in communication interactions	Favourite stories or songs; specific interests (e.g. dinosaurs, trains or soft toys); enthusiasm for painting, sand or water play
Involvement of parents and carers	Providing information about children's specific communication needs or difficulties; using parental knowledge or expertise	Learning some words in the child's first language; parental involvement in specific language activities (e.g. parent teaching the children a well-known nursery rhyme in a different language, or using Makaton gestures)

Are you ready for assessment?

AC	What do you know now?	Assessment task	✓
1.1	How to explain the terms 'speech', 'language', 'communication' and 'speech, language and communication needs'	Page 407	
1.2	How speech, language and communication skills support children's learning, behaviour and their emotional and social development	Page 407	
1.3	The potential impact of speech, language and communication difficulties on the overall development of a child, both currently and in the longer term	Page 407	
2.1 2.2	The ways in which adults can effectively support and extend the speech, language and communication development of children during the early years and the relevant positive effects of adult support for the children and their carers	Page 413	
2.3	How levels of speech and language development vary between children entering early years provision and need to be taken into account during settling in and planning	Page 413	

Your tutor or assessor may need to observe your competence in your placement or work setting.

AC	What can you do now?	Assessment task	✓
3.1	Demonstrate methods of providing support, taking into account age, specific needs, abilities, home language (where this is different from that of the setting) and interests of the children in own setting	Page 417	
3.2	Demonstrate how day-to-day activities within the setting can be used to encourage speech, language and communication development in young children Could you provide actual examples from your own practice to discuss with your assessor?	Page 417	
3.3	Demonstrate in own practice how to work with children to develop speech, language and communication in groups and on a one-to-one basis Could you provide actual examples from your own practice to discuss with your assessor?	Page 417	
3.4	Evaluate the effectiveness of speech, language and communication support for children in your own setting Do you have any evidence of this to share with your assessor?	Page 417	
4.1	Explain the importance of the environment in supporting speech, language and communication development Could you discuss this with your assessor?	Page 418	
4.2	Review evidence about the key factors that provide a supportive speech, language and communication environment Could you give examples of this from your own setting?	Page 418	
4.3	Demonstrate how settings use the environment to provide effective support for speech, language and communication for all children	Page 418	

Index